# VERDI

# FORCE OF DESTINY

## BY DENA HUMPHREYS

*Illustrated by Hans Alexander Mueller*

HENRY HOLT AND COMPANY

*New York*

17242

*To*
**MAESTRO ARTURO TOSCANINI**
*truest of Verdi's interpreters,*
*this book is humbly dedicated*

". . . If there is anything in life to be valued it is the bread earned by the sweat of one's own brow. He is young, let him work. . . . He should imitate no one, especially not the great; and now, now only . . . should he dispense with studying them: let him put his hand on his heart, study that, and, if the true quality of an artist is there, his heart will tell him everything. He must not be puffed up by praise, nor afraid of censure. . . . The critics ply their trade; they judge, and should judge, according to established forms and standards; the artist must peer into the future, see new worlds through the chaos, and if on the new path he sees far, far away a tiny glimmer of light let him not be alarmed by the murk that surrounds him: he must go forward, and if he sometimes stumbles and falls he must pick himself up and keep on his way. . . ."

*(From Verdi's letter written in 1867 to his friend Vincenzo Torelli, whose son Achille stood at the threshold of a career as poet-playwright.)*

# Contents

## Contents

CHAPTER ONE

# *Let Me Learn Music!*

## 1813-1823

LUIGIA would have liked to go to Mass that day. Her Giuseppe, seven years old, had been chosen to serve as an altar boy. Proudly she had scrubbed his face, combed his thick chestnut hair, and sent him up the road to the big, bare church of St. Michael the Archangel, round which clustered the village houses of Le Roncole. Now, as she went about her housework, she pictured him, in his starched white robe, standing beside the priest while the pious villagers knelt in prayer. In her mind she heard the ancient, holy chanting, saw the glowing tapers, and the child's clear gray eyes and solemn face. He was always so good, so serious—her "Peppino"!

At least Carlo, her husband, was there and would tell her all about it. They could not both go, because on Sundays the little tavern that Carlo Verdi kept was always busy and there were preparations to be made. Between Mass and Vespers people dropped in for a glass of wine, a piece of crisp, dark bread, and a slab of cheese. On local Saints' days visiting choirs from other villages gathered at Carlo Verdi's between services. Often there was dancing, since in Italy holy days are for merrymaking as well as for church-going. And the village church was only a few steps from the village inn.

Le Roncole, in the flat plains of the Duchy of Parma, was a tiny place—hardly more than two hundred souls. Far on the southern horizon lay the foothills of the Apennines, and to the north, out of sight, the mighty Alps rose like a wall

[1]

protecting (not always successfully) the peace- and liberty-loving Italians from the seething wars of Europe. Mountain streams poured down to the river Po as it wound through the plain on its way to the Adriatic Sea, keeping the land green and fertile in spite of the parching sun and scanty rainfall. It was dull country—the monotony of endless cultivated fields broken only by a few lean poplars, here and there a clump of silvery willows, an occasional road, and the age-old homes of the hard-working peasant farmers.

Mass must soon be over. Luigia paused in her sweeping to glance toward the church. A man was coming down the road carrying something white and heavy. Why—it was Carlo—with Giuseppe! Ah, what could have happened? She ran to meet them.

"Carlo, what's the matter? My Peppino, what have they done to you?"

The boy, in his now crumpled robe, lay limp and unconscious in his father's arms. "He fell and struck his head," said Carlo.

"Fell? In church? *Dio mio!*"

Quickly they carried the child upstairs to the dark, stuffy, slope-ceilinged rooms under the roof that served the Verdi

[ 2 ]

family as living quarters, and laid him on his bed. An ugly lump was forming on his forehead, but the injury was fortunately only skin-deep. Luigia brought a wet cloth and bathed his face.

"Poor little one!" she murmured. "But Carlo, why should he fall in church? He must be ill!"

Carlo shrugged his shoulders. "It was the strangest thing, Luigia. When the time came for him to hand the holy water to the Padre, he just stood there and did nothing. The Padre whispered to him—I saw it, I was quite close—but Peppino didn't seem to hear. The Padre spoke again. I heard him say 'Water!' quite loud, and again, louder still. People began to shift about trying to see why the Mass didn't go on. But Peppino stood like a statue, and he had the queerest expression on his face! I never saw him look like that before—no, nor anyone else either for that matter. And then the Padre pushed him."

"*Pushed* him!" Luigia was amazed, indignant.

"But he had called for the water three times, Luigia, and maybe he shoved harder than he meant to. Anyhow Peppino lost his balance and rolled down the altar steps and hit his forehead. He was furious! He—" Carlo lowered his voice. "Well, he screamed at the Padre, 'God strike you down!' And then he fainted."

"Oh!" Luigia, shocked, stroked Giuseppe's heavy hair for a moment in silence. Then she said, "If only he didn't have such a frightful temper . . ."

"Yes—his temper. It was a wicked thing for him to say. But he's a good boy, Luigia."

"Yes, yes, he's a good boy. Of course he is! But whatever could have been the matter with him?"

The child stirred and opened his eyes. They were extraordinary eyes, pale gray, luminous, unfathomable—eyes that a noted sculptor would one day describe as "phosphorescent." Luigia bent over him tenderly. He's going to cry, she thought. He's so little—and his head hurts.

But Giuseppe did not cry. He stared at Luigia and Carlo. "Father," he begged, "let me learn music!"

[ 3 ]

"Music!" Often and often the boy had pleaded for it, but that this should be his first thought on regaining consciousness . . . Carlo was surprised. "Well, son, perhaps. You're very young, you know." To himself he added: And we are very poor.

"Tell me, my Peppino,"—Luigia spoke gently—"what happened to you? Why didn't you give the Padre the holy water when you were supposed to? He asked for it three times."

"It—it was the organ. Oh, Mother—I never heard it before! It was like—I don't know—I felt as though I weren't there at all, as though I were somewhere else. I didn't hear the Padre, truly I didn't. Father, let me learn music—please!"

Over the child's head Carlo's eyes met Luigia's, full of wonder. "Very well," he said. "I'll see what can be done about it. At once. I promise. Now I must go—I hear people downstairs."

It seemed as if the whole village had come to the tavern to inquire about Giuseppe. "The boy's all right," Carlo told the customers as he served them. "Just a bruise. He says it was the sound of the organ that upset him."

There were exclamations of surprise. Old Baistrocchi, the village organist, sipping his wine in a corner, leaned forward eagerly. "The organ, you say? Well, just imagine! But the child always *was* fond of music."

"Music's the only thing he ever seems to get excited about," Carlo agreed.

One of the villagers spoke up. "Why, he was practically born to the sound of music, eh, Carlo?"

"That's right!"

Back in the autumn of 1813 a band of traveling musicians had stopped at the inn. "Listen, Luigia," they declared gaily, "when your boy is born" (everyone hoped it would be a boy) "we'll come and play under your window!" And sure enough, a few nights later—it was the tenth of October—as Luigia held in her arms the baby Giuseppe, not yet an hour old, suddenly from the darkness outside came the jubilant sound of brasses celebrating with a lively tune. Now Carlo smiled, remembering the happiness in his wife's strong, brave face and

[4]

his own pride as he had invited the musicians to drink the health of his newborn son.

"He's a fine little fellow, and bright," said Baistrocchi, "but different. He doesn't seem to play much with the other boys."

"Not much. He's quiet," Carlo explained. "Likes to be by himself. But music! You can't keep him away from the organ-grinders; and before he could walk or talk he would stop crawling about and keep perfectly still whenever Bagasset played his fiddle. And as soon as the tune ended the little one would cry for more."

Bagasset was a strolling fiddler who provided music at fairs and weddings, picking up a few pennies as he went from place to place by playing in market squares, by village fountains, at the small roadside inns. His gaunt and ragged figure was a familiar sight all about the countryside. Often he stopped at the Verdis', sometimes bringing with him a friend who was a 'cellist. Then the two shabby musicians would play just for little Giuseppe, and the light that their music brought to his baby eyes more than rewarded them.

"One time," Carlo went on, "I was coming home from Busseto, and I met Bagasset striding along with his fiddle under his arm. Way down the road I saw a tiny figure toddling after him in the dust. It was Peppino. He couldn't have been more than two or three years old, but he had come clear out of the village—like a hungry dog following a man with meat!"

"Who knows?" murmured Baistrocchi. "Perhaps you'll make a fiddler out of him, or an organist. If you can find something for him to play on I'll gladly teach him music!"

For Carlo Verdi it was no easy matter to acquire an instrument. He was a poor man. A tavern in tiny, out-of-the-way Le Roncole could bring small profits at best, even though he combined with it a sort of general store, selling his neighbors their staple groceries, liquors, tobacco, cheap clay pipes, matches, and odds and ends. Once a week he went on foot to Busseto, three miles and a half away, to purchase supplies, trudging home again with his two big baskets laden with bags

[ 5 ]

of coffee and sugar and salt, and bottles of wine and oil.
Sometimes he had to make trips even farther afield; and during his absences Luigia took charge of the inn and store. Even
Giuseppe helped, shouldering responsibility early as peasant
children must. When he was needed, he went to Busseto to
share his father's load on the way back, and there were always
chores to be done at home, too. He did his part in the garden,
planting and tending onions, tomatoes, cabbages, the green
Italian squash, and spicy fennel. The solemn, silent little boy
worked willingly and well, taking a quiet pleasure in making
things grow. He was a lonely child. His only sister, two years
and a half younger than himself, had been born crippled in
both body and mind, and though he loved her dearly she
could not share his healthy activity nor offer him companionship. She was beautiful to look at, but with an empty, sad-
dening beauty.

During Giuseppe's childhood the struggle to make ends
meet was especially bitter for the Verdi family. Times were
hard, and Carlo's grocery business suffered. Even coffee and
sugar were luxuries the neighbors could seldom afford, because the country was ruled by grasping foreigners from beyond the Alps. In those days "Italy" was the name not of a
nation but of a peninsula divided into many separate states—
small kingdoms and duchies, weak, helpless, often ill-gov-

erned, and given to quarreling among themselves. At the end of the eighteenth century the insatiable conqueror Napoleon Bonaparte, seeing that no one in Italy was capable of resistance, had poured his armies over the Alps. Sweeping southward, they gobbled up the little Italian states one by one. Napoleon's generals made fair promises and established efficient government, but the Italians soon found their lives restricted, their beloved land being drained of its wealth, and their most prized heritage—the art treasures of classical Rome and of the cities that had flowered during the Renaissance—being shipped crate by crate to Paris for the glory of the Emperor. In 1813, when Verdi was born, the Duchy of Parma was still under the harsh, oppressive rule of the French, but by that time Napoleon's power had begun to wane. Less than a year later, the Austrians and Russians, now allied against him, sent soldiers into Italy to cut off his Armies of Occupation there.

These soldiers were not patriots fighting for a cause. They were rough, adventurous men who earned their living by waging wars that scarcely concerned them; and the life of hardship, danger, and violence had brutalized them. They had no quarrel with the peace-loving Italians, whose land seems fated every so often to become a battlefield for other peoples. Yet they spread terror wherever they went, especially the hard-riding Cossack regiments, which in those days were famed for wildness and ferocity.

Le Roncole lay in the path of the invaders, and one ghastly day in 1814 the Cossacks rode arrogantly into the quiet village. Those of the peasants who were not off working in the fields, or pasturing the cattle and sheep, fled in terror to the church for sanctuary—among them Luigia and her baby son. The lawless soldiers broke into the abandoned village homes and helped themselves to whatever caught their fancy, especially wine. Then, drunken and reckless, they forced the church door and brutally killed the handful of old people, women, and children huddled in frightened prayer at the altar—all but Luigia. Clutching her baby, she had run to the bell tower and climbed the steep, dark, winding stair to the very top. There she hid for hours, watching through the open arches under the roof until she saw the last of the soldiers ride off down the dust-whitened road. Then, with shaking knees, she had stumbled home with Giuseppe and his glorious, still undreamed-of future safe in her arms.

A year later, in 1815, as everyone knows, Napoleon was defeated forever at Waterloo. But the Italian people were no better off than before. The mighty Emperor had handed out several of the Italian states to members of his family and friends to rule, and now these usurpers were firmly entrenched in their little kingdoms. After his downfall the Duchy of Parma was given to his Austrian wife, the ex-Empress Marie Louise, as her domain. So the proud-spirited Italians, who wanted only to be left alone, found themselves still dominated by hated foreigners; and the Austrian government was just as oppressive as the French and far less efficient. The seeds of a fierce patriotism that was eventually to throw off the alien yoke and unite all Italy were already growing.

Meanwhile times were hard, people had little to spend, and for many years Carlo Verdi's business suffered from the general poverty. He had saved only a small sum, and musical instruments were dear. Nevertheless, by inquiring around he located a spinet belonging to an old priest—a miserable affair so ancient and battered that no one wanted it, and the price was therefore low. Carlo bought it, courageously investing his savings in his little son's future. If only the boy had ability as well as the longing to make music he might some day support himself as a musician.

Giuseppe had never seen a spinet. Speechless, breathless, he watched it being unloaded from the cart and brought into the house. Noticing his eagerness Carlo said quickly, "It won't sound very fine, you know, son. It's out of tune and needs repairs. Better wait till Cavaletti comes to fix it."

But Giuseppe could not wait. He pressed one of the chipped and yellowed keys and listened to the sound—thin, weak, rather metallic, but sweet. Enchanted, he pressed another and another and another. The spinet was wonderful, and it was his, his very own! Till long past bedtime he explored the keyboard, struggling to find the music he heard in his mind. But in vain—only a confused and meaningless jangle resulted.

Luigia saw the growing disappointment in the child's eyes and spoke to him gently. "You can't make music right away, Peppino dear. You must let Baistrocchi show you how. He'll start teaching you tomorrow if you like."

Wisely she dragged him off to bed, but not until he had stumbled, quite by accident, upon the chord of C major. It was a lovely sound—a satisfying sound. A shiver of delight went through him, and he could still hear it as he fell asleep.

In the morning he was back at the spinet the very first thing, eager to find that special sound again. But in his excitement he had failed to notice which keys he had struck the night before, and now they all looked alike. He tried something. Oh, no—that wasn't it. He tried again. Still wrong. In a kind of panic he tried again. Worse, much worse! Losing patience, he began to strike at random, pounding up and down till the old spinet shook. The noise was horrible—it hurt him, and the sound he wanted, the lovely sound, was gone. A wave of helpless fury swept over the boy, and as his temper took possession of him tears of rage blurred his sight. Blindly he beat the instrument with his fists, tore at the strings, then seized a hammer and struck again and again.

The din brought Carlo running. He snatched the hammer away, grabbed the frantic child, boxed his ears, and turned him out of the room. Then, with a sinking heart, he inspected the damage. The spinet had been in bad shape before, but now—could he ever pay for the repairs?

Later Cavaletti, the instrument maker, arrived and with sighs and head-shakings set to work. As he unpacked his tools, Giuseppe, much chastened, crept back into the room and watched in fascinated silence, gradually coming closer and closer.

After a while Cavaletti glanced at the child's tense, serious face. "So it's for you, the spinet, eh, boy?"

"Yes, sir."

"Can you play?"

"Not yet, but I'm going to learn."

"You like music?"

"Yes, sir." Giuseppe's eyes glowed.

When the long, difficult job was done Cavaletti rolled off a few chords and nodded, muttering to himself, "Not bad! Not bad!" He was an old-fashioned craftsman in a land where instrument-making was more than a craft—it was a fine art. Was not Cremona, where all the world's greatest violins came from, only a few miles to the north? One took pride in one's work and, like an artist, one signed one's name to it. Cavaletti sat down and wrote a label to be pasted inside the spinet: "I, Stefano Cavaletti, made over these key-hammers and lined them with leather, and I fitted the pedals . . ."

He paused and looked up. Giuseppe had climbed onto the bench before the spinet and was now cautiously repeating the chords that Cavaletti had just played! The child had watched and listened carefully, determined not to lose the delicious sounds this time. Cavaletti twinkled with pleasure. "Good for you!" he exclaimed, and went on writing. ". . . I fitted the pedals which I gave as a present; likewise I repaired the said key-hammers without charge in view of the good disposition the young Giuseppe Verdi shows to learn how to play this instrument, which is sufficient satisfaction for me. Anno Domini 1821."

Then to Carlo Verdi he said: "There will be no charge. It's a joy to work for so enthusiastic a customer. The boy's so eager—he may turn out to have real talent. I shouldn't be at all surprised!"

Thereafter Giuseppe spent hours with old Baistrocchi in the musty organ loft of St. Michael's, or seated at the precious spinet in his attic home. He did not envy the other boys who were out of doors at play or working in the fields. He had found a new world of his own, and he lived deep in dreams that he could as yet but dimly understand.

Of course he learned rapidly, so rapidly that at the end of a year Baistrocchi felt that he could teach him nothing more. The old fellow was growing feeble, and soon Giuseppe even began to take his master's place, from time to time playing the organ for the villagers at Mass.

Every autumn a boy named Giovanni Biazzi came from Parma to spend the vacation in Le Roncole; and while he was there Giuseppe had a companion of his own age. Music was Giovanni's hobby, and though his interest was superficial he always brought with him the newest compositions then in vogue. Giuseppe, who had quickly exhausted the scanty supply of church music available in the village, pored hungrily over the printed sheets. The two boys were forever at the old spinet, ecstatically sharing their enthusiasm for these fashionable novelties from the outside world.

In 1823 Baistrocchi died, and the villagers insisted that Giuseppe, in spite of his youth, be appointed to fill his place as organist. He would have a regular salary of about ten dollars a year and receive almost as much in extra fees for playing at weddings and funerals. Besides, once a year at harvest time he would be allowed to take up a collection for himself.

This new development set Carlo Verdi to thinking. When he had invested his meager savings in the spinet he had hoped that some day his son might earn something through music. And now, only three years later, Giuseppe was the official organist of Le Roncole. Though the boy was not yet ten years old he had already risen as far as he could rise at home. Through his business Carlo knew something of the world beyond his village, and it seemed to him that Giuseppe might surely aspire to a better position when he grew older. Perhaps it would not be too ambitious to try to give him some sort of general education beyond the little reading, writing, and arithmetic to be learned at the parish school. Carlo talked it over with Luigia and—not knowing what to do—they decided to ask the advice of Signor Barezzi in Busseto.

Antonio Barezzi was a well-to-do dealer in groceries and liquors from whom Carlo had bought supplies for many years. Though their stations in life were vastly different the two men had become friends; for Carlo, though poor and almost illiterate, was a good man and much respected for his honesty and intelligence. The kindly, cultivated Barezzi liked the village innkeeper and frequently asked after his promising young son. The boy sometimes came to the warehouse, and Barezzi had watched him shoulder his share of the weekly load and trudge patiently homeward beside his father. So it was natural that Carlo Verdi should tell Barezzi what was on his mind.

Barezzi, who was passionately fond of music and an accomplished amateur, became interested at once. "Of course the child must have an education," he said. "As yet he's too young for anybody to tell whether his musical ability will amount to anything; but he's bright, and should be given a chance to better himself. Send him here to Busseto to school, and we'll see how he develops. He can work at his music in his spare time. I'll keep an eye on him and do anything I can to help him—you can count on that."

So it was arranged that Giuseppe should live and board with a friend of Carlo's, a poor cobbler named Pugnatta, for three and a half cents a day. This tiny sum meant a real sacrifice for the Verdis—and then, too, Luigia would miss him dreadfully; but for Giuseppe's future it was worth it. At any rate he could walk back to Le Roncole on Sundays and holidays in time for Mass. He would not have to give up his newly won position as organist and the all-important salary that went with it.

On a November day in 1823 the precious spinet was loaded onto a borrowed cart, and Giuseppe, putting his arms around his mother's neck, kissed her goodbye. Then the quiet, serious, lonely boy climbed up beside his father and, with his few belongings in a parcel on his lap, set out in search of education.

"Goodbye, my Peppino—goodbye!" Luigia, in the doorway, called and waved as the cart creaked off down the road.

He was just ten, and he was leaving home to make his way alone in the unknown world. It was the first step on the long, hard, bitter, and incredibly glorious path of his destiny.

# CHAPTER TWO

# *Maestrino*

## 1823-1832

CHRISTMAS morning. Before dawn, under a cloud-laden and starless sky, Giuseppe stumbled in blinding darkness along the road to Le Roncole. He was still half-asleep, and hungry, and cold, too, for the Italian winters, too mild to be invigorating, could nevertheless turn bleak and raw, and there was no shelter from the fierce wind that raged across the plain. Numbly he plodded on, thinking of his mother who was always up waiting for him with a good breakfast ready when he came. He would have just time to eat it before playing the organ at the traditional sunrise Mass.

The boy knew the road by heart. Once a week, sometimes twice, all the year round, he had to make the trip from Busseto against the winter wind or under the scorching summer sun. He had not much farther to go—the sharp bend where the road ran beside a big ditch must be just ahead. He was very tired.

Suddenly—splash! He had missed the turn and stepped off the road into the ditch. Deep and wide and nearly full of water, it was almost like a small canal. His feet did not touch bottom, his arms were just too short to reach the top of the bank. Frantically he clawed at the sides, but the earth crumbled away in his cold fingers. He shouted with all his might— though who would be out at such an hour to hear him? Struggling to keep his head above the icy water he called and called until his strength was almost gone.

[ 13 ]

Someone was bending over him. Someone seized his hands and pulled. It was an old woman on her way to Busseto to spend Christmas with relatives. But she was not strong, and Giuseppe was heavy and nearing exhaustion. Tugging mightily, desperately, she managed at last with a great effort to drag him up onto the bank.

"Why, it's the Verdi boy!" she exclaimed. "Of course. Who else could it be out on the road alone at this hour—and on Christmas day? Lucky for you that I came along! The good God must want you to live, son. His angels must be watching over you, else why should they bring me to this spot just at this very moment? No Paradise for you—not yet! You're meant to stay on earth!"

Trying to squeeze the water out of his sodden clothes, she rattled on. "Now then, go along home as fast as you can and get some dry things on you, and some hot food and drink inside you too. Mercy, child, you're all bones! Don't they feed you enough in Busseto? There, run along. Are you all right now?"

Giuseppe was all right, though still breathless and shivering pitifully. He gratefully reassured the old woman and hurried home, where Luigia soon warmed and revived him. Thanks to her care and his strong constitution he suffered no ill effects from his accident.

Though he was hardy enough, and tall, Giuseppe did not have the broad chest and strong muscles of other peasant boys, and no wonder. During those first years in Busseto he worked constantly, seeming more like a grown man than a child. Besides holding his job as organist—by the time he was twelve his father had got him a tiny raise in salary—he studied his books steadily and well, and pounded his poor spinet whenever he had the chance—sometimes even far into the night. Often he was half-starved. Pugnatta, the cobbler, could seldom afford to fill the pots as full as they might have been, and many times Giuseppe had to take a penny from his pay and slip round the corner to a fruit-seller's for a bag of hot roasted chestnuts. That helped—a little.

If Giuseppe's growing body went hungry there was nevertheless rich food in Busseto for his growing mind. Though the place was typical of northern Italy, perhaps nowhere else in the world could one find a town of the same size so culture-conscious and civil-minded. Its two thousand citizens were proud of their history which they traced back through the great days of the Renaissance to the Middle Ages, and even to ancient Roman times. They were proud of their University, their Library crammed with precious antique volumes, their Monte di Pietà, an ancient charitable and cultural institution. They were proud, too, of the many frescoed churches, and the fine Renaissance buildings with rows of graceful arches offering shade from the bright sun. Above all, they were proud of their music.

In Italy music is not a pastime, a luxury—it is a necessity of life. Busseto, like every other town, had a municipal brass band that played rousing military marches, overtures, and arias weekly in the public square. Everyone turned out to hear them, and on special occasions the concerts were followed by displays of fireworks. Of course there was a great deal of

[15]

church music too, and the town also boasted an amateur orchestra which went by the imposing name of Philharmonic Society. This orchestra rehearsed and gave its concerts at Signor Barezzi's house in a large room known as the Academic Hall. Signor Barezzi himself could play any of the wind instruments, the flute exceptionally well, and besides was the guiding spirit in all the town's musical activities. Provincial and amateurish though these must have been, the Bussetans made up in enthusiasm what they lacked in skill.

Music-hungry Giuseppe was of course soon in the thick of everything, even attending the Philharmonic rehearsals at Barezzi's house. It was heaven for the boy to find himself surrounded by ardent music-lovers, scores, instruments, and orchestral shop talk. Barezzi taught him something of the woodwinds, and let him try the fine Viennese piano—so much richer and more satisfying than the wretched, overworked spinet. Seeing Giuseppe's pleasure the good man said kindly, "Come and play it any time you like, my boy. It's yours to use whenever you want to."

The Philharmonic was under the direction of Ferdinando Provesi, organist of the cathedral, head of the music school, and composer of a number of church works and comic operas that had been locally successful. A man of culture and understanding, something of a poet, and a profound student of music, he might have made quite a name for himself. But the government restrictions imposed on all art in Milan, where he had gone in search of a career, were too much for his independent spirit, and he had returned to his native province, preferring little Busseto and freedom. Now he was growing old; and in the gifted, serious boy from Le Roncole of whom Barezzi spoke so highly he felt that he had perhaps found a disciple to whom he could pass on all that he knew. He offered to give the young Verdi lessons in theory, counterpoint, harmony, instrumentation—in short a thorough grounding in his art.

Giuseppe went to work with a will, absorbing eagerly and quickly all that Provesi taught him, and making himself useful besides by copying parts, accompanying, playing the big drum at band concerts, taking a share in anything and everything that had to do with music. He even taught a blind violinist of the orchestra his parts, by playing them patiently over to him phrase by phrase until the poor fellow had them memorized. Everyone liked and admired the Verdi boy, and in this friendly, stimulating atmosphere he became more talkative, livelier, less withdrawn into himself. At the Palazzo Barezzi (in Italy every big house is a "palace") he came to be treated like a member of the family. Barezzi's children adored him— there were four girls and a boy when he came to Busseto, and another boy was born while he was there. Of them all he liked Margherita the best. She was the eldest, only seven months younger than he, and she studied singing and piano with Provesi. Ghitta, as they called her, was a bright, attractive girl with blue eyes and a mass of golden hair. Giuseppe helped her with her music and played duets with her whenever he could. In her company he seemed to feel no shyness.

Canon Seletti, who taught Giuseppe Latin, realized that the boy had an exceptionally good mind and pushed him rapidly forward in his studies. But Giuseppe gradually took to giving more and more time to music and less to his general education. Seletti and Provesi had had a quarrel and had cordially disliked each other and gone out of their way to annoy each other ever since. Seletti grew jealous of Provesi's influence over the promising young Verdi. One day, when Giuseppe was fourteen, he sent for him.

"Listen to me, my son," he said. "I have some advice to give you. You're a good student and I've been much pleased with your work. I'd like to see you go on to the University, and even to Parma. You should enter the Church—become a priest, a scholar, a teacher, perhaps even head of a school, like myself. That's a fine career for a country boy to aspire to, and you can do it, you have the ability. But lately I see you wasting too much time over music. There's no benefit in that, Giuseppe. By trying to serve two masters you'll only spoil your chances. I know that everyone seems to think you're gifted, but what do people really know about music in a little town like this? Nothing at all! Give it up, my boy, and put your mind on your studies. Otherwise I shall have to consider expelling you from the school!''

Surely Seletti's threat could not have been serious—he was only trying to win the boy away from Provesi. But Giuseppe was stunned. Give up music? It was unthinkable! On the other hand he must not let himself be expelled. His father and mother, who had made sacrifices for his sake, could never bear the disgrace. Even now his parents needed his help, and he knew that in time he would be their sole support. Reluctantly he began to pay more attention to Latin and less to music.

Soon it was Provesi's turn to call him to account. "Giuseppe, what has come over you lately?" he asked. "You're not making as rapid progress as you did, and as I know you can. I have great hopes for you, my boy, but recently I've been disappointed. What's the matter? Are you losing interest in music?"

Giuseppe, who had kept his troubles to himself, now told his master the whole story.

"So that's it!" Provesi exclaimed. "So Don Seletti presumes to suppose that I don't know a musician when I see one, in spite of my years of experience! You have much to learn, but you have a great gift, and may go far. Believe me, my son, I know whereof I speak. If Don Seletti threatens to wash his hands of you, never mind—I'll gladly take charge of your education. I'm an old man now, and not strong. In a few years, if you work hard, it may be that you'll take my place here in Busseto. That would be a fine career for you, Giuseppe, far better than becoming a priest or a teacher of Latin!"

Giuseppe agreed with all his heart. Aside from his love of music he did not want to be a priest; he was too independent of spirit to endure the rigid discipline of the Church. But he dare not risk Seletti's anger. And so, while his two masters fought over him and insulted each other whenever they got the chance, he tried to please them both by working so hard that neither had cause to complain. Under such a heavy burden it was no wonder that he enjoyed none of the high spirits and carefree good times that most young people his age take for granted.

But fate soon stepped in. One day, as Canon Seletti was about to celebrate Mass in the chapel of his school, word was brought to him that the regular organist—a highly incompetent fellow—was ill. Seletti told Giuseppe to take his place. It would be a good joke on the boy—let him find out that to play without warning for a cultured Bussetan congregation was quite different from satisfying the ignorant farmers of Le Roncole in their poor, bare church with its miserable organ. It would teach him a lesson to make a bit of a fool of himself— perhaps cure him of his silly notions.

But at the altar Seletti listened in amazement. Being a man of culture, an Italian, and a Bussetan at that, he knew a good deal about music, and the beauty and power of what he heard astonished him. The congregation, too, listened enthralled. There was no doubt about it—a mysterious something in the young Verdi's playing stirred people and held them spellbound.

When Mass was over, Seletti met the boy at the foot of the organ-loft stairs. "Well done, Giuseppe!" he said with feeling. "Tell me, what was the music you played? I never heard it before. It's a most beautiful thing. Who wrote it?"

"That?" Giuseppe lowered his eyes. "It was nothing. I played just as I felt, making it up as I went along."

Seletti was a good and generous man. "Giuseppe," he said kindly, putting his hands on the boy's shoulders, "I'm an old fool. You have a great gift. Go study music to your heart's content. Make it your life's work, son, and God be with you!"

Giuseppe was free! He did not neglect his general education; on the contrary he spent hour after hour in Busseto's fine old library reading history, which fascinated him, the great classics of literature, and, above all, the Bible. But he now devoted himself with fresh enthusiasm to his studies with Provesi and was soon composing marches for the town band, little overtures, all sorts of instrumental pieces, choir music, and piano duets to play with Margherita. These compositions were quite ordinary, but the Bussetans, because they admired him and took pride in everything he did, thought them marvelous. In Italy a musician, because of the respect in which all musicians are held, still retains his title of *Maestro* (Master) from the days of the medieval Guilds, and young Verdi came to be affectionately known as "our *Maestrino*" (little Master). His services were soon in demand all about the countryside.

One beautiful summer day Giuseppe sang in the choir at High Mass at the Little Madonna of the Meadows, a lovely church near Busseto set quite apart in a field of wild flowers. Afterward he went to the house of a friend who lived near by for his midday meal, and lingered there until he realized suddenly that the time had flown—he would be late to Vespers. The sky had clouded over. Hurrying back to the church he was aware of the ominous hush that comes before a summer storm, and as he reached the door the first drops fell. Since the afternoon service had already begun, Giuseppe, instead of climbing to the singers' gallery where he belonged, stayed down among the congregation. Soon the storm broke right above their heads. The wind howled and the thunder rolled—there was a blinding flash, a stunning noise, and the whole church seemed to shudder. Then all was quiet. But three of the singers in the gallery where Giuseppe should have sat had been killed by lightning, and of the three priests at the altar two lay dead! Giuseppe saw with horror that one of the victims was the man at whom, eight years before on the altar steps at home, he had screamed in fury: "God strike you down!"

When this event occurred Giuseppe was fifteen, and Provesi by then considered him a "finished master" and his own equal. The aging teacher depended on the pupil to help give lessons and even to conduct the orchestra at concerts. The Maestrino's compositions became increasingly numerous and ambitious, and in 1828 he had his first triumph as a composer, at a performance of Rossini's *Barber of Seville*.

Opera in Italy, where it was born, is of all forms of music the best loved. In the big cities, world-famous opera houses were centers of artistic life, and innumerable traveling companies brought the new works and the old favorites even to the smallest towns, where their performances stirred up a frenzy of popular excitement. The audience lived the stories in their imaginations and quickly knew words and music by heart. This was true of the illiterate as well as of the educated classes, since in Italy, land of the world's greatest voices, everybody sings. The young girl drawing water at the well, the shepherd in the fields, the peddler on his rounds, the city tradesman, even the children in the streets—all sing opera. It is a part of every life, grand or humble.

The performance of the beloved *Barber of Seville* was a gala occasion, and the proud Bussetans insisted that their Philharmonic should have a share in it. Giuseppe—already interested in writing for voice on an intensely dramatic subject—composed a work for solo baritone and orchestra, copied the parts, and rehearsed the men in secret so as to surprise everyone, even old Provesi and Barezzi. The piece, a musical setting of Alfieri's poem, *The Madness of Saul*, was presented in the theater on the same evening as the opera, and evoked a clamor of applause such as Busseto had never heard. Immediately the new work was in demand at all the neighboring towns. The good Bussetans raved about it, declaring that it stood up well even beside the great Rossini's masterpiece.

They were thoroughly mistaken. Verdi was no early genius like Mozart or Mendelssohn who, educated for music from the cradle, turned out works of enduring beauty in their 'teens. There was nothing remarkable about his youthful compositions, but the loyal Bussetans were too provincial, too far removed from the world's great musical centers to have real critical judgment. Besides, they were blinded by affection for their Maestrino. Like his teachers, they felt his undeveloped power, and in their possessive local pride they swore that his equal had never been known.

At Soragna, a sizable town near by, the post of organist became vacant, and Giuseppe, aged sixteen, immediately applied for it. The salary looked big to him. Added to what he earned at Le Roncole it would really help his parents in their long struggle against poverty. His local reputation and the recommendations of Provesi and Barezzi were in his favor. Full of hope, he wrote asking to be given a trial. But the authorities in whose hands the appointment lay had their own favorite, a much older man who was musically inferior. Verdi was turned down, thereby learning that success does not depend on ability alone. It was a bitter lesson, since he did not realize that fate had something better in store for him than a career as a church organist.

As time went on, his master, and Barezzi—who advised him in everything—became convinced that Busseto was too small, too limited for his talents. "You were born for greater things," Barezzi told him. "Go to the Conservatory at Parma or, better still, go to Milan. There are no finer professors in all Italy than at the Conservatory there, and you'll have the added advantage of being able to study opera—the best in the world!"

Giuseppe was eager, but his father hesitated. To him it seemed that his son was already learned enough. Let him come back to Le Roncole and help his family—he would surely find something better to do than selling groceries or toiling in the fields. Besides, Carlo could never support him while he studied, either in Parma or in Milan.

But Barezzi soon persuaded the good innkeeper. "With the right training this boy of yours has it in him to make his mark in the world. Maestro Provesi himself says he'll go far. And as for supporting him—you won't have to. Let him apply to the Monte di Pietà for a scholarship. He's sure to get it."

Busseto's benevolent institution, The Monte di Pietà, had at its disposal a fund for furthering the education of a limited number of poor but promising young people. This fund had come into being during the seventeenth century, when an epidemic of cholera that swept through the town had killed, among others, many children. The bereaved parents then set aside the money they had hoped to use for their own dead children to help children who had lost their parents, or were otherwise in need. This public-spirited action was typical of proud little Busseto.

As Giuseppe had the influence of Provesi and Barezzi to back him, there seemed no doubt that his application to the Monte di Pietà would eventually be granted. But, since no scholarship was immediately available, lengthy negotiations were involved. In the meantime he continued to work as before, going more and more often to the Barezzis' hospitable house.

One night in May 1831 a horrible crime shook the virtuous little town and filled its law-abiding citizens with terror. A few doors from the Palazzo Barezzi lived one Isaac Levi, who, having recently sold a piece of property, was thought to have a considerable sum of money on hand. Through the help of one of his servants, a gang of robbers entered his home in the small hours, brutally murdered the old man and beat his little niece, his invalid wife miraculously escaping to safety. Then the criminals got away by a back door, while accomplices in the street shouted and banged with sticks on an iron railing to create a distraction.

Mamà Barezzi, roused from her sleep by the uproar, was terrified, nor did her fears subside the next day.

"Tonino, I'm frightened," she told her husband. "Suppose this gang should break in and attack *us* some night when we're all asleep? And then I don't like to think of Giuseppe going back to Pugnatta's at all hours, alone in those dark, narrow streets. He might be set upon. Why not let him live here? It would be a protection. He's always up so late studying his books or his music—he'd be sure to hear any disturbance and warn us. Anyhow, he's here all day as it is; so why not the night too?"

Giuseppe thus became a member of the Barezzi household, and he was happier than he had ever been before. For the first time he tasted comfort and plenty, in an atmosphere where the strain of poverty was unknown. He was surrounded by culture and refinement, worshipped by Barezzi's lively children, and treated like a favorite son. It was a great step up in the world, but in spite of it he remained loyal to his own parents, whom he loved, and proud of his peasant origin.

Soon he had a special reason for even greater happiness— special and secret. But by autumn Mamà Barezzi's sharp eyes had discovered it, and, a little anxiously, she spoke to her husband.

[ 23 ]

"Tonino, have you noticed anything about Giuseppe lately?"

"Why, no. What do you mean?"

"About him and our Ghitta. They're in love!"

"But they're only children! Maria, my dear, what makes you think so?"

"Tonino, I *know*. The piano duets have been getting longer and longer, and they go for endless walks—as if the boy didn't have enough of that with the trip to Le Roncole every week! Anyhow, you have only to look at them. I've even spoken to Margherita about it, and she admits it."

"Maria, the boy hasn't a cent in the world, but you know how I feel about him—there's no one to whom I'd rather give my daughter. He's honest, good, serious, strong-willed. He has self-confidence without conceit. I love him already like my own son. And he has genius—rare genius. One of these days he'll be a glory to Busseto, and I feel that to be able to help such a young man, to have a part in his destiny, somehow makes my life complete."

"I'm so glad you're not angry, Tonino. I was afraid you might be."

"You should have known me better than that, Maria. But the children are just eighteen—perhaps this is only a passing fancy. They may forget each other if they're no longer together. We must make sure—Giuseppe must go away. Unfortunately there will be no scholarship available for him until 1833. I'll tell you what I'll do, Maria. If the Monte di Pietà will agree to grant him a scholarship *then*, I'll advance him the money so that he can go to Milan at once. He's only wasting time here in Busseto, he can learn nothing more from us, and it will be a good way to put this young love to the test."

Thereupon the negotiations with the authorities began all over again, and it was finally arranged that Signor Barezzi should support the young Verdi in Milan for one year. After that the boy was to receive the scholarship on condition that he should obtain from the Conservatory a certificate of "good conduct, ability, mastery, extraordinary genius, and such progress as to leave no doubt of his fulfilling the greatest hopes."

It was a heavy responsibility for an unknown village youth. But Giuseppe was determined to justify good Papà Barezzi's belief in him. And now that he knew his loving, trusting, golden-haired Margherita was waiting for him, his ambition soared.

CHAPTER THREE

# *The Battle of Busseto*

1832-1836

EXCEPT in rare cases of extraordinary talent, the Milan Conservatory admitted pupils between the ages of nine and fourteen only. Verdi was eighteen, an age at which in his day most professional musicians had already begun to make their mark; and as yet he was completely unknown. Nor was this his only handicap. The school was crowded, only a few students could be admitted every year, and preference was given to the native Milanese. Even this candidate from the neighboring Duchy of Parma was considered a foreigner, and would therefore have to overcome a certain prejudice. His letters of recommendation, to be sure, spoke enthusiastically of both his talents and his character, but who, after all, was Provesi? A gifted man who had chosen years ago to bury himself in the provinces—a back number!

Moreover, Provesi had never been notable as a pianist, so that at the piano young Verdi was self-taught. Knowing nothing of the rival systems in vogue in the great music schools, he had had to find his own way; but since no one in Busseto could compare with him, since he had never even heard his own equal, he considered himself a good pianist. To enter the Conservatory he would have to be very good indeed. In its teaching, the playing of an instrument was all-important, and its graduates more often became virtuosi than composers. Composition might also be studied, of course, but it took

[ 26 ]

second place. Mastery of the piano, the violin, the 'cello, or whatever, must come first.

On June 22, 1832, Verdi, carrying a bundle of his best compositions, neatly copied, went to the Conservatory to be examined for admission. The formal, spacious, ornate building was far grander than anything in Busseto, as was to be expected in a vast city where music was the most honored of all professions. Its atmosphere was awe-inspiring. In its halls, crowds of students eyed the somber stranger inquisitively and whispered "Who's that?" He looked, and felt, self-conscious, ill-at-ease.

He was directed to an austere room in which four elderly gentlemen, seated on high-backed chairs behind a heavily carved table, faced him in dignity. They were Maestro Basily, head of the Conservatory; Maestro Piantanida, Professor of Counterpoint; Maestro Angeleri, Professor of Piano; and, as Verdi's sponsor, Maestro Rolla, Professor of Violin and Viola. Rolla had been a fellow-student of Provesi's at Parma, and in spite of failing health Provesi had made the tiring trip by stage-coach from Busseto to introduce his beloved pupil to his old friend. "The boy's a genius—take good care of him for me!" Provesi had begged; and with Rolla's assurance that he would do what he could the old man had returned home full of confidence.

The professors were courtly in manner and elegant in dress. Their double-breasted coats had velvet collars, their shirts were delicately starched and ruffled, and they carried gold-headed canes. As their four pairs of eyes turned on him searchingly, Verdi stiffened with nervousness.

The four pairs of eyes beheld a tall, lean, unsmiling youth with a quantity of chestnut hair and, as was then the custom, a short beard. In his pale, expressionless face, his deep-set eyes shone with peculiar intensity. His clothes were coarse and ill-fitting, his manner awkward and hesitant. Did this young man have it in him to bring glory to the Conservatory? It seemed unlikely. Basily did not care for his appearance. In those days a musician was expected to look and act like a musician; he must show feeling, temperament, a fiery, vivid

personality. But this frozen-faced youngster seemed to have no feeling whatsoever. Without a word the Maestro motioned him to the piano.

Verdi had chosen to play a technically difficult *Capriccio* by Herz, a composer highly esteemed at the time. It was a dull work at best, and he went through it correctly, meticulously, but with an empty dryness. The professors, alert for any weakness, leaned forward listening intently. And watching, too, especially Maestro Angeleri, who had developed and published a piano method of his own. According to his theory, the position of Verdi's hands was wrong—a fault that at eighteen could no longer be corrected.

The *Capriccio* ended. The professors made no comment. Verdi rose and diffidently put the music he had brought on the table in front of Basily. "My compositions," he said.

"Ah, yes, thank you. We shall give them our careful consideration. Good afternoon." The four masters bowed. Verdi bowed, and clumsily took his departure.

There followed a conference during which his music passed from hand to hand. The work was crude, but it showed imagination, originality. The professors agreed that with a few years' serious study the young man might well achieve some success as a composer. But as for admitting him to the Conservatory—it was his performance at the piano that counted.

Back in his little room, Verdi felt anxious and depressed for the first time since he had come to Milan three weeks before. The journey had been a great event—it was not often that a peasant came to the city to study. Even Carlo had proudly traveled the sixty miles with his promising son and stayed to see him comfortably settled at the house of Professor Seletti, nephew of Giuseppe's former Latin teacher. After the tranquil fields of Le Roncole, and Busseto with its small, local interests, young Verdi had found big, busy, noisy, flourishing Milan an exciting place. He seemed suddenly to become part of the great world, his ideas expanded, and he looked forward to his work with the keenest impatience. Margherita, good Papà Barezzi, his parents, Maestro Provesi, all took his success for granted. He was responsible to them and to the Monte di Pietà. He knew himself to be capable of big things, great things. That he should fail now was unthinkable.

In his eagerness he expected to learn the result of his examination at once; but the days dragged on, and no word came from the Conservatory. A week went by, a grim, endless week during which he kept his growing anxiety to himself. At last, unable to bear it longer, he gathered his courage and called on Professor Rolla.

"Maestro," he said, "I've heard nothing from the Conservatory. I don't know what to do."

Rolla was aware that eventually, when the formalities had all been attended to, Signor Barezzi would be officially notified of the result of Verdi's examination. Meantime the boy was in suspense, and Rolla guessed that his pale face hid a spirit both sensitive and proud. "My young friend," said the Maestro gently, "if I were you I would forget all about the Conservatory."

The blow had fallen—Verdi had been rejected! His future seemed to come tumbling down in ruins. What was to become of him? One thing only was certain: all hope of a career as a concert pianist was now shattered forever.

"But there's no reason to be discouraged," went on Rolla

[ 29 ]

quickly. "In your application you said that you desired 'to perfect yourself in the art of music.' There are many ways of doing that. Why don't you study privately? We have excellent teachers here, and with the right man you might learn more than you could in any other way. In your place I should try Negri, or Lavigna."

Verdi thanked Maestro Rolla and left. Knowing himself to be worthy of the Conservatory, his failure hurt him deeply and was to leave a lasting scar. But his Ghitta and her father believed in him. Silently he crushed his disappointment, and lost no time in asking Professor Seletti's advice.

"Maestro Negri is organist at the Cathedral," Seletti told him, "and he's written some fine church works himself. If your interest lies in ecclesiastical music you couldn't have a better teacher. But if you're more drawn to secular music— opera, for instance—then Lavigna's your man. He's a sound musician, and his own operas were quite successful at one time. Besides, he was for many years conductor at La Scala."

La Scala! Milan's great opera house—one of the most famous in the world! Verdi chose Lavigna.

Then began months, years, of the most arduous and intensive study imaginable. Day and night, shut in his little room, the young man labored at harmony and counterpoint, struggling to master the intricate laws by which sounds are made into music. He analyzed the works of the old Italians: Palestrina, Marcello, and Lavigna's favorite, the more recent Paisiello. He composed, not what he felt like, but set exercises of the most difficult and complicated kind. As fast as it was finished he took his work to his teacher for correction, and came back with a new and more advanced assignment. Sometimes it seemed to him that his whole waking life consisted of nothing but "fugues and canons, canons and fugues." It was grueling, yet it taught him, as he himself said later, to "bend the notes to his will."

Conscious of his debt to Barezzi, longing to hasten the day of his independence' so that he might marry his Ghitta, he permitted himself not even a single holiday. At La Scala during the season he attended opera as part of his training;

but he had neither time nor money for the usual amusements of a large city, and he made no friends. Lavigna, however, took a fancy to his gruff, lonely pupil and often kept him chatting long after the lesson was over, sometimes till late at night. Time and again the Maestro would take out the score of *Don Giovanni*, saying, "Let's go over this passage once more," and together they would pick Mozart's great masterpiece apart, to find the structure of the music beneath its life and glow and sparkle.

To satisfy his own curiosity Verdi explored the works of the German composers, even copying out quartets that he liked by Haydn, Mozart, Beethoven, and Mendelssohn. When he had time he also composed just to please himself. Once he showed Lavigna a symphony that he had written, only to have his master alter it with the remark, "Paisiello would have done it this way." Verdi, however, was not Paisiello, and did not want to be. He said nothing, but thereafter he kept his spontaneous compositions to himself. Once he had mastered his tools, he intended to use them in his own way.

At the beginning of Verdi's second year in Milan, old Provesi, who had prayed during a long illness that he might live to see his dear pupil succeed him, died. Verdi, though saddened by the loss of the teacher and friend who had done so much for him, did not attend the funeral. He had no money for the journey, nor could he spare the time. In spite of his grief he stuck to his "fugues and canons" even when, a month later, death also took his beautiful, pitiful, and much-loved sister.

What with Provesi's illness and Verdi's absence, Busseto's musical activities had deteriorated from lack of direction. Now the members of its ardent little orchestra suggested to the Rector of the Cathedral, a man named Ballarini, that he install some pupil of Provesi's as temporary organist until Verdi's studies in Milan should be completed. But Ballarini had never got on well with Provesi, and his resentment turned against "this Verdi," as he called him. Without consulting anyone he appointed a total stranger who played so badly that the critical Bussetans were outraged. The Philharmonic held an indignation meeting. "This fellow's hopeless!" they declared. "We'll fix him!" And marching furiously into the Cathedral they carried off all the scores! Since these scores had belonged to Provesi himself, and after his death had been bought by one of their members, the Philharmonic could not be forced to return them. Thereafter Mass had to be celebrated without music, and the unfortunate would-be organist vanished from Busseto in disgrace.

The men of the orchestra considered this prank a glorious victory, but it was only the opening skirmish in a long and complicated battle. The town talked of nothing else; and while Verdi, far away from the uproar, concentrated on his work, other candidates for the position arrived in Busseto. Among them was a mediocre musician named Ferrari, backed by two powerful bishops who knew him to be a worthy man but did not appreciate the musical aspect of the situation. Ballarini, impressed by the recommendation of these high dignitaries, of course gave the incompetent Ferrari his support, warning him, however, that before the matter could be settled Barezzi and his Philharmonic would have to be won over. Ferrari duly handed in a formal application, but, having a wife and six children to support, he took temporary work elsewhere while awaiting a decision.

Provesi had really held two positions—that of organist and master of music at the Cathedral of St. Bartholomew, appointed and paid by the Parish, and that of music teacher for the town and director of the Philharmonic, appointed and paid by the Monte di Pietà. For generations these duties had been fulfilled by one man, for whom the two salaries combined to make a comfortable living. It was therefore necessary that the Parish, the Monte di Pietà, and the Philharmonic should agree as to the appointment. Ballarini's followers, though few in number, had the power and influence of the Church behind them. The Philharmonic—young, reckless, and music-mad—counted among their supporters most of the townspeople. Friction between the two groups was of long standing, and now, over Verdi, flared into open war.

The Philharmonic wanted the question settled, as Verdi

himself would wish, not by intrigue, but on merit. They insisted that the candidates must compete for the position, and both the Monte di Pietà and the Parish agreed that a contest should be held. But Ballarini, knowing as well as everybody else that Verdi would be sure to win, secretly objected. He sent a friend of his to call on Signor Barezzi.

"Young Verdi forwarded his application to you, to be submitted whenever you felt that the right moment had come, didn't he?" said Ballarini's friend. "If I were you I should withhold it for the present. Wait until the contest is officially announced—that will make a much better impression!" This was wicked, treacherous advice, but honest Barezzi took it in good faith and acted accordingly.

What of the certificate from the Milan Conservatory that Verdi was supposed to procure for the Monte di Pietà? Instead, he hastened to send a glowing report from Lavigna, who declared that in another year his pupil would be a full-fledged master composer. A few months later, in February, came another enthusiastic statement from Lavigna, for Verdi, aware of danger at home, had increased the tempo of his work and was making remarkably rapid progress. The Verdians hailed these reports with the wildest joy. The Ferrarians, on the other hand, began to feel seriously worried. Hostility between the rival factions deepened. Hitherto tranquil and well-behaved Bussetans eyed one another with growing hatred. Little groups whispered together in the cafés and even shouted insults at each other in the streets.

Suddenly, in April 1834, fortune smiled on Verdi, and the turmoil in Busseto, of which Barezzi kept him constantly informed, faded for a while into the background of his life. There was in Milan a musical organization of fashionable, aristocratic amateurs who called themselves the Philodramatic Society and gave concerts and operas in their own theater. They were preparing a performance of Haydn's oratorio, *The Creation*, and at Lavigna's suggestion Verdi, who did not know the music, dropped in at a rehearsal hoping to learn thereby. Since the members of the Society were amateurs and therefore busy with other things besides music, it was necessary to have,

[ 33 ]

not one, but three director-accompanists who took charge of rehearsals in turn. By a curious twist of fate, on this particular evening not one of the three showed up. The chorus stood ready on the stage, the members of the small orchestra had taken their places, but there was no one at the most important post of all—the piano. It would not do to call the rehearsal off, for time was short and practice essential. Massini, head of the Society, was not enough of a musician to act as a substitute himself. At his wits' end, he suddenly caught sight of Lavigna's pupil sitting quietly at the back of the hall. Perhaps he could help them out—at least it would be better than nothing!

Verdi shyly agreed, and Massini, as he handed him the music, said reassuringly, "Don't worry—it'll be all right if you just fill in the bass."

Verdi glanced at him quickly and suppressed a smile. Did Massini really suppose that he couldn't even read a score? But as he took his place at the piano he was conscious of whispering, raised eyebrows, and concealed amusement among the chorus and orchestra. And no wonder. In that elegant, worldly, self-assured gathering, the gaunt youth in his cheap, clumsy suit looked like a scarecrow. Only manners kept these fashionable people from tittering openly.

The rehearsal began. At first Verdi tried modestly to follow rather than to lead; but it was dreadful—half the meaning, the beauty, of the music seemed to be thrown away. He could not bear it, and, deeply absorbed, he began unconsciously to take control, playing with his left hand alone while with his right he conducted. He knew exactly what he wanted, and the performers, their mirth forgotten, responded to his authority eagerly. Soon the chorus was singing as it had never sung before. *The Creation* itself seemed to become a different work—grander and more inspiring.

When it was over, there was deafening applause. With cries of "Bravo! Bravo!" everyone crowded round the queer young stranger to shake his hand and clap him on the shoulder. "Of course, Maestro, you'll take charge of our concert?" they clamored. Massini, beaming with pleasure and relief, exclaimed, "But of course—you *must!*"

So Verdi made his first public appearance in Milan, with such overwhelming success that two extra performances of *The Creation* had to be given by request: one for an Italian Archduke and all the nobility of the land, the other for the Austrian Viceroy and his court. More important, Verdi found a good friend in Massini, who invited him to conduct a number of operas for the Society. Of course he received no pay, but he was winning the respect and admiration of influential people, he was making himself known and establishing a musical reputation. A prominent Count even asked him to compose a wedding cantata; Verdi obliged, but without enthusiasm. He was musically, not socially, ambitious and now, and throughout his life, he disliked writing to order unless he found the subject inspiring.

By June, when Verdi had begun to feel that here in Milan he had a toe-hold on the ladder of success, a distressing letter from Barezzi reminded him of Busseto and its troubles. Although there had been no news of the proposed contest, Ferrari had suddenly reappeared in town! An ugly rumor had it that the Rector, alarmed by reports of Verdi's progress, had sent for Ferrari and was planning somehow to steal a march on the Verdians. There was danger in the air, Barezzi said, and Giuseppe should come home at once. Reluctantly, Lavigna agreed that the studies would not suffer from interruption at this point.

It was hard to leave Milan just when the door of opportunity seemed to be opening, but Verdi was in duty bound to Papà Barezzi, to the loyal Philharmonic, and to the Monte di Pietà. Besides, there was Margherita—he had not seen her for two whole years! He found on his return that she meant more to him than ever. They had parted as boy and girl—now they were man and woman, and time had only strengthened their love.

But the joy of Verdi's home-coming, of his reunion with family and friends, was marred by a staggering development. On that very same day, June 18, 1834, Ballarini, thrown into a panic by the arrival of his enemy, officially appointed Ferrari organist of the Cathedral! There had been no contest, no examination, no trial of any kind.

And now the Rector's crafty double-dealing became apparent. To the stunned Barezzi he said, "Too bad young Verdi never applied for the position. If he had, I'm sure he would have been favorably considered." It was an insult, an outrage. "Treachery!" howled the Philharmonic, while the Monte di Pietà flatly refused to pay its share of Ferrari's salary unless he first submitted to an examination, which of course he dared not do.

The fury of the Verdians knew no bounds. As soon as Ferrari took up his duties as organist, the congregation abandoned the Cathedral in protest, while outside in the public square a cheering crowd thronged to hear the Philharmonic conducted by Verdi. Even the neighboring towns became involved in the dispute. They invited the Philharmonic to give performances, sending horse-drawn omnibuses to transport the musicians and their instruments. But though Verdi made a triumphal tour of all the surrounding countryside, he was still unpaid and penniless, forced to depend on Papà Barezzi's generous hospitality. Meantime the miserable Ferrari, struggling on his half salary, sought to establish himself by offering to take pupils free of charge. In vain—no one went near him. The situation was deadlocked, and from both parties a stream of frantic appeals and protests sped to the Government in Parma.

But the Government acted slowly, as governments usually do; and, while it dallied and deliberated, the Battle of Busseto grew more intense. Neighbors who had been friendly no longer spoke to each other. There were angry parades and demonstrations. Street-corner arguments led to brawls. Any casual remark—that Verdi had not yet finished his studies, for instance—was likely to start a riot. People insulted and threatened each other, the threats grew into fist fights, and lawsuits for damages followed. Time and again the police had to be called out, and the Mayor, weary of being roused in the middle of the night to restore order, scolded the townspeople like naughty children. It was no use—this was Italy, where music is a vital matter. One would have thought a kingdom was at stake.

So the summer passed, and the autumn. At last, in December, word came that the Government had reached a decision: Ferrari's appointment as organist must be considered legal and binding, but the post of music teacher and director of the Philharmonic would be awarded to the winner of a contest to be held at a later date. This was at least a partial victory, and Busseto's streets echoed to the rejoicing of the Verdians.

Now Verdi could safely return to Lavigna. Though he had with dignity kept aloof from all the frenzied uproar, it had distressed him. He was too big for Busseto and its petty squabbles, and he knew it. With relief he turned toward Milan. If only he could have taken Margherita with him . . .

Being back in the city was refreshing, stimulating. Through his friend Massini, Verdi now began to take part in the artistic life that centered at La Scala. The palatial opera house, second largest in Italy, dominated one of the city's squares, to which it had attracted all business that had to do with music. Here the most important publishers had their offices, here were the instrument-makers and the music stores. Two cafés opposite La Scala were famous as the favorite haunts of composers, conductors, singers, poets, scene designers—artists and writers of all sorts plus their friends and hangers-on. The atmosphere was thoroughly professional, and endlessly, all day and all night, the fascinating shoptalk of opera was to be heard. To Verdi this was a new world, but in spite of his retiring nature he knew that he belonged to it. He was instinctively, as he later remarked, "a man of the theater."

He now spent more time than ever at his master's house. One day Maestro Basily dropped in to see his friend Lavigna; and Verdi, who was present, had a chance to take a small revenge on the man who had rejected him nearly three years before.

Basily was depressed. "Times are changing!" he sighed. "I begin to wonder what will become of the beautiful art of music. Lately I had to examine twenty-eight candidates for the position of organist at Monza. I gave them a subject on which to write a four-part fugue—certainly nothing could be more fundamental than the ability to write a respectable fugue—but would you believe it, Maestro? Not one of these so-called musicians could do it even correctly, let alone well!"

Lavigna smiled. "Verdi could do it," he said.

"Verdi? You don't mean it!"

"You remember the subject?"

"Yes, certainly."

"Good. Jot it down, and we'll see."

Basily wrote out a few measures. "Here," said Lavigna, handing the music to Verdi. "Sit down at the table there and see what you can do with this."

Quietly Verdi went to work, while for a long time the two Maestri talked on and on, forgetting all about him. Finally, as Basily was about to leave, Verdi rose. "It's finished," he said.

Basily took the fugue and looked it over. "Why, this is excellent!" he exclaimed. "Extraordinary! Frankly, I'm amazed. But tell me, why did you double the subject? You only made your task that much more difficult."

Verdi shrugged. "It struck me as a little thin—I wanted to embellish it," he said. He was showing off, and, quite humanly, he enjoyed it. The position at Monza might have been his, but, being bound to Busseto, he could not apply for it.

At the end of six months Verdi left Milan with a written statement from Lavigna—the equivalent of a modern diploma —declaring him an accredited master composer. Lavigna had grown fond of him and was sorry to see him go. This young man, he felt, was destined for greatness. But in art the first steps are hard. Like many another before him, Verdi would have to make a start in the limited sphere of a small town. Eventually, Lavigna was confident, his genius would find wider opportunities.

Back in Busseto the battle raged more furiously than ever. In spite of the Government decision the Ferrarians would not hear of a contest. Why should Ferrari compete? The position was by rights already his, they argued. And as for Verdi— "He doesn't need to work!" they sneered. "He's marrying a rich man's daughter!" Savagely they called him "the fashionable Maestrino" and swore that he knew nothing about religious music. As nobody pretended that Ferrari knew anything about any kind of music, the Verdians retaliated by accusing the poor fellow of everything else they could think of—even of being a bad husband and father! And because of Ferrari's organ playing they still refused to go to the Cathedral.

The Council of Elders, hoping to restore peace, decided to put the matter of the contest to a vote, and made preliminary speeches referring in flowery language to justice, art, and the glory of Busseto. But, when it came to voting, ten of the sixteen Councilmen were in favor of the contest. The other six, too frightened of both Verdians and Ferrarians to express an opinion either way, simply left the room—thereby invalidating the votes already cast. The affair was back where it had started!

Weeks went by. On Sundays, Ferrari played to the shadowy spaces of St. Bartholomew's, while the church of St. Mary of the Angels was jammed to the doors because Verdi's music was to be heard there, or he himself was at the organ. Hostilities grew still more bitter. The town seethed with rumor, intrigue, and violence. Parma, thoroughly shocked, sent extra police, officially rebuked Ballarini, and warned the townspeople to behave themselves. Worse yet, the Government forbade all music in Busseto's churches until order should have been restored. This was a scandal, a disgrace! But the promised contest seemed to have been forgotten.

As the weeks dragged into months and nothing decisive happened, both Verdi and Barezzi grew ready to give up the struggle in disgust. Verdi could not, would not, continue to burden Papà Barezzi indefinitely. He must earn a livelihood; but in Busseto there seemed to be no hope, so he would have to try elsewhere. He knew that at Monza the post of organist was still vacant. Monza was a sizable town, offering a far better salary than Busseto; and since it was only a few miles from Milan he would be able to keep in touch with the city's musical life, which meant so much to him. With recommendations from Lavigna and Massini, he applied and was immediately accepted. His troubles, he thought, were over at last.

But the authorities at Monza waited in vain for his arrival. When he obtained the necessary passport for the journey, word of his approaching departure got around, and he promptly found himself the center of a raging storm. The Philharmonic turned on him in fury. How could he desert them now when they had fought and struggled for him all these years? It was for the glory of Busseto, not Monza, that he had been given his musical education. He was accused of rank ingratitude!

Surprised and dismayed, poor Verdi saw that there was no escape—he could not honorably abandon his friends and well-wishers. Monza meant security, independence, peace of mind, but he gave it up even though the sacrifice seemed ruinous.

The Philharmonic thereupon offered to raise a handsome sum for him. Verdi refused it. He wanted not charity but a chance to work. The loyal orchestra then agreed to add to the amount paid by the Monte di Pietà so that his salary, if he were appointed director of the Philharmonic and music teacher of Busseto, would at least equal Ferrari's as organist. But how was he to obtain the position?

In despair, he made one final effort—he appealed directly to the Archduchess Marie Louise herself. And this time he got results. The contest at last became a reality. The Government declared that candidates would be examined by Maestro Alinovi of Parma, and even the date was announced.

On the afternoon of February 27, 1836, Verdi presented himself for the examination. He was no longer the tense and timid youth who had sought to enter the Milan Conservatory nearly four years earlier. With assurance, power, and spirit he played his own new *Variations*, twice through because of Alinovi's pleasure. To test his sight reading he was given some opera music. "But I already know these," he said glancing at the scores. So Alinovi brought out an unpublished work of his own instead. Then Verdi accompanied a quartet of Donizetti's from a piano part purposely full of errors, so that he was forced to make corrections as he played. Last came some duets with Alinovi, who showered him with praise, even calling him "the Paganini of the pianoforte."

At eight the next morning Verdi was given a subject on which to write a four-part fugue, and by seven at night it was finished. "Magnificent! Stupendous!" exclaimed Alinovi. "This is worthy to be printed. I myself could not have done as well in the time." And Alinovi was an accomplished composer.

For Verdi, the contest was over. He had friends in Parma, and that evening at a party he played his *Variations* with brilliant success. Then one Rossi, a new candidate for the long-disputed post, was asked to play, but he refused, much embarrassed. He would not have come, he said, had he known there was such a competitor from Busseto. And the next morning, instead of going to be examined, Rossi quietly left Parma. Ferrari of course never showed up at all. So Verdi, having frightened away all other contestants, won by default.

On his return, the Verdians staged a gala welcome for him. Banners fluttered from the balconies, a cheering crowd paraded, and there was singing and dancing in the streets. The town band blared forth in noisy triumph while the members of the Philharmonic, in a delirium of joy, crowned their victorious hero with a wreath of laurel.

Ballarini nevertheless tried to have the contest declared illegal on the ground that it had not been properly announced. But this was a futile gesture. The Battle of Busseto was over, and Verdi soon signed a formal contract as town music teacher and director of the Philharmonic.

He had a position, a means of livelihood at last. There was nothing now to prevent his marrying the beloved Margherita for whom he had worked and waited so many years. And from Milan he had brought another cause for happiness: the libretto of an opera that Massini had asked him to compose. Opera— for every Italian it was the dream, the highest goal, the ultimate glory! In spite of his worries he had already begun to work on it. Now, with his mind at rest, he would be free to give it his best efforts. It was this opera, he knew, which held the key to the future.

# CHAPTER FOUR

# *Oberto*

## 1836-1840

ON May 4, 1836, Margherita Barezzi was twenty-two
years old, and that very day she and Giuseppe Verdi
were married. It was the proudest, happiest moment of his
life. His origin was humble, his poverty acute, his ultimate
future entirely uncertain; yet the Barezzis found him worthy
of their beloved daughter. That so upright, so admirable a
citizen as Signor Barezzi should have such faith not only in
his genius but in his integrity was the brightest feather in
Verdi's cap. All his new in-laws felt for the young Maestro an
almost worshipful affection, and to Carlo and Luigia their
loyal, devoted son seemed to be entering a bigger, brighter
world than they had dared to dream of.

For Busseto the wedding was a joyful event, and the Verdians outdid each other in wishing the bride and groom happiness, long life, prosperity, and all good things. As the smiling
young couple, fearless and confident, left the church as husband and wife no cloud, no evil omen, no shadow of the days
to come marred the festivity.

It was to Milan that Verdi took his Ghitta for their brief
wedding trip—Milan that could make or break a composer,
where his dreams would or would not come true. Ever since
her pigtail days she had understood those dreams, perhaps
even before he himself had understood them. She was eager
to see the city of her Peppino's hopes.

They stayed with Professor Seletti and his wife, who had grown fond of Verdi during the years that he lived with them, and were delighted to see him so happily married. Certainly Margherita was a lovely creature. Signora Seletti, watching her loosen and comb out the elaborate twists of her coiffure, said that her hair poured down her shoulders like a torrent of gold. And how sweet, how good-natured, how warm-hearted she was! Best of all, it was clear that she loved her Verdi deeply and was as proud of him as he of her.

Back in Busseto, Papà Barezzi, generous as always, set the young people up in the Palazzo Rusca, a large house near his own that was conveniently spacious for music lessons. There Verdi, in accordance with his contract, taught the town's musical children for three hours a day five days a week. Besides these youngsters, who were being educated at the expense of the Monte di Pietà, he also took a number of private pupils. And of course the Philharmonic kept him busy; under his leadership it became more active than ever, with innumerable rehearsals, performances, and excursions to other towns. For these affairs Verdi composed a number of small works which, though really quite insignificant, the enthusiastic little orchestra declared "divine." The ill-feeling between the Verdians and the Ferrarians had not yet died out, but it bothered Verdi no more than the after-rumbles of a thunderstorm. For the first time in his life he was completely, radiantly happy.

True, Busseto did not now and never could offer sufficient scope for his growing ambition, and in spite of all the demands on him he managed to work with concentrated zeal at his opera, *Oberto, Count of St. Boniface*, the libretto of which he had brought from Milan. This libretto, by an obscure poet named Piazza, was rather weak, but at least the improbable story had dramatic moments, and the picturesque medieval setting was sure to appeal to the romantic taste of the time. Verdi, putting his best efforts into the music, finished it by the end of the year. But luck turned against him. His friend Massini, for whom he had undertaken the work, had resigned as head of the Philodramatic Society and was therefore no longer in a position to produce *Oberto*. Someone else would have to be persuaded to stage the new opera, and then, as now, it was difficult for an unknown composer to obtain a hearing. Verdi, however, had confidence in his score. Though disappointed, he was not yet discouraged.

In March 1837 his first child, a girl, was born. According to the Italian custom she was christened Maria Luigia after her two grandmothers, and for her first name Verdi chose Virginia. Perhaps because he himself had always lived under foreign domination, the passion for liberty was strong in him, and he named his little daughter for the young heroine of ancient Rome who had preferred death to slavery. Verdi, now twenty-three, was a proud and adoring father. The rosy baby, with a wreath of soft gold curls like her mother's, held him spellbound. Often, between lessons, he would disappear from the music room, but when the next pupil arrived Ghitta knew where to look for him. He was sure to be in the nursery, his dark head bent over the child in his arms, while in his deep, sweet voice he sang a lullaby—a *ninna-nanna*, as the Italians say: "Virginia mine, art thou alone . . ."

Meantime the score of *Oberto* lay idle on his desk. Though Verdi's contract with the Monte di Pietà ran for nine years there was a clause permitting him, provided he gave six months' notice, to leave at the end of the first three years if he so desired. Of course he could not think of giving up his work in Busseto until he had reasonable hope of being able to support his family as a composer. But if only he could get his *Oberto* before the public it might lead to other opportunities. So much depended on this first opera.

Verdi's annual vacation came during September and October, and at the earliest possible moment he set out for Parma, where he knew he was well thought of, with the precious score under his arm. His hopes were high and rose still higher when his many friends in Parma, including members of the town's orchestra, grew enthusiastic about *Oberto*. But to his consternation the theater manager refused even to consider the new work. It was one thing, he told Verdi, to write a good fugue or play the piano brilliantly at a social gathering. It was quite another to compose a successful opera. And suppose the opera should fail—think of the expense for scenery, costumes, musicians and, most costly item of all, singers. No, the manager could not and would not take the risk.

Many an unknown composer, in order to get his work produced, had undertaken to foot the bills himself; but this, Verdi could not afford to do. It was clear that the manager was not going to change his mind; he would not even glance at the score! Verdi went home again, angry, hurt, discouraged. How was one ever to get a chance? "A lot of good it does a young man to study!" he wrote Massini bitterly in a letter asking his friend to try to persuade Merelli, the great Merelli of La Scala, to consider *Oberto*.

This Merelli was a celebrated personage and difficult to approach. He had made a fortune as manager of La Scala and other theaters, and he lived like a prince. What would he, a power in the opera world who could pick and choose among the most famous composers of the day, care about a youth from provincial, unheard-of Busseto? What if the young fellow did have a new score to submit? People sent Merelli scores

[45]

every day, more than he could ever look at. Verdi's good friend and master, Lavigna, might have helped, but he had lately died. Massini could do nothing, and the year slipped away without bringing Verdi nearer to his goal.

Early in 1838 six songs of his were accepted by one of the lesser music publishers of Milan. It was the first time that Verdi had had anything printed, and this was at least a step in the right direction. He was young, he had genius, energy, confidence, ambition. He was surrounded by admiring friends. His dearly loved wife adored him and believed in him completely. And so, although hard luck seemed to thwart him, he did not lose hope. He planned to go to Milan himself during his next vacation and try by his own efforts to get a hearing for his work.

That summer, in July, to his great joy, Margherita bore him a son, and this child too was given a heroic ancient name. Icilio Romano they called him, and of course Carlo Antonio after his grandfathers. To Verdi life seemed good. He and Ghitta looked forward eagerly to their autumn trip to Milan, convinced that fortune would at last be kind.

But when September came they made the journey with fresh, sharp sorrow in their hearts. Only a month after their son was born, little Virginia had been taken ill. The doctor shook his head. For lack of our modern medical knowledge he could not tell what ailed her; he knew only that the mysterious disease was serious, very serious. Two days later the child died.

It was a cruel blow. The grieving parents turned toward Milan hoping to find there distraction, relief from the thought of that tiny, tragic coffin. But the city was topsy-turvy over the visit of Ferdinand, the new Austrian monarch. Though he turned out to be a weak and stupid ruler, the Milanese nevertheless had great hopes of him at the beginning of his reign and did all they could to win his favor. With a fine show of pomp and splendor they held a coronation ceremony in the cathedral, followed by parades, troop reviews, festivity of all sorts. The celebrations went on for days and of course included gala performances at La Scala. Milan was so crowded that the young Verdis had trouble finding a lodging. They felt bewildered and out of tune with all the gaiety round them.

Verdi had brought with him the full score of *Oberto* and all the parts neatly, painstakingly copied in his own hand. He busied himself trying in every way he could think of to bring his opera to the great Merelli's notice. After all, he sought no special favors. Whenever he had applied for a position—at Soragna, at Monza, in Busseto itself—he asked only to be given a trial, and now all he wanted was that Merelli should read his score. He called on his friends to help him: Piazza, the librettist; Pasetti, an engineer who knew Merelli well; Merighi, first 'cellist of La Scala; the influential noblemen whom he had met through the Philodramatic Society; and of course loyal Massini. All promised to do their best. But there was too much excitement in the city—people had too much on their minds to give any thought to the unknown work of an unknown composer. Nothing happened, and Verdi's vacation dwindled away.

Just as he was about to return, sad and discouraged, to Busseto, word came that Massini and Merighi had at last succeeded in getting the unapproachable Merelli's attention and had even extracted from him a promise to produce *Oberto* the following spring, not as part of the regular season, to be sure, but as a benefit performance. Since there was little risk of financial loss, new operas were often given in this way for some charity. It was a sort of back-door entrance to the composers' world, but Verdi was more than satisfied. At least his work would have a hearing.

Back in Busseto, he and Papà Barezzi talked over the good news. Verdi's salary was barely adequate—he had even had to borrow money for the trip to Milan. As a composer of operas he might vastly increase his income, but he must be free to give all his time to composing. Encouraged by his father-in-law, he bravely decided to give up his job and stake his whole future on the success of *Oberto*. The Monte di Pietà regretfully accepted his resignation, and even gave him a few months' leave of absence in advance.

In February 1839, therefore, Verdi moved to Milan taking

Ghitta, the baby son, and their faithful servant girl with him, since this time he hoped to settle there for good. Patiently he waited for word from La Scala; but weeks passed, the spring opera season got under way, and still, to his growing anxiety, there was no news of *Oberto*. Apparently Merelli, preoccupied as usual with his many-faceted affairs, had forgotten all about it. For Verdi this was serious. He saw that he would have to take steps before too late. Perhaps the famous singer Strepponi would help him. With his friend Massini he called on her.

Giuseppina Strepponi, now twenty-three years old, was the daughter of the organist at Monza whose death had left the post vacant in Verdi's student days. Trained at the Milan Conservatory, her fine soprano voice had been in great demand from the time of her graduation. She was a thoroughly lovable person, not selfish, frivolous, and vain like many opera singers. Ever since her father died she had shouldered all responsibility for her family, supporting her widowed mother and sending the younger children to the best schools. Her success was deserved. She managed her voice with real musicianship, and as an actress had imagination and the power to move her audience. Merelli thought the world of her, gave her all the best parts, and was known often to seek and act upon her advice.

It was because of her influence with the great man that Verdi turned to her in his difficulty. He had never seen the famous soprano off the stage and he found her charming— not strictly beautiful perhaps, but strikingly attractive with her dark hair parted in the middle and drawn down to frame a wide, lovely brow. Small and slender, she dressed simply and in exquisite taste, and there was grace in all her motions. She had intelligence, animation, kindliness, humor. No wonder the public adored her.

As Verdi played *Oberto* and explained the action, Strepponi listened with keen interest. Yes, she liked it, she liked the role that was intended for her, very much indeed. She would speak to Merelli about it.

Only a few days later came the news that *Oberto* was to be produced as soon as possible! The cast was agreed upon, the parts given out, the rehearsals scheduled. Verdi walked on air. Now, now at last, his real career was about to begin. For him and Ghitta, after all their worries, this was the sunrise.

And then, once again, disappointment. Before the rehearsals had actually started, the tenor was suddenly taken ill. He was irreplaceable. Postponement was out of the question—the season was almost over. The performance of *Oberto* had to be canceled.

Verdi was in despair. For three years he had struggled to get his opera before the public, and he had no sooner come within reach of his goal than he found himself back where he started—only worse off. Because of his high ambition, he had given up his safe little job. Now his money was almost gone, and the future seemed to hold nothing at all. Fate mocked him, and he did not know which way to turn.

Half ill with worry, he lingered on in the city, undecided. His friends in Busseto had been convinced that in no time he would have all Milan at his feet. He was reluctant to return to them—a failure, still dependent, with nothing accomplished and no prospects. Yet he realized that his family would have to live at the ever-loyal Barezzis until he should find some new means of support. But it was a bitter pill to swallow, and he put off his departure as long as he could.

One morning when his spirits were at their lowest ebb there came an abrupt knock at the door. No one was expected, and Verdi, rather startled, went to see who it was. A stranger, somewhat out of breath, spoke to him gruffly.

"Where's the Maestro from Parma who was to have had an opera produced for charity?"

"I am he," answered Verdi.

"All right. Come along with me. Signor Merelli ordered me to fetch you at once."

Merelli! Verdi's heart gave a great bound. "Ghitta!" he called, "Ghitta, I'm going out—Merelli's sent for me!" Quick, where was his hat?

"Hurry up, he's waiting," said the unceremonious messenger.

Verdi needed no urging. He arrived breathless at La Scala

and was immediately shown into the manager's private office.

Merelli was a big man with clever, kind brown eyes. He greeted Verdi warmly. "Ah, Maestro, I'm glad to see you. Sit down, sit down. About your *Oberto*—too bad it had to be called off. Strepponi has given me no peace ever since—keeps telling me that the music is really remarkable, and so on, and so on. She has good judgment, you know, and besides she's not the only one. The other singers have been talking enthusiastically about it too. Well, they can't all be wrong, eh? Anyhow I've decided to produce it next autumn, not as a benefit, mind you, but as part of the regular season. I'll be responsible for all expenses, and you and I shall share equally in the proceeds. How does that strike you? Is it fair?"

Fair? It was generous! Verdi was well aware that he might have been asked to pay the costs himself. The great manager must have real faith in him to offer such good terms to a beginner.

"Of course," Merelli went on, "the libretto will not do as it stands. It will have to be strengthened. I want a duel in the last act, and other changes, so I'm getting Solera, the poet, to rewrite it. That means revising the music too; you can work on it during the summer."

A new Verdi, exultant and confident, rushed back with the good news to his Ghitta waiting for him in a flutter of excitement. Now they could look ahead with courage; the future was no longer blank. No need to go back to Busseto—Milan was to be their home. Near the edge of the acres of brown-tiled roofs, far from the center of town where the cathedral towered frosty and majestic, they took a modest apartment. Though small, and several flights up, it was the best that Verdi could afford. He even had to borrow for the advance payment on the rent. How he hated this constant borrowing! But it would soon be over now—forever, he hoped. He longed to give his uncomplaining Ghitta a better place to live. Some day she should have everything she could desire. Some day she should drive through the streets in a fine carriage, and people would say, "Look, there goes the Signora Verdi!" Soon, now, he would make her proud to be his wife.

That summer while he revised *Oberto* Verdi's horizon widened. He had never before met anyone like the young poet with whom he worked. Themistocle Solera, huge, talented, reckless, and unstable, was a soldier of fortune, brilliant but erratic. As a boy he ran away from home to join a circus, and his life ever since had been a series of fantastic escapades. There were no such breezy fellows in Busseto, and Verdi found the contact stimulating.

With Solera he produced a new version of the opera, which Merelli approved. The cast was chosen (unfortunately Strepponi was not now available), and the performance scheduled for November 17, 1839. By mid-October, Verdi was fully occupied with the myriad details of the production. It was an absorbing, exciting time.

One morning Ghitta came to him with fear in her eyes. "The baby," she said; "there's something wrong—he's not well."

It was impossible not to think of little Virginia. In anxious haste Verdi summoned the doctor. But, as before, the doctor could make nothing of the mysterious illness. He was certain only that it was dangerous—and the child grew steadily weaker.

Verdi and Ghitta, homesick in their distress, longed for the comfort of family and friends about them. Desperate letters went to Busseto. Mamà Barezzi secretly sent money; sickness was so expensive, and she knew that Verdi, with his meager salary, had never been able to save for emergencies. But in spite of everything that anyone could do, the tragic story repeated itself. After a few ghastly days—more ghastly for the poor young parents because they had been through it all before—their beloved little son was dead.

At least in this crushing sorrow they still had each other. Ghitta, though ill with grief, forced herself to strengthen and encourage her husband. He must master his heartbreak. Rehearsals were about to start, and he must give all his attention, his energy, to the opera on which so much depended. The precious opportunity would not recur. The success they had so long struggled and hoped for must come now or never.

On the night of the great event the whole Barezzi clan and many other loyal friends from Busseto eagerly took their places among the audience. Most excited of them all was young Giovanni, Margherita's brother, who idolized his brother-in-law. Only Ghitta herself was absent. In mourning, she could not face the crowd so soon after the death of her child.

To present a new work in those days was even more of an ordeal than it is now, especially in Italy where the public expressed either approval or disapproval wildly, violently, without restraint. It was the custom for the composer to await the verdict hidden among the musicians of the orchestra, for whom he pretended to act as page turner. As Verdi inconspicuously seated himself between the 'cellos and the violins he heard the rustle of programs, late-comers settling in their places, the babble of animated voices filling the huge auditorium. For the first time that vast, incalculable throng out front was to pass judgment on a work of his. No wonder that he seemed more solemn, tense, and hollow-eyed than ever.

Then the performance began, and as it proceeded he breathed more easily. Though he saw little from where he sat he could feel the audience's growing interest and approval. As the curtain came down at the end of the first act there was good, solid applause and the composer was even called onto the stage a number of times to take a bow.

Meantime Ghitta, all alone, waited anxiously for news. As soon as he could get away Verdi slipped out the stage door and ran home to her through the dark streets. "It's all right," he panted. "Everything's all right. It's going well. They like it!" And, rewarded by the relief in Ghitta's face, he tore back to La Scala for the second act.

For a first opera *Oberto* had a very fair success indeed. Fourteen performances were given, and Giovanni Ricordi, an important music-publisher, bought the score. This was significant—it meant that Ricordi shrewdly saw in the new composer a man with a future. The critics, to be sure, were not entirely in accord. One called *Oberto* "most beautiful, entirely original, sublime," and declared that the young Verdi had "nothing more to fear." Another, however, found it imitative, humdrum, uninspired—the work of a greenhorn, and as the Italian word for "green" is *verde* he even made a pun about it.

Now, later, and always, Verdi paid little heed to the critics. It was the public he hoped to please—the public and Merelli. If they approved then indeed he had nothing to fear.

And approve they did. Merelli, in fact, lost no time in offering him a contract for three more operas, to be finished at intervals of eight months. The long spell of bad luck and uncertainty appeared to have ended. Now Verdi's future, he felt, would depend on his own efforts. The way was open for him. Though his path so far had been difficult he had come out onto the high road at last. Or so it seemed. . . .

# CHAPTER FIVE

# I'll Never Compose Again

## 1840

NOT long after the performance of *Oberto*, Merelli went to Vienna, where he was manager of the Imperial Theater, and before leaving he gave Verdi a new libretto to set to music, a tragedy called *The Exile* (*Il Proscritto*). Unfortunately Verdi did not like it. He found the situations uninteresting and the poetry unimpressive. *The Exile* failed to grip his imagination, and, waiting for ideas, he put off getting to work on it from day to day. Merelli, returning from his business trip a few weeks later, was not sorry to find that Verdi had written nothing. On the contrary, he informed Verdi that he had changed his mind. In order to balance the next season's repertory he needed not a tragedy but a comic opera, and as he had nothing suitable on hand Verdi would have to supply one. There was no time to have a new comic libretto written to order, so Merelli hunted through the shelves at La Scala, found a handful of long-since discarded works by the poet Romani, and forwarded them to Verdi telling him to take his choice.

Though Verdi was willing enough to set *The Exile* aside, he found to his disappointment that Romani's stale comedies appealed to him even less. Young though he was, he had no experience of frivolity, and his somber nature inclined toward intense, even violent, drama. His interest, his ambition, lay in serious opera, not *opera buffa*, as it was called, which ranged

[ 54 ]

from courtly high comedy to slapstick farce and had its own set of rules and traditions. Nevertheless he had to make the best of it. After studying all the librettos carefully he selected *King for a Day* as the least bad, and began without enthusiasm to compose. The play was leaden-footed and its humor lagged. To contrive music with life, gaiety, sparkle around its foolish plot was a tedious chore, especially for him.

Verdi had barely tackled his task when he was interrupted by illness. In spite of the strong constitution that had seen him through his childhood hardships he often suffered from sore throat, and now a severe infection kept him in pain for many days and left him weak and weary. But the fever subsided at last, his strength began to return, and he set himself to work at *King for a Day* in earnest. The opera was to be produced early in September, and already more than half of March had slipped away.

Lying on his couch one day, with music paper spread all about him, he realized with a start that it was March twenty-sixth, and on the twenty-ninth the quarterly payment of his rent would be due. What with his illness, he had forgotten all about it until that moment. The sum—only fifty *écus*—did not seriously worry him; thanks to *Oberto* and his new contract with Merelli he was more prosperous these days than he had been. But he had not enough cash on hand. It was too late to send to Busseto for it; the mail went only twice a week. What was to be done?

Another man would surely have asked the landlord for a few days' grace. But not Verdi. His sense of honor would not permit him to neglect his obligation even for a single day. He had agreed to pay his rent at a given time, and the proud, stubborn honesty that was part of his being forced him, now and throughout his life, to live up to his word. Since he was still convalescent and not able to go out, he asked the engineer Pasetti, who was Merelli's friend, to help him.

"I want you to do me a great favor," Verdi told him. "Go to Merelli, explain the situation, and ask him to advance me the fifty *écus*. If he prefers not to wait until my next opera is produced, tell him I'll repay him in six or eight days—as soon as I can get the money from Busseto. Make him understand that but for my illness I would of course have been provided with the funds in time. But such a small sum means nothing to him. Go and ask him for it, there's a good fellow. I'm sure he won't fail me."

Pasetti, seeing Verdi so wrought up and anxious, agreed at once. But he was a timid man, and as he descended the many flights of stairs to the street he thought to himself: "How can I bother Merelli with such a silly matter? Fifty *écus*! He'd think me a fool! Let Verdi be late with his payment. Even if the landlord has to be patient for a few days there's no harm done." And he dismissed the whole thing from his mind.

Meantime Verdi waited in vain for the expected messenger from La Scala. It was a small and simple favor that he asked, and Merelli had always seemed to him kind, generous, sympathetic. The manager could have no possible reason to refuse; but hour after hour passed, and still no knock came at the door. Verdi was at first puzzled, then hurt and distressed. By the afternoon of the twenty-eighth his hope had entirely faded.

[ 56 ]

Toward evening Margherita put on her bonnet. "I'm going out for a little while, Peppino," she told him as she rearranged the blanket over his lanky legs. "I have an errand to do. Are you all right? I won't be long."

Left alone, Verdi tried to compose, but the work went badly. Too troubled about the rent to put his mind on the comic opera, he was glad when he heard Ghitta at the door.

She ran to him with cheeks flushed and eyes sparkling. "I have something for you!" she said. And onto his lap she poured a heap of coins—exactly fifty *écus!*

"Ghitta! Why—what—? But Ghitta, how did you ever—?" Verdi looked up at her in delighted amazement. Suddenly he understood. "Oh, Ghitta, your cameo brooch—it's gone! I'm sure you had it on when you went out. But that wouldn't have been enough. Where's the gold mesh bracelet? And your coral earrings? Are they in your jewel box?" Smiling, she shook her head. "And the other things, are they all gone too?" She nodded. "Oh, Ghitta, you've pawned all your precious trinkets—how could you?" To think of her, a Barezzi, going alone to a pawnshop with her handful of little treasures!

Ghitta laughed happily. "Never mind, Peppino. Now you can pay the rent. That's all that matters."

Verdi was deeply touched. "Ghitta, you shall have every one of your jewels back. I'll get them all for you, I swear it. And soon, very soon—I'm almost strong enough to go out now. And one of these days we'll find ourselves well off, and never have to worry about paying for things anymore. You'll see—I'm going to write many more operas, and better ones. I know it!"

Never once had Ghitta complained of the pinch of poverty; never, when bad luck dogged them like a persistent evil fate, had she lost courage. Her faith in him had not wavered, and she had borne her sorrows bravely for his sake. Ever since, as boy and girl, they had sat together at her father's fine Viennese piano, she had always understood him, loved him. What would he ever do without her?

Of course Verdi recovered Ghitta's treasures for her at the first possible moment. But he often wondered why Merelli had not helped him out. "I can't understand it," he told Pasetti. "Why should he refuse me?" Pasetti chose the coward's answer. "I don't know," he mumbled, with a shrug. And Verdi, who could never have treated anyone so shabbily, felt in spite of himself a bit less friendly toward the great manager.

Now that Verdi was well again he plugged away steadily at the music for *King for a Day* even though his heart was not in it. But, after all, his contract called for three new operas. Surely one of them would inspire him with enthusiasm, bring him a sense of achievement as he worked. Meantime he must do the best he could with the task at hand. Some day he knew he would write something really fine. He must be patient, hope a little longer.

It was for Margherita's sake that Verdi yearned to hasten the day of his success. Pale, wan, listless, she had for some time past not been herself. Their endless worries and, above all, grief for her lost children had undermined her health and broken down her physical resistance. In June she became acutely ill. "Brain fever," the doctor said—frightening words. Desperately Verdi wrote to Busseto, and Papà Barezzi, seriously alarmed, dropped everything and rushed in all haste to Milan.

It was the evening of June 17 when he climbed the long stairs to the Verdis' flat. Margherita lay white and quiet, as if asleep, her bright gold hair spilling over the pillow. Verdi, unable to sit still, paced the floor with clenched fists and burning eyes. The doctor came and went away again, looking grave. There was nothing that he could do.

All night long, with the lamp turned low, the two men watched by the bedside in silent torment—hoping . . . hoping . . . hoping . . .

At noon the next day Margherita died.

For Verdi there was nothing left, nothing. He was alone in the world. Death had taken his baby daughter and his little son. Now his wife. What had he to work for, to live for even? Music? He could not bear to think of it. Success, fame, glory?

It was for Ghitta's sake that he had dreamed of these. What good was anything to him—alone?

Bare-headed, like a man in a trance, he followed Margherita's coffin to a forlorn cemetery in Milan and saw her buried there, in alien soil. Then he returned home to Busseto with poor Papà Barezzi. But the grief-stricken Barezzi family could not comfort him. In their well-loved house, wherever he was— on the stairs, in the halls, by the sun-flooded windows, at the piano—Verdi saw only one thing: that Ghitta was not there. His parents, though they suffered with him, were helpless to ease his sorrow. He could find no escape, no relief from the intolerable pain that he carried within himself. For a time it seemed as though he must lose his mind.

Suddenly from Merelli came a reminder that the half-finished *King for a Day* was to be ready by autumn. Verdi was expected to compose a comic opera—light-hearted music, full of fun, to set a glittering, carefree audience laughing and humming as it left the theater! It was impossible. From the depths of his grief he wrote to Pasetti: "Tell Merelli I can't do it— not now. Beg him to let me off."

This time Pasetti did as Verdi asked, but Merelli would not listen. Though individuals died every day, the public was immortal; and opera, therefore, went on no matter what happened. La Scala could not wait. Merelli insisted that the comedy be finished on schedule, and for Verdi there was no honorable way out. Since Merelli refused to release him, he must live up to their agreement. He went back to Milan, to the humble apartment into which he and Margherita had moved with such bright hopes, and alone there, by an inhuman effort of will, forced himself to complete the score. For several weeks he worked day and night, sleeping but little, eating almost nothing, drinking strong black coffee. All the time he had to fight down his sorrow—not let it take control of him. The strain exhausted him nervously and physically, but he was too conscientious to do less than his best. Unfortunately, though naturally enough, his best under the circumstances was not good.

The performance took place on September 5, 1840, a day

that Verdi was never to forget. The singers, lacking enthusiasm, went through their parts in a sloppy and perfunctory manner, and the opera had barely got under way before the audience began to snicker. Soon there was unmistakable hissing, and it came more and more often and grew steadily louder. At last the crowd got entirely out of hand and the noise swelled to loud guffaws and jeers. Verdi, hot and sick with angry shame, had to listen to roar after roar of cruel laughter. La Scala, where violent demonstrations were the rule, had never been the scene of a more ghastly, ridiculous, humiliating failure.

Behind his mask of reserve Verdi was always sensitive, and now, less than three months after Ghitta's death, more acutely so than ever. He had looked forward to no great success with *King for a Day;* the libretto was too forced and dull, the music too obviously uninspired. But it was not quite hopeless; certainly worse operas had enjoyed a brief popularity in their time. And in his youth, his inexperience, Verdi had expected some consideration because of his personal tragedy, which was, of course, common knowledge. He had thought of the public as a friend who would appreciate the appalling effort this comedy had cost, and instead it had mocked him. He could forgive the people in the audience for not liking his work—after all, this was their right. But if only they had had the decency to keep quiet! He, whose sympathetic imagination was so powerful, could not understand the lack of it in others. It seemed to him that the audience deliberately made fun of his grief, and this was more than he could bear. It taught him a never-to-be-forgotten lesson: individuals with normal human sympathies, when poured together into a theater, become a single, unpredictable, and utterly heartless monster. Clearly, a composer must make no excuses and can expect no mercy. He must be willing and able to stand up and take whatever comes with detachment, almost with indifference. Verdi, deeply wounded and disgusted with everything and everybody, vowed that he would never go through such an experience again. Why should he?

The critics were not quite so brutal as the public. They

blamed the fiasco more on the performance than on the music, which, they said, even had occasional charming moments. One critic, moreover, had the heart to point out that Verdi had written it when under a severe strain. But the ill-starred *King for a Day* was not repeated, and except for a few odd numbers it was not even printed.

In October, Merelli hastily revived *Oberto* in an effort to erase the bad impression made by Verdi's second attempt. It was no use. The fickle public had lost interest, and *Oberto* drew only listless applause from half-empty houses.

There were in Italy at that time composers by the dozen, by the hundred. But then, as now, an authentic genius was a rarity and from an opera manager's point of view the most priceless of all treasures. In spite of what had happened Merelli was shrewd enough to see in Verdi more than a promising country boy who had had bad luck. He still believed firmly in this strange young man's future.

The manager was stunned, therefore, when Pasetti brought him a message from Verdi who asked that his contract, by which he was bound to compose two more operas, be canceled. "He insists that he's through," Pasetti said. "He's made up his mind to write nothing more."

"Impossible!" exclaimed Merelli. "Surely he can't mean it!"

"But I'm afraid he does," Pasetti told him.

Merelli sent for Verdi at once and suggested that he revise *King for a Day*, assuring him that, remodeled, it might yet succeed. Verdi refused. Merelli then scolded him as though he were a naughty child who did not know what he wanted. "You can't be serious," he said. "Your present mood is understandable, of course, and believe me, I know how you feel. But everything passes, even dark days like these. Why, you're a musician, man, and by and by you'll find you can't give it up! A failure like this means nothing at all, especially at your age. Forget it, and get back to work. You have a brilliant career to look forward to, I tell you. You can't just throw it away!"

Verdi shook his head.

[ 61 ]

Patiently Merelli tried another tack. "But you're trained for music. What else can you do? How do you propose to live?"

"I can always become a schoolteacher, I suppose," Verdi answered indifferently.

It was aggravating, incredible, absurd. Composers without a spark of talent constantly clamored, begging Merelli to produce their works. And here was a man on whose ability he could count running away from him, ready to give up. He, Merelli, had hitched his wagon to this new star only to have its light suddenly go out. But Verdi, for all that he seemed scarcely alive, was young, vigorous, and more than talented. Real genius, Merelli knew, is a driving, compelling power that can neither be resisted nor escaped. He saw that he would have to be patient. He must give the composer time to heal his wounds.

"Listen, Verdi," he said quietly, "I can't force you to write and, since you insist, I'll tear up your contract. But I still believe in you, and some day you may change your mind. If that time ever comes you have only to give me two months' warning before the season opens, and I promise to produce any opera that you bring me."

To Verdi, not so long ago, in the days of his struggles to get a hearing, such an offer from the great Merelli would have seemed like heaven itself. Now it was too late—it did not matter any more. Nothing mattered. "Thank you," he said. "You're very kind. But I shan't change my mind."

Merelli sighed. "Very well. Only remember my promise."

Verdi rose to leave. "I shan't forget it," he said. "But it's no use. I'll never compose again."

Wearily he went back to his lonely flat. At twenty-seven years of age he was a man without work, without love, without hope—with only bitterness and sorrow to make him conscious of living. He would have nothing more to do with music. After all, except for the small, brief success of *Oberto*, what had it brought him but misery, hardship, failure, ridicule? He was determined never to give it another thought.

# CHAPTER SIX

# Go, Thought, on Golden Wings

## 1840-1842

VERDI had no intention of returning to Busseto, where everybody knew and pitied him. Instinctively, like a wounded animal, he wanted rather to hide himself away. But the home in Milan that he had shared with Margherita and his little son was full of memories that hurt him. So now that his ill-fated *King for a Day* was done with, and he had leisure, he packed his meager household belongings, sent them back to Busseto, and moved into a cheap and dreary furnished room in Milan. Here he was quite alone, not caring to see even his few city friends, and he became more silent, more withdrawn into himself than ever.

His days were much alike. Often he stayed indoors devouring popular novels one after the other. Since his tastes were scholarly, literary, he had never read such trash before. Now it served a purpose, holding his attention without stirring his mind or his feelings. His broken spirit needed repose. He slept but fitfully, woke unrefreshed, and was always tired.

When he felt restless he walked the streets for hours. Milan was a lively city. Everywhere there was bustle and animation: the rattle of wheels, the clop-clop of horses' hooves, peddlers' cries, street-corner arguments, snatches of song, and children's noisy games. But Verdi was unaware of the life around him and of its background—quiet, gracious Renaissance "palaces," rows of little shops, and here and there, oddly embedded in the modern buildings, a weathered column from the days of Rome's greatness. He walked at random, with bowed head, and if he looked at anything at all it was with unseeing eyes. The neighborhood of La Scala, where he had once felt so at home, he now avoided.

Every day he went to an old-fashioned restaurant not far from his lodgings for his main meal, though half the time, absorbed in bitter thoughts, he forgot to eat the food that was served to him. On his way there he passed regularly through a newly built arcade that was like a small street entirely roofed over with glass, but for pedestrians only. Because of its novelty this place was the talk of Milan. Here, sheltered from the weather, people strolled and gazed at the windows of the fashionable shops, or sipped their coffee in the smart cafés while they watched the crowds go by. It was the thing to meet one's friends here and idle away a little time in a gay exchange of greetings and gossip. But Verdi always strode through this sociable scene lonely as a ghost, looking neither to right nor to left and speaking to no one.

One evening late in December 1840—the year that had brought him so much sorrow—he came out of the arcade on his way home and turned down a dark, quiet street. Big flakes of snow spun slowly through the chilly air. Verdi, with the collar of his shabby coat turned up and his broad hat pulled low over his face, rounded the corner of a building and bumped square into a hurrying passer-by. He stepped back to apologize. It was Merelli!

"Verdi! It's good to see you!" exclaimed the manager warmly as he shook hands. "Funny thing—running into you like this. I was thinking about you only the other day. It's been an age since I heard from you."

Verdi looked gaunt as a skeleton, his pale young face drawn and lined with sadness, his strange eyes glittering from deep shadow. Merelli took in his suffering at a glance but was too wise to offer sympathy or ask questions. Instead he slipped his arm through the younger man's. "I'm on my way to La Scala. Come, walk along with me. I need company. We managers lead a dog's life—work and worry at all hours—always trouble

of some sort. Just now I'm in such a jam—got to find a libretto
for the composer Nicolai at once—heaven knows how. I
commissioned him to write an opera for me, you know, and
I gave him a libretto about Nebuchadnezzar—by your friend
Solera—a magnificent thing, superb! Would you believe it?
Nicolai has turned it down! Won't have anything to do with
it—says it doesn't appeal to him. What am I to do? I've got
to provide the man with a book, and there's no time to have

anything new written. I'd give my head to get hold of something for him right away. And here's this extraordinary work of Solera's going to waste—such a pity!"

All this friendly shop talk caught Verdi's interest, thawed his reserve. "What about *The Exile?*" he asked. "You remember, you gave it to me, but I never wrote a note of it. Couldn't Nicolai use that?"

"*The Exile!* Splendid—just the thing! I'd forgotten all about it. But you might want to set it to music yourself."

Instantly Verdi was on his guard. "I'm not composing," he said stiffly.

"As you wish. I only thought perhaps you'd changed your mind."

They had reached the opera house, and Merelli pushed open the door. "Come in, come in," he said. "I must have a look at *The Exile* right away. There's sure to be a copy here somewhere."

While Merelli's assistant searched through the library for the forgotten libretto, Verdi, half against his will, followed the manager to his office—that venerable room to which sooner or later all the great ones of opera found their way.

*The Exile* was soon unearthed, and together Verdi and Merelli glanced through it. Yes, it would do for Nicolai very well.

"That *is* a relief!" exclaimed Merelli. "You can't think how grateful I am for this idea. What luck that we should happen to run into each other just at this time, eh? Now that you're here, do take a look at *Nabucco.*" He held up Solera's *Nabucodonosor*, which was always spoken of as *Nabucco* for short.

"Thanks," said Verdi gruffly. "I don't want it."

"Nonsense, man! Take it home with you and read it."

"What is it to me? I'm not interested in operas."

"I know, I know. But it won't hurt you to read it and bring it back to me, will it? Such dramatic situations—such magnificent poetry! It's really extraordinary. Here, take it." Merelli thrust the manuscript into Verdi's unwilling hands. There was no getting away from his insistence, and Verdi, rather than argue, rolled it up and said goodbye. "I'll return it to you immediately," he added.

Once outside the opera house and alone again, a feeling of immense sorrow engulfed him, and with it a vague dread, almost fear, of he knew not what. It was painful, this stirring of his buried dreams. By the time he reached his lodging he was thoroughly angry. He would not read the thing—Merelli should have left him alone. With a gesture of exasperation he flung the libretto away from him.

The manuscript, unrolling as it fell, lay open on the table. Verdi glanced down and caught his breath. "*Va, pensiero, sull' ali dorate*," he read. "Go, thought, on golden wings"— beautiful words, magical words, like music. Rapidly he skimmed through the whole chorus of which this was the opening line: the homesick lament of a captive, exiled people. Based on a passage from the Old Testament that Verdi knew and loved so well, it seemed to him deeply moving. His spirit, always keenly responsive to the poetic, had long been starved. For weary, barren months no beauty had crossed his path. Now his dormant imagination quickened. It was like coming home after a journey in an alien land.

What was he thinking of? He closed the manuscript abruptly and shoved it aside. He would not read it. It must go back to Merelli first thing in the morning. All too vividly Verdi remembered the strain, the intense, soul-shaking effort of writing music. And what was the reward? Nothing but bitterness. No, he would never compose again. Forget it. He undressed and went to bed.

But not to sleep. "Go, thought, on golden wings." The haunting phrase drifted through his consciousness, leaving him no peace. Again and again he settled himself and resolutely closed his eyes only to find that he was staring into the darkness, wide awake. "On golden wings—golden wings." Without his willing it the words sang themselves. . . . He must forget it . . . sleep. . . . But insistently a pattern of music shaped itself, moved through his mind. "Go, thought . . ."

It was no use. He sat up, lit his lamp, and drawing a blanket over his shoulders reached for the manuscript. . . .

When Verdi raised his head it was daylight, and he had not even been aware of the dawn! He stretched himself and rubbed his burning eyes. Three times, from beginning to end, he had read *Nabucco* so intently that now he practically knew it by heart. Yes, Merelli was right, the libretto was magnificent. But he, Verdi, was through with it. After all, it was no concern of his. He drank the morning coffee that the landlord's servant brought him and set out for La Scala with the manuscript under his arm.

"Ah, Verdi! Good morning," said Merelli cheerfully. "Have you read it, so soon?"

"Yes, I've read it."

"Tell me, what do you think of it? It's a fine work, eh?"

"Very fine."

"Well, then—set it to music!"

Verdi protested. "I wouldn't dream of such a thing. I don't want anything to do with it!"

Merelli rose, smiling. "Set it to music, I tell you, set it to music!" With that, he shoved the manuscript into Verdi's overcoat pocket, seized him by the shoulders, and pushed him bodily out of the office. It happened so quickly that Verdi had no chance to object; and as he stood bewildered in the hall he heard the key turn in the office door behind him. He was locked out! There was nothing for him to do but go back to his lodging, with *Nabucco*.

At first Verdi paid no attention to this libretto that he could not get rid of. Intending to ignore it for good, he put it aside, and with Giovanni Barezzi traveled to Genoa and to Venice, where his *Oberto* was being produced. In both cities the applause was tepid, the critical notices downright bad. By the time he returned to Milan he was growing accustomed, even hardened, to public disapproval.

Shut away in his room, he took up his lonely existence again, seeing no one and eating almost nothing for days on

[ 68 ]

end. But he could not get *Nabucco* out of his mind. Persistently, snatches of music occurred to him and haunted him, until at last he jotted them down. By and by he developed a phrase or two, adding a note here, a cluster of notes there. Soon he found to his surprise that he had a whole scene finished, then another. Before he knew it he was completely absorbed and working hard.

In those days opera music conformed to a rigidly fixed pattern that had been evolved through the centuries. In a sense it was the ancient Greeks who invented opera, for the great classical dramas were certainly produced with music—music that would sound strange to our ears, and unfortunately has long since been lost. During early medieval times, opera ceased to exist, but with the coming of the Renaissance "the glory that was Greece and the grandeur that was Rome" were rediscovered. People worshipped the Greek way of life (often not as it was, but as they imagined it) and hungered to do all that the Greeks had done. Back in the sixteenth century a little group of pioneers in Italy began to stage ancient dramas in what they considered the true Greek manner; and since the original music had vanished they had to create something to take its place. There was no model for what they needed; the popular music that had grown out of the strumming of the troubadours was too commonplace, and the church music of the period, with its elaborately patterned counterpoint, was too stiff, cold, and formal. So these pioneers sought to develop a new kind of singing that should express emotion directly and thus serve to intensify the drama. Through their primitive, experimental efforts opera was born.

The new idea expanded rapidly. At one time opera wagons toured all over Italy giving crude performances on street corners and in market places before delighted crowds. Soon opera became the favorite form of court entertainment, and composers were kept busy supplying royal demands. Each prince tried to outdo the neighboring rulers in splendor; and the primitive singing dramas, to which the simplest of instrumental accompaniments had been added, rapidly developed into grand, lavish spectacles. No royal wedding could be properly celebrated without a specially magnificent opera written and staged for the occasion. There was even a time, about a hundred years before Verdi's day, when drama and music were overshadowed by pure pageantry. Colossal theaters were built, with intricate machinery by which stage effects at least as elaborate as anything we see today could be achieved, and the greatest architects and artists designed scenery and costumes. Mere size was part of the show, and the stages were so big that they sloped up toward the back in order to improve the visibility. Hundreds of people took part in these spectacles, fantastic ballets were introduced, and sometimes animals were used to add to the thrill. Exotic oriental scenes with live elephants and leopards on parade were popular, and on one occasion a troop of huntsmen on horseback even chased real bears and wild boars across the stage.

Opera soon outgrew this circus phase and once again became drama with music. But the tradition of grandeur persisted for many years—Verdi's Nebuchadnezzar, for instance, was to make his entrance riding on horseback at the head of an armed throng. The atmosphere of courtly elegance survived too, almost down to the present. In Europe every great opera house has to this day a gorgeous royal box, and even in democratic America society prefers to attend opera dressed in its most formal finery.

As time went on, the music of course changed and developed greatly. The Italians, who love melody, had introduced songs or arias to vary the somewhat tuneless singing dialogue, which was called "recitative." These arias, which naturally interrupted the dramatic action, were supposed to express the character's feelings, and were governed by certain musical rules. They had a definite form, much as a sonata has. The first part, called the cavatina, was slow and often melancholy; the second part, or cabaletta, had to be rapid and vigorous for contrast. This sudden change of mood did not always fit the story, but no matter—it was the musical law. In this land of the world's greatest voices, singers were all-important, and their arias, which they embroidered to suit themselves, sometimes became mere showing off—displays of meaningless vocal fireworks. In every opera there were concerted numbers too: duets, trios, quartets, etc., and big choruses, all distributed so as to avoid monotony. These set pieces became, and for a long time remained, more important musically than the framework of action on which they were hung; for the Italian composers were slow to realize the possibilities of recitative, and of orchestration too. At one period they even abandoned music altogether for the in-between parts and let the dialogue be spoken, especially in comedies. But this did not prove satisfying; such works tended to become plays-with-songs rather than operas. Thereafter, only singing was permitted; and gradually the recitative became more interesting and the orchestration richer, fuller, more vivid.

By the time Verdi's career began, the conventions of opera had become so fixed and formal that originality was being stifled. Of the new works produced in Italy—sometimes as many as five hundred in ten years—only a handful had any lasting vitality. Even the greatest composers—Rossini, now retired, Bellini, who had died some years earlier, and Donizetti, still active though his star was soon to wane—wrote much that was overelegant, artificial, mannered and empty, leaving only a few masterpieces that are still played and loved today. The vast bulk of the operatic music of the period was commonplace and lifeless. It needed new feeling, new vigor, and above all new sincerity.

Like everyone else, Verdi accepted the deep-rooted conventions of opera without question, but he had a powerful imagination and a strong dramatic instinct. Putting notes down on paper in solitude hour after hour, day after day, he saw his characters not as singing puppets, but as flesh-and-blood human beings capable of the most intense emotions. The older composers had often written music that, since it fitted no story, would fit any story, and they had been known to transplant whole numbers from one opera to another. For Verdi this was unthinkable. To him it seemed obvious that the music should inevitably bring the words and the situation to mind, and vice versa, all blending to form a single, strong, dramatic whole. But it was no easy task to knit action, words, and music together within the established operatic pattern.

As the score of *Nabucco* grew, Verdi realized that certain passages of the libretto did not suit the music that seemed right to him. "Look," he explained to Solera; "here I must have a different meter, like this"—he played a few bars—"and here I need a word with the same meaning but with the accent on the last syllable."

Solera, who had done some composing himself, understood what Verdi wanted, but he was a lazy fellow. He grumbled and delayed before he finally made the changes. Verdi, however, was still not satisfied and sent for the poet again.

"This duet won't do here," he told him. "It has no point, it's trivial, and it slows up the action. The audience will lose interest. Write me a prophecy for Zacharias instead. Let him foretell the doom of Babylon. It'll be tremendously effective."

The thought of more work irritated Solera. "Oh, very well," he muttered. "I'll do it for you by and by." And he moved toward the door.

Verdi stepped in front of him, blocking the way. "I need it at once," he said.

"But it can't be done so fast—you must give me time!"

"I've got to have it immediately," Verdi repeated firmly, knowing that the poet would postpone the task forever if he had the chance.

Solera was a huge man with an ungovernable temper. He spluttered furiously, "All right then, I'll bring it to you to-morrow!"

"No, not tomorrow, now." Verdi looked lank and brittle facing the poet's angry bulk, but he was apparently calm. "There are pens, ink, and paper on the table," he said. Then he locked the door and put the key in his pocket.

It was a dangerous moment. Solera, who was quite capable of violence, glared at Verdi like a bull about to charge. But Verdi stood his ground, and suddenly the poet's rage collapsed. Meekly enough, he sat down and went to work, and in a quarter of an hour the prophecy was ready to be set to music.

The incident was characteristic. Never was there a composer surer of what he wanted than Verdi, or more stubborn when it came to getting it. Where his work was concerned he could not compromise, could never accept second best. His courage was limitless and his determination granite.

In October, 1841, Verdi brought the completed score of *Nabucco* to Merelli and reminded him of his promise. The manager was taken by surprise. He had not expected Verdi to come to life so quickly. For the gala Carnival season, which ran from after Christmas until Lent, he had already arranged to put on three new operas by well-known composers. A fourth, especially by a beginner whose former failure might not yet be forgotten, was more than he dared risk. He offered to produce *Nabucco* later, in the spring.

Verdi was not satisfied. The spring opera season, after Lent, was comparatively unimportant, and the best singers, including Strepponi, would no longer be available. He declared that *Nabucco* must be given at Carnival time or not at all.

"Very well," said Merelli. "Ask Strepponi about it. If she wants to do it we'll put it on. If not, it will have to be postponed."

With his score under his arm, Verdi called on the famous soprano as he had done once before about *Oberto*, and this time his friend Pasetti went with him. Strepponi became even more enthusiastic than she had been over *Oberto* and, putting on her bonnet, insisted on driving off at once with them in Pasetti's carriage to tell the other singers of the cast about the new work. On hearing the music all were delighted and eager to take part. Verdi considered the performance settled. He was exultant. For months he had lived *Nabucco* and it meant a world to him.

In December the customary bulletin announcing the operas for the Carnival season was posted outside La Scala. *Nabucco* was not on the list!

Verdi's temper, long dormant, suddenly flared uncontrollably. He dashed off a furious letter to Merelli calling him names, accusing him of bad faith, reminding him of how he, Verdi, had lived up to his agreement in finishing *King for a*

*Day*. No sooner was this hot-headed outburst on its way than his rage melted, leaving him empty and ashamed. Surely he had ruined his chances forever! How could Merelli ever speak to him again? If only he could get the dreadful letter back— but it was too late.

The next day he received a curt summons to Merelli's office, and, sick with anxiety, he went to take the consequences of his foolishness.

"Now, now, now," scolded Merelli, "I ask you, is that the way to treat a friend? But you're quite right. Listen, Verdi, I'll put on *Nabucco* for the Carnival if you insist, but I advise against it. I can't afford new scenery and costumes. We'd have to use old sets—you remember the ballet about Nebuchadnezzar several years ago? The scenery for that could be renovated a bit, and the costumes refurbished. But if you'll wait till spring you shall have brand-new sets, new costumes— everything of the best."

To Verdi it was the singers, not the scenery, that mattered, and without hesitation he chose the Carnival season. Soon a new poster went up, and on it in large letters he read: "*Nabucodonosor*, by G. Verdi." All was well.

Toward the end of February the first rehearsal was called. On the vast, bare stage, principals and chorus, looking a little weary and drab in their street clothes, grouped themselves round the piano from which Verdi himself was to direct. In the background workmen were busy dressing up the shabby old sets under the supervision of a scene-designer. The great curtain had been raised, and in the front of the house a handful of friends of the management sat quietly in semi-darkness. Here and there in the tiers of gilded boxes charwomen puttered at their endless cleaning. But for these tiny, scattered figures, the huge auditorium was empty, hushed, and eerie as a banquet hall after the guests have gone.

The music began. The charwomen, so used to the sound of opera that as a rule they were scarcely conscious of it, one by one stopped dusting. The few spectators leaned forward in their seats. A carpenter, crossing the stage, set down the lumber he carried and stood still. The painters, quietly at work on the sets, turned round on their ladders, their dripping brushes forgotten in midair. The stage-manager at his little table looked up from his prompt book. From their workroom a couple of wardrobe mistresses, pincushions swinging at their belts, crept into the wings. Stagehands came down from the flies, engineers came up from the basement, workmen appeared at the rear of the auditorium. All over the building activity came to a standstill while the vast backstage crew gathered and stood transfixed in open-mouthed wonder. Opera was the daily accompaniment of these people's lives; yet never, never before had they heard anything like this.

At the second rehearsal, at every rehearsal, it was the same story: when the music began, all work stopped. The managers scolded, and the men dutifully picked up their tools—only to put them down again. Here was an opera that *compelled* one to listen, and word of it quickly spread through the city. At the end of the day the singers spoke of it in the fashionable drawing rooms, and in the cheap cafés the stagehands told their cronies. It was new, it was different, they said, but not outlandish. On the contrary, it seemed somehow familiar, satisfying, right. And, unable to explain the music's power, they added, "You must hear it for yourself."

Curiosity throughout Milan grew daily more intense. The current operatic standbys, with their empty, mannered grace, were wearing thin. None of the three other novelties—including Nicolai's *The Exile*—that Merelli had offered that season met with the audience's approval. The public longed for something new on which to lavish its enthusiasm.

To be with Verdi during these tense days young Giovanni Barezzi came from Busseto, bringing in secret a sack of gold pieces. He could not bear to think that his brother-in-law might face another such ordeal as the première of *King for a Day*, so he arrived prepared to buy at least temporary success for the new work. At every large opera house there was in those days (and still is, in Europe) an organization known as "the claque" whose members, scattered among the standees, were paid by the singers to applaud. So strong was this organization that, by creating disturbances, it could ruin the reputation of any who refused its fee. Applause money was therefore a part of every singer's regular expenses. Composers feared the claque less, for though it might stimulate artificial enthusiasm for an undeserving work it was powerless to prevent a genuine success. Giovanni, however, intended to leave no stone unturned. He planned to circulate among the standees during the performance and, if things appeared to be going badly, to hand out his gold pieces with instructions to drown out any hisses by hearty clapping. But, knowing Verdi's temper, he took care that his friend should hear nothing of this scheme.

One evening after rehearsal Giovanni sat with Verdi in a crowded café. "Tell me," he asked modestly, "why didn't you write an overture for *Nabucco?* To my mind it would be an improvement."

"I wanted the action to begin at once," said Verdi, "but perhaps it was a mistake. Yes, I'm sure you're right, but what can I do? With the performance only two days off, it's too late to write an overture now."

But was it? Verdi could never be satisfied with second best. After a little thought he went to work then and there, with such concentration that in spite of the noise and bustle all round him he soon had the overture ready.

On March 9, 1842, Verdi took his place in the orchestra pit, as he had done twice before, to await the verdict of the public. But this evening was not like those other occasions. Now the musicians smiled at him with eager anticipation in their eyes, and his friend Merighi, the 'cellist, leaned over and whispered, "I wish I were in your shoes tonight!" The air was electric with expectancy, as before some great event.

And a great event it was—one of the memorable days in opera history. The overture, though written hastily as an afterthought, produced a mighty burst of applause. After the curtain rose, spontaneous clapping broke out again and again, and the rousing first-act choruses even brought forth cheers. As the act swept to its climax the whole exultant audience, carried away by a single impulse, surged shouting to its feet. So appalling was the uproar that Verdi, in his hiding place,

[ 76 ]

had a moment of sickening panic—he thought the mob must be after his skin! Then, in the tumult, his ears caught the cries of "Bravo! Bravo!" and all at once he realized that this was the sound, the very sound, of glory. . . .

*Nabucco* is a long opera, but throughout its four acts the enthusiasm, the excitement, increased. Many numbers had to be repeated, some of them several times. In the third act the chorus, "Go, thought, on golden wings," sent a shiver of emotion through the audience—to them it was not the lament of the captive Hebrews of old that they heard, but the voice of the oppressed Italian people themselves, longing for freedom. What they felt could not be told in words, only in music —*this* music that was new and strange, yet by some magic seemed to come from the listeners' own hearts.

The opera ended. "Verdi! Verdi! *Verdi!* VERDI!" roared the crowd. Pale, gaunt, dignified, a little dazzled, he came before the glowing footlights. In front of him, in the huge, dim cavern of the auditorium, the people clapped until their hands were sore and stinging. They stamped, they waved, they hugged each other, they even wept. The string-players beat on their desks with their bows and cheered. With tears in their eyes the singers, who had performed magnificently, pressed forward to shake the composer's hand. Strepponi was radiant. As for Merelli, he was beside himself with joy—had he not seen all along that this queer, gruff young fellow from the country was a great man in the making? Verdi bowed and bowed. Time after time he was called back onto the stage. It seemed as though the audience would never let him go. They had found their own composer at last—the man who felt for them all, spoke for them all.

Afterward, in Verdi's humble room, Giovanni Barezzi thought of his untouched sack of gold pieces and laughed aloud, though even now he dared not mention it. "Why didn't you tell me *Nabucco* would be such a triumph?" he asked. "Surely you must have known!"

Verdi shook his head. "I wasn't afraid of failure—not after the rehearsals. But I never dreamed of anything like this!"

And truly it was bewildering, miraculous. Only a few hours earlier he had been utterly obscure, his one small success forgotten, his second attempt ridiculed into oblivion. Now he found himself in the front rank of Italy's idols, side by side with Rossini and Donizetti who, each in his day, had been the public's god.

As time went on, it became clear that Verdi was there to stay. After the graceful elegancies to which Italian ears were then attuned, *Nabucco* might seem rough, in places even clumsy. But it had sincerity, strength, and power such as had not been heard before. This opera was no courtiers' entertainment—it spoke directly, irresistibly to the people. The chorus, "Go, thought, on golden wings," which expressed Italy's own sorrow, spread rapidly to every town and village, and the Austrians, aware of the hatred their Italian subjects felt for them, understood its meaning only too well. The foreign rulers had suppressed all public demonstrations; they had clamped a rigid censorship on press, drama, and speeches—even on music and art. But this song, since it was on the surface about a far-off Biblical event, they were powerless to stop, and they came to dread the very sound of it. Bands of students, passing the government buildings, sang it boldly with a new feeling of strength and unity, and the Austrian sentries tightened their grip uneasily on their guns. At night in the unfriendly streets Austrian officers glanced over their shoulders and quickened their pace as "Go, thought, on golden wings" floated down from some dark window. But they hurried in vain. The song followed their nervous footsteps as from every courtyard, from every passageway, other voices joined in. It was everywhere, haunting and inescapable, and, hearing it, the conquerors—not the conquered—were afraid. In this Italy that was not yet a nation Verdi's chorus became a sort of national anthem, and Verdi himself was more than a beloved composer—he was the patriots' spokesman.

At La Scala *Nabucco* ran for fifty-seven performances, longer than any opera had ever done before. But this work, with which Verdi considered that his career really began, is no more given outside of Italy, and rarely there. Yet for the reopening of La Scala in December 1946, rebuilt after its bombing in the Second World War, *Nabucco* was chosen as the opera most fitting for so proud an occasion. Parts of it are crude and noisy; parts, conforming to a convention now outworn, would strike our modern ears as dull. We, who know the later, greater Verdi, fail to discover in this score the novelty that so impressed its first hearers. We forget that the ruggedness, the power, the sincerity so typical of the composer were new to opera in that stilted period. And if there are weaknesses in the music there is also much that is fine. Even today, a full century afterward, it would be hard to find an Italian who does not know, or who can hear unmoved, the great chorus, "Go, thought, on golden wings."

# CHAPTER SEVEN

# Ernani "Goes to the Stars"

## 1842-1844

THOUGH in his twenty-nine years Verdi had known only struggle and misfortune, though a hard road still stretched before him, he was never to taste obscurity again. No longer could he stalk lonely and unrecognized through the bustling streets of Milan. From that first performance of *Nabucco* until the end of his days he must live in the full glare of fame—fame so tremendous as to fetter and burden him. Literally overnight he found himself the object of a new, fervent hero-worship. Shop windows that he used to stride past in bitter solitude now displayed "Verdi hats" and "Verdi ties," and in the fine restaurants white-clad chefs concocted new sauces to name after him. He was showered with invitations from the world of fashion. Aristocrats rivaled each other to do him favors, offering him the use of their carriages (often he had as many as six at his disposal) and sending him elaborate gifts. All Milan, rich and poor, was at his feet.

A weaker man might well have lost his head. How easy, under these circumstances, to feel important, to let complacency creep in, to fritter time and energy away accepting admiration! But Verdi, whom honest praise made humble and flattery disgusted, continued unchanged to hold the world at arm's length. Inevitably the circle of his acquaintances was soon vastly enlarged, and he made new friends whom he was to keep for life—thoughtful, sincere people whose integrity matched his own; but society in general, though every door was now open to him, he avoided. He had no taste for frivolity, no small talk, no easy laughter, and he was never tempted to dissipation. Time and success were to polish away the gruff shyness of his early days, yet he continued aloof and, except with his closest friends, almost forbidding. Above all, never did he permit anyone to forget that he was a man of the people, peasant-born and proud of it.

With *Nabucco*, Merelli's faith in the strange young composer was justified beyond his wildest dreams; there was no longer any doubt that Verdi could make an impresario's fortune. Meeting the new hero the day after the première, Merelli threw his arms around him and, in true Italian fashion, kissed him on both cheeks.

Verdi eyed him askance. "That's all very well—now," he remarked. "But when I was poor, unknown, sick and in need, you wouldn't even advance me fifty *écus!*"

"I wouldn't—what? What on earth are you talking about? What on earth do you mean?"

"So you've forgotten? I haven't."

As Verdi told the story Merelli actually turned pale with distress. "But this is terrible!" he exclaimed. "I swear, I swear this is the first I've heard of it! Verdi, you *must* believe me—come, we'll find that wretched Pasetti now, at once, and settle the matter!" Grabbing the composer by the arm, Merelli rushed him off to confront the miserable engineer, who sheepishly confessed that he had not thought Verdi's message worth delivering.

In those days every manager was required each season to present at least one *opera d'obbligo*, or "obligatory opera," written to order for his theater. Other new works might of course be produced, but an *opera d'obbligo* was a truly gala event for which the most prominent composers felt honored to supply the score. During the third performance of *Nabucco*, Merelli sought out Verdi backstage, led him into his office and handed him a piece of paper.

"Here's the contract for next season's *opera d'obbligo*," he said. "It's all drawn up, all but the amount you're to receive. That I've left blank for you to fill in."

Verdi, surprised and elated, felt quite at a loss. His success was only three days old, and, unlike Merelli, he had not as yet grasped all that it meant for the future. What was his triumph worth? He had no idea. He must not belittle himself by asking too small a sum, nor must he take advantage of his sudden popularity by asking too much. Muttering that he wanted to think it over, he took the contract and went straight to Strepponi's dressing-room. Loyal Strepponi who had so often helped him before—she was theater-wise, she would know what to do.

"The highest price ever paid for an opera was 6800 francs," she told him. "Everyone knows that's what Bellini received for *Norma*. Of course you can ask no more, but surely you have a right to the same amount."

Bellini! *Norma!* Suddenly, with amazement, Verdi realized how fully he had "arrived." He would not have dreamed of naming so large a sum, but Strepponi's advice, as always, proved sound. This was not the first time that he thanked heaven for her friendship, nor was it to be the last.

It was the expression of patriotism that the public most eagerly awaited from the new composer, and for this his next subject, *The Lombards at the First Crusade*, offered splendid opportunities. Moreover Solera again prepared the libretto, and the poet, whose father was a political prisoner in Austria, hated the Austrian oppressors with all the violence of his stormy nature. His influence fanned the flame of Verdi's own ardent love of freedom. Perhaps, too, Verdi knew that the great patriot Mazzini, who from exile was inspiring his countrymen to resist their conquerors, had said that "an ideal and unknown young man" should arise in Italy to write the music of the revolution. It may be that in all humility Verdi strove to fulfill Mazzini's prophecy. In any case, whether deliberately or not, he succeeded.

Of course the foreign rulers saw in Verdi and his inflammatory music a new menace, and before *The Lombards* reached the stage the Archbishop of Milan, an Austrian related to the Imperial Family, found a way to make trouble for him. One of the scenes was to take place in the Valley of Jehoshaphat

before Jerusalem, with the Mount of Olives in the background. "Sacrilege!" declared the Archbishop. "To represent
so holy a spot in a theater! Besides, there are churches, religious processions, a baptism. It must not be allowed!" To
Baron Torresani, Chief of the Milan Police, he wrote a furious
letter threatening, unless the opera were modified, to appeal
directly to the Austrian Emperor himself. And so, just as the
rehearsals were about to start, Verdi, Solera, and Merelli
were summoned before the Baron in order to hear the Archbishop's objections and make the changes that he required.

The poet and the manager, thoroughly alarmed, hastened
to obey, but they went to the dreaded interview without the
composer. Verdi was not to be intimidated. "*The Lombards*
will be given as it is written or it will not be given at all," he
told them, and, ignoring the summons, he remained at home.

Tactfully, anxiously, Merelli and Solera pointed out to the
Baron that they quite understood: it was indeed daring to set
a scene in the Holy Land's most hallowed spot. But what
could they do? "You don't know the Maestro," they said.
"No power on earth can force him to change a single note
against his convictions. Rather than that, he'll forbid the
performance altogether, and the singers know their parts, the
scenery is built, the costumes are finished, everything is ready.
Think of the waste! But worse, far worse than that, you will
be depriving the public of a magnificent work!"

In spite of himself, Torresani was impressed by Verdi's defiant attitude. Moreover, he was an Italian first and a policeman second—he could not bear to think that, through his
doing, an opera of which so much was expected might never
be heard. "I shan't be the one to clip the wings of so promising
a genius!" he declared. And, shouldering the responsibility
himself, he undertook to talk the Archbishop around.

Shortly thereafter Verdi received word that the opera might
be produced complete with Valley of Jehoshaphat, churches,
baptism and all, provided that at one point the words "Ave
Maria" were changed to "Salve Maria"! This was ridiculous
—merely a face-saver for the Archbishop who must not appear
to have given in—and Verdi of course agreed at once. He

had won the skirmish, but it was only the first in a feud with the censors that was to plague him for years.

Rehearsals of *The Lombards* began at once and progressed smoothly; the singers were enthusiastic, especially Erminia Frezzolini, the young and beautiful soprano. Nevertheless Verdi's nerves were on edge. If he should fail now, after *Nabucco!* And yet, dare he hope for a second triumph only eleven months later? It was impossible—such miracles did not occur. As each passing day brought the performance nearer, his anxiety increased.

On the fateful evening, just before the rise of the curtain, Verdi called at Frezzolini's dressing-room to wish her luck. The young singer was radiant with expectation, and his tenseness, his distraught and worried look, amazed her.

"Maestro, surely you have no misgivings? Either the opera will be a triumph," she exclaimed, "or I'll die on the stage!"

When the performance ended, Frezzolini was still very much alive, for the miracle Verdi dared not expect had actually occurred. The applause for *The Lombards* was, if possible, even greater than that for *Nabucco*. What matter that the libretto was confusing, the music less inspired? There were the strong rhythms and vivid contrasts—so effective, so dramatic, so typically Verdian. Above all, there was the patriotic thrill. In the Crusaders, who, far away in the Holy Land, had fought and died for their beliefs, the Italians saw themselves. The prayer, "Lord, from our homes," seemed to come from their own hearts, just as "Go, thought, on golden wings" had done before. This new chorus was less fine, perhaps, but no one noticed or cared. Once again it expressed what the listeners felt. Once again Verdi had read their souls.

Two dazzling, incredible triumphs within one year! Of course Merelli begged for more, again offering to let Verdi name his own terms. But audiences are fickle—it would be folly, Verdi knew, to risk a third opera now in Milan. He would write for La Scala later. Meantime he agreed instead to provide the next *opera d'obbligo* for La Fenice, the famous opera house of Venice, and to open the season there with *The Lombards*.

All his life Verdi had worked hard; now success brought with it the necessity to work still harder. In his search for new subjects he read enormously and with the most careful analysis. He had to find a story that appealed to him, that, as he put it, he could "feel," that the managers considered suitable, and that would pass the suspicious eye of the censor. He must make sure that singers whose talents and personalities fitted the parts were available; if not, the subject chosen would have to be discarded in favor of another. Thinking, not of posterity, but of the immediate performance, he often wrote for a particular voice, and even made occasional trips to hear some singer who was unknown to him. Often he disagreed with a manager over questions of casting or setting. In that case Verdi never argued. Always clear and decided in his own mind, he stated his reasons and then simply did not give in. There were business matters too, such as the terms of his contracts with managers and publishers; these Verdi drew up himself with a clarity, simplicity, and fairness that could scarcely be surpassed. And he must find and inspire a poet to put the libretto, which he himself worked out in minute detail, into verse line for line, word for word, as he wanted it. Then, and only then, could he begin the actual composing.

Nor did his labors end with the completion of the score. Though he rarely conducted, Verdi directed rehearsals himself, taking infinite pains over matters that most composers were content to leave to others. Every scene that he set to music was vivid and complete in his mind's eye; he *saw* the characters, knew how they looked and stood and moved; he even saw background, costumes, colors, lights. With a sure theatrical instinct he described to scene designers just what he pictured, and persuaded artist friends, of whom he had many, to supply sketches of costumes and headdresses copied from famous paintings of historical events. It was Verdi who coached the company in the techniques of acting and singing —he himself sang exceptionally well. More difficult, and more important, he strove to fire the singers' imaginations, make them see what he saw, feel what he felt. For him, every performance must be as fine as it was humanly possible to make it; intolerant of any attitude less zealous than his own, he drove everyone hard, but himself hardest of all. To each who shared in the many-faceted undertaking he must communicate his inspiration. How simple, in comparison, to compose for solo instrument, or even for full orchestra!

For his fifth opera, after long delays and innumerable letters, Victor Hugo's play, *Hernani*, was agreed upon. Hernani himself, however, was an outlaw, a sort of Spanish Robin Hood, and the spirit of rebellion personified. Would such a hero pass the censor? It seemed unlikely, and Verdi half expected to have to do an opera about Oliver Cromwell instead. His new librettist, obliging, stage-struck young Piave— a facile verse-maker, less gifted but more reliable than Solera —even prepared the book for Cromwell in case of need. But Verdi had set his heart on *Ernani*, as the Italians called it; he persisted, and in the end he got his way.

This story that appealed to him so strongly was perfectly suited to the taste of the period. People were turning away in boredom from delicate formality—from the elegance of the minuet in the gilded ballroom under the twinkling chandelier. They preferred to let their imaginations dwell in dark medieval castles where were enacted deeds of chivalry and passion. Europe, casting off the cool spell of classical Greece and Rome, had rediscovered its own past and was fascinated by color, violence, glory. The works of Victor Hugo, literary standard-bearer of this romantic movement, had created a furor.

His *Ernani*, set in sixteenth-century Spain, follows a pattern now stale, but new and thrilling at the time. There is the lovely Elvira, the typical fair maiden in distress, about to be married against her will to Silva, her villainous elderly guardian. There is the unwelcome suitor who turns out to be the King in disguise and who, in order to capture Elvira, lays siege to Silva's castle. There is Ernani himself, the chivalrous outlaw—nobly born of course—who seeks to rescue the maiden and avenge his wrongs upon the King. There are all the trappings of romance, even a secret hiding place behind an ancestral portrait, and a meeting of conspirators at the subterranean tomb of Charlemagne in Aachen.

Ernani, taken prisoner by Silva, the wicked guardian, buys his freedom at a terrible price: he gives Silva a hunting horn and vows that whenever Silva shall sound it, he (Ernani) will take his own life. But the King, who has just been elected Holy Roman Emperor (Charles V), overhears the conspirators plotting against him and captures them, including Ernani. Whereupon, instead of ordering Ernani's execution, he has a sudden change of heart, forgives him, and even presents him with the fair Elvira as bride. There is general rejoicing, with a fine chorus in praise of the new Emperor's magnanimity.

Ernani's life, however, is still forfeit to Silva. In the midst of the wedding festivities the old man, mad with jealousy, sounds the fatal horn off stage. And Ernani, though happiness is at last within his grasp, is true to his vow. He stabs himself, and as he dies Elvira falls in a despairing swoon across his body.

A fantastic tale—but not to Verdi, nor to his audiences. They saw in it only the essential drama of the hero-lover who, with everything to live for, gives up life itself rather than break his word. They put themselves in Ernani's place and felt the nobler for it. No wonder Verdi, with his powerful imagination, had felt inspired.

In December 1843, taking his new and still unfinished score, Verdi went to Venice to direct *The Lombards*. There was no spot on earth quite like this city on the sea, with its exquisite buildings, mellowed by time and gilded by sunlight, reflected in the placid waters of the canals. He watched the gliding of the gondolas, listened to the swish of oars and the melodious voices of the gondoliers. It was wonderful, he admitted, poetic, divine. But he missed the familiar bustle of Milan, and the few friends whom he held dear. He had no heart for all this beauty, no thought for anything but work.

Then came a blow, unexpected and severe. *The Lombards*, which had set all Milan cheering, was an utter failure in Venice! Verdi took the setback quietly. On the night of the performance he wrote to a friend: "You are impatient for news of *The Lombards* and I send it to you still fresh—the

[ 87 ]

curtain fell not a quarter of an hour ago. *The Lombards* was a great fiasco, one of the really classic fiascos. . . . Simply and truly, that is the whole story, and I tell it with neither pleasure nor pain. . . ." He had come a long way since *King for a Day*. Now the discouragement he must have felt was well controlled.

With *Ernani*, too, he had his troubles. The manager of La Fenice, Count Mocenigo, found much to object to, especially the horn call. Verdi had written a lovely theme, haunting and ominous—but for the horn! A vulgar instrument used by hunters and postmen! Nervously the Count protested, "From the stage of La Fenice such a thing has never been heard!"

"It will be," said Verdi. And it was.

Verdi had been warned that Sophia Loewe, the German soprano who sang Elvira, was conceited, willful, and quick to anger. Anxious to avoid trouble, he treated her with more than his usual aloofness, but in vain. During rehearsals she made no secret of being displeased with her part, declaring that it gave her no opportunity to display the full brilliance of her voice. Her public, she insisted, would be disappointed. Verdi ignored her complaints.

Loewe then turned to Piave, the librettist. A soprano solo,

she told him, must replace the trio with which Verdi brought his opera to a close. Could Piave write new verses for it? Piave, always a "yes-man," could and did. Quite cheerfully he handed them to the Maestro.

Verdi, taken by surprise, was thrown into a cold fury. If he had composed a trio it was because musically and dramatically the opera required a trio at that point. These vain, stupid singers—why did they not write operas themselves if they knew so much better than he how it should be done? Would they never realize that it was the whole work, not the single aria, nor even the individual role, that mattered? Their imaginations were so self-bound that they could see an opera only as a vehicle for their own glorification. He had no patience with them.

This uncompromising attitude was all the more to Verdi's credit in that many composers flattered the singers, gave in to them, and even encouraged them to embellish their arias to suit themselves. Verdi, however, fought all his life against vanity and ignorance, and he won his battles. The trio remained, though as a result composer and prima donna were scarcely on speaking terms. But some months later Loewe admitted that the Maestro had been right; they made up their quarrel and thereafter she became one of his best interpreters.

It was on March 9, 1844, two years to the day after *Nabucco*, that *Ernani* was presented to the public but, unlike *Nabucco*, the new opera got off to a poor start. Loewe, angry and nervous, sang consistently off-key. The tenor flatted almost as badly, and he was hoarse besides. Neither cast nor audience seemed to understand the score. The delicate grace of Donizetti, the sparkle of Rossini, were not to be found in this music which, old-fashioned though it may sound to us, struck their ears as violent and noisy. It was puzzling, and at the première the applause was only lukewarm. But at the second performance things went better, and at the third better still. Soon *Ernani* became what we call a "smash hit"—the Italians said it "went to the stars." Again and again people returned to hear it, nor had they had enough when La Fenice closed

[ 89 ]

for the season. Another Venetian theater promptly put it on with huge success, and meantime twenty cities clamored for it. Throughout Italy immense crowds waited, often for hours, for the tickets to go on sale. Everywhere people talked of *Ernani* and hummed the music. It influenced current fashions much as Hollywood hits do in our day. And, as *Nabucco* had not done, it carried Verdi's reputation beyond the borders of his own land to all of Europe. Eventually it even found its way as far as that outpost of civilization which Europeans still pictured as a barbarous encampment surrounded by wild Indians—New York. Or, as Verdi himself wrote the incredible-sounding name, "Nuova Jork"!

In its own day *Ernani* was a great opera. Its melodies were unforgettable, and if the music was sometimes crude it was also passionately, irresistibly sincere. The strength, the intensity of feeling, left people breathless, and coming, as it did, at the end of an era of stilted and mannered restraint, *Ernani* swept the opera-loving world like a fresh, reviving breeze. For many years it held the stage. And if it is seldom to be heard in our time that is because we have outgrown it, as Verdi himself was to do.

# CHAPTER EIGHT

# Leave Italy for Me

## 1844-1847

VERDI had seen five of his operas reach the stage in as many years. Now, with his mounting fame, the pace quickened and in the next five years he was to produce nine more. This was not record-breaking; both Rossini and Donizetti had turned out a greater number in less time. But their labors were lighter than Verdi's and they took them more lightly; nor did they work under quite such intense pressure as he had to contend with. So keen was the demand for his music that even *King for a Day*, under the title of *The False Stanislas*, was revived (though not in Milan) with mild success. The public became insatiable, while publishers and managers, quick to see Verdi as the goose that lays the golden egg, pursued him relentlessly. Bound by contract often for two and three seasons ahead, he must always be planning an opera, even two, in advance of the one he was currently composing. Each involved complicated and tedious negotiations, not to mention travel, as did the repeated revivals of his earlier works which he himself frequently directed. It was not unusual for Verdi to rise day after day at four in the morning and work until nightfall, pausing only for a cup of black coffee hastily swallowed. He had no leisure, no chance to draw his breath in peace. As an old man, he was to refer to this period of his life as "the galley-slave years."

His health was wretched. The strain of each new opera

seemed to bring on recurring sore throat, fever, headaches, and severe digestive trouble. Sometimes he struggled on with his task in spite of pain and weakness. Now and again he was unable to leave his bed for days or even weeks, and these stretches of enforced idleness increased the tension under which he lived. His fatigue became chronic; only his sense of obligation and the strength of his will enabled him to fight it down.

Fortunately Verdi was not alone. In 1844, shortly after *Ernani*, a red-headed youth named Emanuele Muzio came from Busseto to Milan to be his pupil. Like Verdi himself, this Muzio was a poor boy who showed musical ability, was befriended by the ever-generous Signor Barezzi, and held a scholarship from the Monte di Pietà. Unlike Verdi, however, he was destined to become a competent musician and nothing more, for Muzio was no genius. And unlike Verdi he studied, not with the excellent but comparatively obscure Lavigna, but with a public idol, the best-loved composer in the land. For young Emanuele the wonder of this privilege never faded.

Daily Verdi gave the boy a brief lesson, then hour after hour master and pupil faced each other across a wide work table, each absorbed in his own task. Occasionally the older man would interrupt his labors to look over the youngster's progress and offer a word of criticism or encouragement. As a teacher Verdi was thorough, strict, and hard to please, yet kindly. Remembering the barren loneliness of his own student days, he tried to brighten Muzio's path with companionship, advice, and even a sort of fatherly affection. The boy, full of awestruck, limitless devotion, soon made himself useful in return by acting as secretary and assistant. Verdi's correspondence was vast and growing. Besides keeping faithfully in touch with friends, besides business affairs, he had to deal with strangers, cranks, and crackpots. (There was even a would-be composer who wrote him to stop work on his next opera at once because he, the unknown, was planning one on the same subject and did not wish to be eclipsed!) Muzio answered for Verdi such letters as he could, copied music, went shopping, delivered messages, and, in rare moments of relaxation, played bowls or billiards with his adored Maestro. They say that no man is a hero to his valet, yet through years of the closest association the pupil looked upon his master not only as a genius but as a saint.

Attending opera was of course an essential part of Muzio's education; but "little Redhead," as Verdi called him, was short of pocket money, and to offer to pay his way would hurt his pride. "Go only when I tell you to," said Verdi. "Then you'll be sure to learn from what you hear." Conscientiously, Muzio wrote to Signor Barezzi, "The money isn't spent in vain," for afterward Verdi would quiz the boy to make sure that he had listened well, and together they would analyze the different works. How unerringly could Verdi put his finger on a weak spot! How much he knew, about drama as well as music! How unfailing was his kindness! To young Emanuele such teaching was a revelation.

It was Muzio who kept Barezzi, and thus all Busseto, informed of the state of the Maestro's health and the progress of each new opera. Verdi himself was far too busy, though he did manage to visit his old home from time to time. Comparatively prosperous now, he had of course long since seen to it that all his debts were paid and that his toil-weary father and mother should spend the rest of their days in comfort and contentment. Seeing them, he could not help contrasting the peace of their little lives with the incessant turmoil of his own. "They are happier than I," he said. Once or twice he took an unfinished score to Busseto hoping that the placid countryside would refresh his spirit. But in vain—he had grown accustomed to the clamor of big cities and the kaleidoscopic tensions, the urgency of theater life. His self-important little home town irritated him, and the wide skies and tranquil, sun-baked fields of his boyhood only increased his driving restlessness. Being Verdi, he tried to hide his heart, yet it is clear that through all these crowded days, in spite of wealth, popularity and fame he was a deeply unhappy man.

What of the operas of these "galley-slave" years—the long procession of old-fashioned works that, except for an occasional overture or aria, are now forgotten? There was *The Two*

*Foscari*, based on a play of Byron's and composed for Rome—a brilliant but not lasting success. There was *Joan of Arc* for La Scala—a disappointment that never caught the public fancy, though Frezzolini's glorious singing and dark beauty in her white robe with the golden Fleur de Lys were much admired. Solera's libretto, introducing a love story for popular appeal, preposterously distorted history just as the movies often do now. The music, too, was for the most part weak, though for a while, since it was Verdi, every hurdy-gurdy in the land ground out the tunes.

Then came an opera for Naples, *Alzira*, written after an illness in just twenty days. Though Naples gave him a gala welcome Verdi took a dislike to the city, which was rife with gossip and intrigue. As a celebrity his every move was spied upon: "Look, he's going into the café!" or, "See, he's coming out onto his balcony!" Moreover he saw with contempt the host of minor composers who, "gnawing their fingers," as Muzio put it, in jealousy of the great man, made a practice of toadying to critics and other influential people. "I never spoke to a journalist or paid court to the wealthy," Verdi declared. "I disdain such methods. I do my operas as best I can and let public opinion take its course."

The singers liked *Alzira*, and after the final rehearsal the orchestra accompanied the Maestro home with cheers. At the première the public clapped (was it not Verdi?) but thereafter they stayed away. The opera failed. Verdi was indifferent; for once he had not been able to put his heart into his work. He had written, he admitted, "almost unconsciously" and "without much effort." Shortly afterward he himself realized the worthlessness of the score, and his artistic conscience forced him to seek a way to improve it. In the end, however, he wisely decided that it was hopeless and best forgotten. Years later he shook his head over *Alzira*. "That one," he said, "was really terrible!"

Not since *Nabucco* had Verdi felt such enthusiasm as his next subject, *Attila*, inspired in him. Piave seemed to him too mild a fellow to put the fearsome Hun, the "Scourge of God," into verse, so for the libretto Verdi turned once again to his old friend, fiery Solera. But Solera was difficult to deal with. Muzio, sent to spur him on, would find the lazy creature sound asleep in bed at high noon, and nothing done in spite of promises. To make matters worse, the poet raced off to Barcelona on one of his escapades before his work was completed, so it was Piave after all who wrote in the finishing touches. Verdi himself, though plagued by unusually severe illness, strove zealously to make this opera his finest.

For a time it seemed as though he had succeeded. At La Fenice, where *Attila* first appeared the applause was "almost too much for a sick man," Verdi said. And after the ovation at the theater Venice's dark waters shone as a throng of singing, cheering admirers escorted the tired composer to his hotel by torchlight. Yet the popularity of *Attila* did not spread beyond Italy, and was not lasting even there. By now a first audience's reaction no longer spelled success or failure. Verdi's presence alone was enough to set off the most frenzied demonstrations.

These early, less important operas of Verdi's often aroused an excitement which the music in itself, for all its crude energy and thumping rhythms, might not warrant. In those days, when to whisper the word "Italy" on the street was to risk imprisonment or worse, it was only in the safety of a crowded theater that the people dared give vent to their suppressed patriotism, their longing for freedom, their hunger for revolt. They looked to Verdi for the kindling spark—some situation, perhaps only one scene or even a single phrase, to spur their ardor and set them cheering. While *Attila* vividly brought to life on the stage their heroic ancestral stand against the Hun invaders, the audience repeatedly leapt to its feet, shouting "Italia! Italia!" When, with a grand gesture and in ringing tones, the baritone sang "Take the whole universe, but leave Italy for me!" the crowds of course went mad. In every theater in the land this line was breathlessly awaited, and it became the favorite catchword of the day.

*Attila* soon appeared at La Scala, but the production there was so inadequate that the Milanese raised a hubbub of protest. Through mismanagement, Merelli's fortunes had de-

clined, and the magnificent white and gold opera house, the pride of the city, had fallen upon evil days. Overpaying his favorites among the stars, Merelli skimped on all other expenses, and both orchestra and chorus, now shrunken and incompetent, were no longer equal to the demands of Verdi's music. In spite of La Scala's tradition of splendor, settings and costumes appeared worn, shoddy, and cheap. The singers, their fervor lost, squabbled incessantly both with Merelli and among themselves. Verdi, who had already struggled against hopeless odds while directing a revival of *The Lombards*, felt that the standard of performance was no longer worthy of this theater that had been (and fortunately was again to be) the greatest in the world. Even the public now indignantly declared that the staging of *Attila* was a disgrace to all Milan. When the composer protested, Merelli, on the verge of bankruptcy, turned against him, and their long association ended in bitterness on both sides. Not for many years thereafter would Verdi write expressly for the theater of his first triumph, and for a long time his contracts even stated at his insistence that his works might be given in any theater in Italy *except* La Scala.

There were plenty of other theaters—more than he could possibly supply. For lack of time he had to turn down innumerable requests, even from such far away places as St. Petersburg and Madrid. But the Parisian editor, Escudier, and Lumley, director of Her Majesty's Theatre in London, were not to be put off. Traveling all the way to Italy, they patiently pursued the Maestro from place to place with tempting offers. Escudier, who had had a statuette of Verdi made to stand in his study beside those of Bellini and Rossini, used every inducement to persuade him to come to Paris, artistic headquarters of the world. Verdi would go—when he could. Lumley wanted an opera a year for the next ten years. Verdi agreed to provide him with one.

Though Verdi was now comparatively well off, he was actually not so wealthy as might be supposed. Under the system then in use, he himself often profited less from his operas than did the editors who bought his scores in advance and among whom there naturally was keen competition. A certain editor named Lucca had pestered him for years, and Verdi at last contracted to write two new works for him. In the first days of the Maestro's renown, this Lucca's wife, a clever and ambitious woman, had even thrown herself on her knees before the composer and declared, weeping, that her husband faced financial ruin—nothing but a Verdi opera could save him! Verdi, however, was not the man to be swayed by such antics, and only much later did he give in. Now, through Lucca, it was arranged that one of the two new operas should be for London, the other for Naples. And there was a score for Florence to be produced besides.

Verdi, who had been very ill while finishing *Attila*, needed to build up his strength, for with so much ahead of him he could no longer carry his burden of weakness and exhaustion. So, holding the managers off as best he could, he spent a few weeks that summer of 1846 deliberately loafing. It was not easy. From London and Naples came frantic letters making light of his symptoms, implying them to be imaginary and insisting that the fine air of London or of Naples (as the case might be) would do wonders for him. Verdi, the most honest, considerate, and conscientious of men, was of course indignant. Bitterly he remarked, "It seems an artist has no right to be ill!" and forwarded doctors' certificates stating that he was in no condition either to work or to travel. Then, his breathing space won, he continued in determined idleness, driving almost daily to the outskirts of Milan to stroll through quiet lanes or to rest in sunny meadows. As the shadows lengthened he would return to the city and, after dinner and a game of billiards with his faithful Muzio, go early to bed. He even spent some time taking the waters at a health resort, where he grew stronger though thoroughly bored. Everything that concerned him was news throughout Italy; it was soon known that he was not working, and rumors of course flew: the Maestro had been poisoned, he was dying of consumption, he was already dead! Stupid lies, Muzio hastened to assure the anxious Bussetans. The truth was that their Verdi had gained

[ 98 ]

a little weight and looked less pale. Yet all during his so-called holiday he was considering new subjects, corresponding with managers as to which singers would be available where, and planning, and thinking.

Back in Milan, he began to write the opera for Florence, slowly and reluctantly at first, but with increasing fervor as his subject, Shakespeare's *Macbeth*, took hold of his imagination. At that time in Italy, Shakespeare was looked down upon as a horror writer; his gory plots, stripped of the poetry, the insight, the magic of his language, gave him the reputation of a not quite respectable lowbrow who broke every rule of classic drama. Verdi, however, had his own opinion. For years he had felt a special admiration for the English poet whom he was later to call "the greatest searcher of the human heart" that the world has everknown. Macbeth, Lady Macbeth, Banquo—these were no puppets, no stock heroes and villains to whom he, Verdi, must try to give the breath of life. These were real human beings, but more vivid, more marvelously revealed than human beings can ever be. Day after day, at his work table from eight in the morning until after midnight, he lived their story.

Soon Muzio, watching his progress, wrote to Papà Barezzi: "Macbeth is going better and better. What sublime music! I tell you there are things in it that thrill you! It costs him a great deal of hard work to write music like that, but he succeeds very, very well." Muzio added that the recitatives were about finished and only the arias remained to be done.

In the preceding century recitative had been considered such a bore that audiences often chattered aloud throughout, settling down to listen only when a singer stepped to the footlights to launch into a favorite air. Since then this music that linked the set pieces had grown more interesting, but it was still of secondary importance, and the time-honored procedure was to compose the arias first. Yet here was Verdi suddenly working the other way about! He could not now foresee the day when the edges of the arias were to melt away, when the singers would be obliged to act all the time, and the music, tight-woven with the drama, would flow continuously from curtain rise to curtain fall. Still, with *Macbeth*, recitative took on a new significance in his mind.

Though Verdi, always preoccupied, always rushed, had not yet brought to light the best that was in him, these weary years were not wasted. Each of his operas, whatever its faults, showed somewhere the flash of genius, and with each, whether success or failure, he taught himself something of value. The least self-important of men, he was not given to dreams of immortality, and—since his popularity was now secure, since he already had no rival in Italy—he might well have been content to repeat himself without making further progress. But the desire to write *good* operas—better operas—better and better—was too strong, and with *Macbeth*, his tenth work, he took his biggest forward stride so far.

Arriving in Florence in February 1847 to take charge of rehearsals, he was warmly welcomed, for nowhere was his music better loved. The city on the winding river Arno—so rich in the art and architecture of bygone centuries that the Renaissance seemed still to flourish there—delighted him. Humbly, almost devoutly, he visited the picture galleries, and, though he was no church-goer, would spend a quarter of an hour in a chapel on his knees as if in prayer, contemplating a favorite Michelangelo. In Florence, too, he enjoyed the stimulating company of writers, sculptors, painters, and such kindred spirits, many of whom became his lifelong friends.

But the *Macbeth* rehearsals—what a nightmare! Verdi, always hard to please, with this opera became relentless. Never had he cared so intensely about every detail. He himself had even written the entire libretto in prose for Piave to versify, and his instructions as to staging were minute. Now he struggled tirelessly to bring the drama, so real to him, to life in the singers' minds. In those days every singer was trained in standard attitudes and gestures designed to carry to the farthest spectator, and could be counted on to use these gestures at the appropriate moments. Moreover, those who took leading parts practised alone with the director in advance, so that three or four complete rehearsals were generally considered ample. For *Macbeth*, Verdi was not to be satisfied with this conventional approach. He made the singers work as they had never worked before, and bitterly did they resent it.

"Anyone would think we don't know our business," they grumbled. "He wears us out, and never a word of praise or encouragement no matter how hard we try. He's so severe, so unfriendly!" They even dreaded to see the Maestro arrive at the theater smiling—that always meant that he was full of energy and would keep them long over time.

Barbieri-Nini, the Lady Macbeth, had already practised her sleep-walking scene for three whole months, so eager was she to be convincing. Verdi was not satisfied. Again and again and again he made her go over it. She must be a woman half-mad with guilt, caught in a ghastly dream. She must move as though her feet did not touch the ground. Her face must be rigid, mask-like, drained of all expression, the eyes half-closed. Hardest of all, she must sing with her mouth motionless and almost shut. It was enough, she told her friends, to drive one crazy.

And then there was the great duet between her and the baritone Varesi, who sang Macbeth. They must forget the opera, the stage, Verdi told them. They must not consider their voices. This was no time to treat the audience to pure, golden tones. In a gloomy Scottish castle, in the dead of night, they had just murdered a king! Softly—still more softly—it was the secret terror in their hearts that he wanted to hear. Over and over he made them go through it, only to go back once more to the beginning. It was never quite right.

The stage was set for the final rehearsal, which Verdi had insisted should be in costume—a thing unheard of in those casual days. From the auditorium came the hushed and eager chatter of the invited spectators as they settled into their places. The orchestra tuned up. Backstage, nerves were on edge. Verdi, silent and unapproachable, stood in the wings in a characteristic attitude, his head bowed as if by the intensity of his thoughts.

Suddenly he looked up and, calling a stage-manager, had

Macbeth and Lady Macbeth summoned from their dressing-rooms. "We must go through the duet once more," he told them. "Come with me to the lobby."

Varesi's hand tightened on Macbeth's dagger at his belt, and there was active hatred in his eyes. "Impossible!" he spluttered. "This is too much! We've already been over it a hundred and fifty times! And besides, we're in costume—the audience will see us!"

"Then you will put a coat over your costume and go over it for the hundred and fifty-first time," said Verdi calmly. There was nothing to do but obey.

At the première the effect of the great duet was indescribable. Never before in opera had there been anything quite like it, and its novelty, its dramatic power, took the audience by storm. The singers, forced thereafter to repeat it at every performance two, three, four, even five times, soon forgave Verdi the ordeal of the rehearsals.

And the sleep-walking scene! That first night Barbieri-Nini, waiting backstage in the shadows for her cue, was conscious of Verdi hovering nearby. Tense, speechless, his phosphorescent eyes glowing, he kept circling about her as if in her hands she held all his hopes. Nor did she disappoint him. The applause still thundered as she fled to her dressing-room and stood there alone, trying to catch her breath and quiet her pounding heart.

Abruptly the door flew open and there was Verdi, his face transfigured with relief, admiration, gratitude. Tears brimmed in his eyes. His lips moved, but no words came. Never in his life could he bring himself to pay trite, empty compliments; now, deeply moved, he was unable to speak at all. With a helpless gesture he took the soprano's hand, pressed it, and was gone. In Barbieri-Nini's career this was a memorable moment. Never, she felt, never, had singer been so richly rewarded as by the Maestro's wordless thanks.

That night Papà Barezzi, who had come all the way to Florence for the occasion, sat out front, proudly counting the curtain calls. Thirty-eight times Verdi was forced to take a bow! What a glory for Busseto!

This was in 1847, more than half a century after the French Revolution, but the embers of that mighty conflagration still smouldered and were about to burst once more into flame. Throughout Europe the day of revolt against oppression was almost at hand. In Italy the Secret Societies (nowadays we should call them the Underground Movement) were growing bigger, stronger, more eager for action. By this time when *Ernani* was performed, the soldiers of the chorus boldly wore red-white-and-green scarves and cockades, and even carried tricolor banners—flags of a nation not yet born. It was just part of the costume, they insisted. Everyone knew better, but how could the Austrians object? The new, liberal Pope, Pius IX, openly opposed the foreign rule, and many Italians hoped (though in vain, as Verdi prophesied) that through him their freedom would at last be won. In the streets people sang a new version of a chorus from *Ernani:* "Glory and honor to Charles Fifth" became "Glory and honor to Pius Ninth." *Carlo Quinto, Pio Nono*—the words were interchangeable. Even in *Macbeth* the patriots found fuel for their fire. Macduffo (as he is called in Italy) had these lines to sing:

> Betrayed, in tears,
> Our country calls to us;
> Brothers, let us hasten
> To succor the oppressed!

In Venice the tenor stepped out of his part at this point, stuck the tricolor cockade in his hat, and, advancing to the footlights, threw wide his arms in a direct appeal to the public. The uproar that followed so alarmed the Austrians that thereafter at every performance they stationed not only police but soldiers inside the theater to maintain order!

Today parts of *Macbeth* sound old-fashioned, stilted, quaint. Much of it is magnificent, however, and can bring even modern hearers to the edge of their chairs. But in its own time, in spite of its novelty and the sensation it caused, it failed to find its way to the public heart—and understandably. The atmosphere of gloom was unrelieved. There was no glittering décor, no spectacular processions, no pageantry. The murky heath, the weird witches and ghosts, belonged to a northern legend unfamiliar in Italy. There was no love story. How could an opera become popular without a love story? Such a thing had never been heard of. Worse still, there was no heroic tenor part: Macbeth was a baritone, and Macduff's role was small and secondary. Nor was there a single flowery, sweet soprano air. Instead of a lovely lady in distress here was an evil, tigerish woman who suffered retribution for her crimes. And the music? It was thrilling but—different. One would have to get used to it.

Public opinion, however, did not influence Verdi's own judgment. At the time *Macbeth* first appeared, he preferred it to any of his works that had gone before. Whenever and wherever it was revived he took special pains over every detail of its staging, and after eighteen years he still thought enough of the score to produce the revised version that is occasionally heard today. Especially notable and appropriate were the performances at the great Edinburgh Music Festival held during the summer of 1947.

On March 25, 1847, eleven days after the first performance, Verdi wrote to Antonio Barezzi:

Dear Father-in-law:
I have long intended to dedicate an opera to you who have been my father, benefactor, and friend. It was a duty that I should have fulfilled sooner had not unavoidable circumstances prevented me. Now I send you *Macbeth* which I prize above all my other operas and therefore consider most worthy to be presented to you. My heart offers it; may your heart accept it as testimony to my eternal gratitude and love.
With deepest affection, your—
G. VERDI

It was a fitting gift for the man who had started him on his way. As yet, for all his fame, Verdi had written little that would long survive him. Now, with *Macbeth*, he had found the road that was to lead to immortality.

# CHAPTER NINE

## Maestro of the Revolution

1847-1849

"THE steam engine flew over the land, the steamboat flew over the water!" Thus wrote Muzio on his way to London with Verdi early in the summer of 1847. Country lad that he was, he marveled at everything, especially this new magic of steam. And the tunnels! Between Cologne and Brussels there were twenty-four of them, some three, some even five, miles long. In the train the oil lamps had to be kept burning all the time!

From Strassburg the travelers were to have proceeded by stagecoach direct to Paris, but they arrived just too late—the coach had left. Rather than spend a day in idle waiting, Verdi, restless as usual, decided on the longer route down the legend-haunted Rhine and through Brussels, even though, as Muzio exclaimed in amazement, this cost four times as much! From a little chugging steamer they watched the steep shores of the river glide by, vineyard-clad and castle-studded. At Bonn, Beethoven's birthplace, they paused to admire the newly erected monument in honor of the great German master whom Verdi always specially revered. All that he saw moved Muzio to wide-eyed wonder; Verdi, however, was less impressionable. He had with him the not quite completed score for London, *I masnadieri*, based on *The Robbers* by Schiller. Never before had an opera of his been first presented beyond the borders of Italy, and he dreaded the ordeal of facing a foreign public.

Business detained Verdi in Paris for a few days, so Muzio was sent ahead to secure suitable lodgings in London. And very cramped these lodgings seemed after the roomy, thick-walled Italian "palaces." But what a city it was, this English capital! How neat, how spacious, in contrast to the picturesque, haphazard towns of Italy. The wide, clean streets, the well-kept buildings, the flowing crowds, the air of power and prosperity had to be seen to be believed. And then its size—to go from one end of the place to the other you would have to change horses three times! Such splendor, such activity, such wealth—London would have been Paradise but for the climate. Verdi's bones, soon saturated with clammy English fog, ached for his native sunshine. He hated the pall of smoke that hung forever in the sky, and the eternal smell of burning coal.

The city would gladly have fêted the visiting celebrity, but he declined all invitations to balls, dinners, receptions, concerts. Only once did he dine out, at Lumley's, where he met his great fellow-countryman, Mazzini. Exiled and persecuted, Mazzini by his writings and by his example had become an inspiration to lovers of human freedom everywhere, and the composer was proud to make his acquaintance. On the whole, however, Verdi kept to a hard routine, rising at five every morning and working all day to finish his new score, while Muzio beside him copied out the parts. Occasionally, in the evening, the two would drop in at the opera, but with little pleasure. The performances struck them as mediocre, and besides, Verdi was sure to be recognized. Why could not people listen to his music without wanting to know what he looked like or to pry into his life? When heads turned in his direction and curious stares clung to him, his face grew somber.

Verdi's music was already well known in England for *Ernani* had been followed there by others of his works. In fact, *Nino of Assyria* and *Anato* had once played simultaneously at different London theaters. Since in England it was forbidden to represent anything from the Bible on the stage, both these operas were simply *Nabucco* in disguise. The story of Nebuchadnezzar had been lifted out of the Old Testament and given new names and new settings.

Between these two theaters—Her Majesty's, which Lumley directed, and Covent Garden—there existed a fierce rivalry. Lumley's best conductor, Michael Costa, had recently deserted to Covent Garden, and to offset this loss Lumley had secured that season not only Verdi, but also Jenny Lind. All England was infatuated with the "Swedish Nightingale." On her way to and from the opera her carriage passed with difficulty through the throng of her admirers blocking the streets. Verdi had made certain beforehand that she should sing in *The Robbers*, but he himself was not much taken with her. She was a plain little woman with heavy features and dull blond hair, and the charm that had brought the British to her feet made little impression on him. Though her voice, her musicianship, were extraordinary, she was at her best in the elaborate arias of the older composers, full of trills and vocal pirouettes. This cool style of singing, thanks largely to Verdi himself, was already beginning to be outmoded in Italy. Meaningless flourishes and embellishments were giving way to simpler, smoothly flowing melody, and Verdi preferred the marvelously sustained tones and emotional warmth of the Italian voices.

It was Queen Victoria herself who set the date of the first performance of *The Robbers*, so that she and all the Royal Family might attend. Never before had an Italian composer of Verdi's eminence written an opera especially for England, and the public was impatient for the great event. By half-past four on the afternoon of the première the crowd could be held back no longer. Bursting open the doors, it poured into the auditorium and sat down to wait. Though Verdi had declined to conduct, he was obliged to do so in spite of himself—a letter from the Russian Ambassador with a long list of glittering signatures made it impossible for him to refuse graciously. When at last, with cold dignity, he stepped to his place at the conductor's desk, the audience could not guess the intense nervousness hidden behind his solemn and unbending demeanor.

Present that evening beside Her Majesty were Albert, the Prince Consort; Prince Louis Napoleon (soon to become President, then Emperor, of France); the Duke of Wellington; and, as Muzio said, "an infinity" of other Dukes and Lords. Satins gleamed, fans waved, jewels flashed in the brilliant gathering. Seldom had the great English capital been treated to such a gala event, and everyone was determined to make the most of it.

The performance of *The Robbers* did not call forth the sort of delirious ovation that Verdi had become accustomed to at home. To shout and weep in public was not the British way. There was, however, tremendous applause both for Verdi and for the beloved Jenny Lind. The critics, for the most part, were politely enthusiastic, although one or two of them lashed out against the new opera. "Mediocre" was too good a word for it, they said. Verdi was clumsy, vulgar, noisy, given to coarse exaggeration. His popularity in his own country must be merely a passing fad. Never could such a composer achieve anything worth while.

This response was not surprising. Musical taste in England at that time leaned toward the dainty, the elegant, the ultra-refined, and the English considered beautiful what nowadays we should call merely pretty or oversweet. At his best, Verdi was strong meat for such a public, and *The Robbers* was by no means his best. His detractors, seeing his faults—he was at times all that they said of him—remained blind to his sincerity, his strength, his enlivening power. They wanted music like that which they then admired: music for the most part long since forgotten for lack of the very vitality which in Verdi's work so shocked them.

On Verdi himself harsh words from the critics had no effect. He could only, would only, write in his own way despite the sneers of the learned, which even at home in Italy he did not always escape. He was a new kind of opera composer—neither an intellectual nor a society man, but one of the ordinary people. Other musicians of humble birth had acquired aristocratic leanings with success. Not so Verdi. He remained a peasant. It was to the crowd rather than to the connoisseurs that his music appealed. In him the crowd heard the voice of its own heart, and it was the crowd that made him famous.

*The Robbers*, however, was a disappointment. Clearly the excitement, the applause, had been due to the presence of a great celebrity, to the glamor of the occasion, and to Jenny Lind, rather than to the opera itself. After only three performances, it vanished from the repertory—one more in the lengthening procession of hollow triumphs. Nevertheless, in spite of (or perhaps because of) the critical controversy, Lumley saw in Verdi a drawing card and made him an offer that might have changed the whole course of his life. Would the Maestro become conductor of Her Majesty's Theatre for the next ten years, providing for it one new opera each season?

For three years, not ten, Verdi was willing to consider it. Could he stand the depressing London climate, he wondered? Could he be satisfied to compose so little and spend his best energies merely conducting? Notwithstanding the drawbacks, the offer tempted him, for by Italian standards the salary seemed enormous. Here, far more rapidly than elsewhere, he could set aside a sum against his retirement, and Verdi, tired, sick, restless and lonely, at thirty-three already dreamed of retiring. Pressed on all sides, preoccupied with endless details, pulled hither and thither by his eternal contracts, he had no home, no life that he could call his own. "Ah, what a wretched fate is mine!" he exclaimed in a letter to a friend—a rare outburst for one so reserved as he. More and more he longed to live as other men, and to be free to write what and when he chose. Above all things he needed leisure to think and feel and grow. By staying in England he could sooner achieve this.

He would accept Lumley's offer. But first he must rid himself of his obligation to supply a second opera for Lucca of Milan. Foreseeing no difficulty, Verdi wrote to Lucca, explained the situation, and promised him 10,000 francs for canceling their contract.

Verdi, however, was not destined to become a conductor first and a composer second. Lucca, who had waited so long to secure a Verdi score, did not intend to relinquish his prize for any consideration on earth. He answered the request with a flat refusal, thereby incurring the Maestro's lasting enmity. Verdi, always reasonable and fair, often extremely generous, expected from others a standard of conduct as high as his own. Had Lucca been less short-sighted he might have won the composer's gratitude and friendship. Instead Verdi angrily lived up to the letter of his agreement and never again had anything to do with Lucca. Henceforth he would deal only with the house of Ricordi, which, thanks to the profits from his operas, rapidly became the wealthiest and most important music-publishing firm in Italy—a position it still holds today.

Wearily Verdi settled in Paris and, sending Muzio back to Milan to attend to his affairs, took up his next task—the revision of *The Lombards*, about to be produced under its French title, *Jérusalem*, at the Opéra. This great theater, most glamorous and impressive in the world, had its own formidable set of rules and traditions. Only grand opera (that is, serious and imposing works with none of the spoken dialogue often allowed in comic opera) could be given there, and only in French. There must be five acts, and above all there had to be a ballet. Verdi, with no time to write an entirely new work, was obliged, in spite of his longing for rest, to make many changes and additions in the score of *The Lombards* to conform to French requirements. *Jérusalem*, produced with all the magnificence of which Paris was capable, and superbly sung, brought the usual applause—and then failed to draw the public. One more empty success!

Though the French capital seemed less splendid to Verdi than London and he hated the noise and bustle of its famous boulevards, he stayed on there. Paris was for all Europeans the center of the universe. As by a magnet, the great of the earth were drawn to this "city of light," and the Parisians, preoccupied with their own affairs, hardly gave a passing glance to the countless foreign celebrities in their midst. Here Verdi for once could go where he pleased, do as he chose, unrecognized. At first he was bored, weary, and homesick, but at least he had privacy.

At the appointed time he sent Lucca the finished score of

*Il corsaro*, based on Byron's *The Corsair*. Having composed it rapidly, mechanically, and with distaste, Verdi took not the slightest interest in the fate of this opera, leaving the rehearsals entirely in Muzio's capable hands. Produced at Trieste, *Il corsaro* was a total failure, never to be revived.

With negotiations for his next work delayed, and no libretto on hand, Verdi could for a short while almost forget that he was a composer. He lingered on in Paris—Giuseppina Strepponi was now quietly living there, supporting herself by giving singing lessons. She, like Verdi, had borne heavy burdens in her youth. Though she was only thirty-three, her voice already showed signs of wear, and, rather than face a bitter decline, she had retired from the stage while her reputation was still at its height. Lonely and disillusioned, she saw before her a future of such emptiness that on dark days even the thought of suicide had crossed her mind. But that was over now that Verdi had come to Paris. He had always liked her, admired her, treasured her friendship; now he discovered that he was deeply in love with her and she with him. Eight years had passed since Ghitta and the babies had died, eight hectic, rootless, frozen-hearted years. Giuseppina at last healed the old wounds of sorrow and despair. From this time on she lived for his sake only.

Hereafter it was Peppina, as he called her, who read and translated foreign plays for him—she was a better linguist than he. It was she who first sang his new arias to him, with the ink still wet on the page; she who advised and helped him in everything he undertook. She knew his moods, his sensitiveness, his inner strength, and her devotion was wise, patient, and selfless. Warmed in the glow of her bright and gentle humor, he began to come out of his shell, to enjoy himself. With her, though he protested a bit, he even went to an occasional party.

Characteristically, Verdi said nothing about Peppina to his friends, but something of his high spirits spilled over in his letters. "I can't conceal from you that I am having a wonderful time," he wrote. "I do nothing, go walking, listen to the most ridiculous nonsense, buy nearly twenty papers a day (without reading them of course) to escape the persecutions of the newsboys, for when they see me coming with a whole bundle of papers in my hand they don't offer me any. And I laugh, and laugh, and laugh." There had been little enough cause for merriment in Verdi's life, yet these days his stern face was always breaking mysteriously into a smile, at anything, at nothing. Peppina noticed that his laughter, when it came, was like himself—like his courage, like his anger, like his love, and like his music—big and whole-hearted.

But why twenty newspapers? This was 1848, the year of revolution. Europe seethed with discontent. The working people of Paris, their patience exhausted by the misrule of King Louis Philippe and his minister, Guizot, muttered and grumbled more and more loudly against injustice, oppression, unbearable taxes. On February 22 an angry mob got out of control; and the soldiers summoned to restore order sided, not with the government, but with the people. The next day Guizot resigned, but too late: the tide of rebellion was rising fast and Paris already echoed, as it had done before and was to do again and again, to the battle that never ends, the battle for liberty. Verdi watched crowds in full revolt surge shouting through the streets, saw men and women rip out paving blocks and cobblestones and pile them high to form crude barricades. He saw the fierce, flushed faces, heard running feet, hoarse cries, and the sickening sound of shots. And late that night he watched an endless, shapeless procession of revolutionists as by torchlight they accompanied the bodies of their dead silently through the silent streets. Next day the fight was won—the King abdicated and a republic was proclaimed, France's "Second Republic." Frantically the populace rejoiced; yet Verdi, seeing the new government stumble confused and disunited into power, without idealism or common sense, could not believe that this republic would endure, and history was to prove him right.

Tidings of the upheaval in France shook the whole European continent, and everywhere the downtrodden took heart. A wave of rioting and insurrection swirled through Berlin, through Hungary, and even broke out in Vienna. Prince

Metternich, the Austrian minister who had maintained the Empire's stranglehold on its vast subject territories, hastily fled to England for his life.

By March came the electrifying news that Lombardy, too, was in revolt. The Milanese Secret Societies had stepped boldly into the open, bringing long-treasured weapons out of hiding and looting gunsmiths' stores. For five famous, terrible, heroic days the improvised army fought the well-armed and -organized Austrian regiments. Everyone joined in the battle. Even untrained young Muzio grabbed a gun and spent those sleepless nights and days shooting, running, hiding, shooting, running, hiding. Verdi, though barely recovered from an illness, sped to Milan. He was no longer a skeptical spectator; he must be on the spot, he must do something, anything, to help.

But he arrived too late to take part—the pent-up fury of the Milanese had routed the enemy. Milan was free! Venice, too, had joined in the uprising, and the Austrians were driven back and back to the Quadrilateral—a great square of Lombard territory where they finally entrenched themselves and held firm.

One of the towns that formed the corners of this Quadrilateral was Legnano, scene of a twelfth-century battle in which the Lombards had defeated the Hapsburg emperor Frederick Barbarossa, ancestor of their present Austrian foes. Verdi, back in Paris, chose this battle as the subject for his next opera. Since his wretched health prevented him from being a soldier, he must aid as best he could the cause that he had so much at heart. He would compose a work that should inspire his countrymen with patriotism and the heroic spirit of sacrifice.

They were to need inspiration. Though courage glowed and hope rode high, theirs could be but a losing fight. Unassisted, the Italian states, weakened by long bondage as they were, could not permanently withstand the might of Austria, especially since they lacked unity among themselves. Without help from their powerful neighbor, France, the cause of Italy was doomed; nor was this help forthcoming. By midsummer the tide of battle inevitably turned; and though Venice, despite starvation and disease, was to hold out heroically for another year, Milan fell once more into Austrian hands.

In Paris a group of distinguished Italians sent an eloquent and touching petition to members of the French government, imploring assistance in the struggle for liberty. Verdi of course signed it, but without hope. Though he always insisted that he knew nothing about politics, he was too clear-headed for wishful thinking. Nothing, he felt, could be expected from a France unsettled and distraught with her own troubles, and once again history was to prove him right.

From Milan came shocking rumors of imprisonment, torture, and even death sentences, for the Austrians were taking a terrible revenge on the reconquered city. In Paris, too, there had been new outbreaks of rioting, with further bloodshed and bitterness. Verdi, disillusioned and heartsick as the light of hope grew dim, felt that the simple people of the earth had once more been betrayed and beaten down. How ridiculous that at a time like this he should have to busy himself with opera, entertainment! And yet he must. There was nothing else that he could do. He resolved that his music should become a weapon in his hands. Impatiently he waited for Cammarano, the distinguished Neapolitan poet, to send him his new libretto. In the meantime, at Mazzini's request, he composed a battle hymn called *Sound the Trumpet*, which he hoped would be sung to the tramp of marching feet. But already it was too late—the fighting had almost petered out.

Verdi was now settled at Passy, just outside of Paris. Though he believed that he hated country life, he had taken a little house there to please Peppina, who insisted the change would do him good. Passy was quiet. Stretched at ease in the sunlight, one heard only the distant laughter of homeward-bound schoolboys, or the occasional placid rumble of a cart. Bees hummed among the flowers. Warm winds stirred lazily through the trees. In the mornings the grass twinkled with dew and the air was fresh and cool. Peppina was right—Verdi found that he could work better here than in the roar and dust of the city. He had almost forgotten that he was a farmer's son. Now he dreamed of owning land—some corner of the earth where he could plant things and watch them grow, where he could build and farm and think, where he could create his own small, peaceful world and live in it the life he longed for. Hearing of a large piece of property for sale not far from his birthplace, Le Roncole, he bought it. Sant' Agata, the estate was called. As soon as he had time he would have the old house altered to suit himself. Meanwhile, *The Battle of Legnano*.

In Rome the Italians were still their own masters, and there in January 1849—just a few days before the birth of the short-lived Roman Republic—*The Battle of Legnano* was first performed. At the final rehearsal a huge uninvited crowd, hysterically excited, forced its way into the auditorium. Not since *Nabucco* and *The Lombards* had Verdi had such an overwhelming, uproarious triumph. And no wonder! Arrigo, hero of the opera, imprisoned for years in enemy land and long given up for lost, returns to Milan just as Barbarossa's invading army threatens Lombardy. At once he is made a member of the Death Riders, a band of brave knights who have sworn to defend their country to the last drop of their blood. Leader of this noble company is Arrigo's old friend Rolando, now married to Arrigo's former sweetheart. Rolando is unjustly led to suspect a love affair between his wife and his friend and, to punish Arrigo, locks him in a castle room while the Death Riders march forth to battle. Thus Arrigo, forced to break his oath, will be forever branded a traitor and a coward. Such dishonor is not to be endured. With a cry, "Viva l'Italia!" he leaps at peril of his life from the castle window into the swirling river below and, swimming to safety, joins his comrades at arms. In the last act tidings of victory are brought to the anxious people of Milan and great is the rejoicing. But Arrigo, who has distinguished himself by dragging the mighty Barbarossa from his horse, is mortally wounded, and at his own wish is borne home to breathe his last in the cathedral. There he and Rolando are reconciled, and, kissing his country's flag, Arrigo dies.

Of course all Rome went mad, and in the deafening applause, in the hoarse shouts of "Viva l'Italia! Viva Verdi!"

was to be heard a new note of fierce resolution. After thirty dangerous years, when even to speak their minds was to court death, these people had seen their long underground activity culminate in a heroic effort—and a crushing defeat. Had all their passionate idealism, their courage, their sacrifices been in vain? No—Rome was still free, and though the fight might not be won yet, never, never would they admit that it was lost. And Verdi's music—one could not hear it and remain quietly seated: it quickened the pulse and fired the blood. As it lashed the crowd to frenzy there was not a man in the house but longed to prove on the spot his willingness to die for his country. In the balcony one soldier, who had perhaps stayed too long at some tavern, was so stirred that, springing to his feet, he hurled his helmet onto the throng below. His coat and spurs followed. Then his unsheathed sword arched through the air to land quivering in the glow of the footlights. Next he began tearing up the seats and throwing them down piece by piece. Just as he seemed about to leap over the railing himself and crash onto the heads of the terrified people beneath, he was forcibly subdued by the police and dragged from the theater.

At every performance of *The Battle of Legnano* the entire last act had to be repeated while the audiences wept and thundered. The "Oath of the Death Riders" became a sort of national hymn, nor was it a plaintive lament as "Go, thought, on golden wings" had been. This new chorus was a song of determination, a fighting song. Now, more than ever before, Verdi became the spokesman of his people. He had been affectionately known as the *Papà dei Cori*—Father of Choruses. With *Legnano* he acquired a prouder nickname: Maestro of the Revolution:

In spite of the blaze of glory, Verdi returned to Paris sick at heart over the sufferings of his country and worried by rumors of the Austrian rule of terror in Milan. Young Muzio, like many others, had had to flee the city and was now in Switzerland—a refugee. Verdi, hearing indirectly that he was desperately short of money, sent him a handsome sum enclosed with a graceful, bantering letter that made light of the gift. He understood his "Redhead" and would not for the world offend his pride.

During that summer of 1849 came the grim news that the last strongholds of independence had fallen, leaving all Italy once more in total darkness. To his close friend, the sculptor Luccardi, Verdi wrote bitterly: "Force still rules the world! Justice? What can justice do against bayonets?" and anxiously he added: "Tell me about my friends. Write quickly, quickly, don't lose a minute. I bear an inferno within me."

He must do another opera, this time for Naples. Weary and disillusioned, Verdi turned from battles and heroism to *Luisa Miller*, a simple love story taken from one of Schiller's plays. There was nothing grandiose about it. No great cause was at stake in this tale of two ill-starred lovers, a peasant girl and a nobleman's son. The nobleman and Luisa's villainous rejected suitor oppose the match. Kidnapping both her and her father, they threaten to kill the old man unless Luisa agrees to marry the villain. Moreover she must write her lover that she will have nothing further to do with him, that all her vows of love were false. Poor Luisa is forced to send the fatal letter or see her father put to death. Whereupon her lover, in despair, poisons both her and himself—only to learn too late that she was true to him. Verdi's music for this pitiful tale had a touching, intimate quality his work had never shown before. No one had guessed that the Maestro of the Revolution was capable of such delicacy, such warmth, such tenderness.

That summer an epidemic of cholera swept over Europe, striking Paris with special violence; and Verdi's frightened parents begged him to come home, where the danger was less. So it was in a fine "palazzo" which he acquired on the main street of Busseto that *Luisa Miller* was finished. In spite of his dear Barezzi family, Verdi had no love for the narrow-minded little town—he could never quite forgive it his early trials and frustrations. By settling there, however, he could plan and watch the building on his new property at near-by Sant' Agata, which meant so much to him.

Of Naples, where *Alzira* had failed, he had only disagreeable

memories, and in October 1849 he returned there with reluctance to put on *Luisa Miller*. Verdi always paid his librettists out of his own pocket, and this opera had been undertaken
largely to help the poet Cammarano, whom he knew to be
in need of money. He had no sooner arrived in Naples than
Cammarano gave him a useful hint.

"It's been kept secret," he said, "but I happen to know that
the opera house is on the brink of bankruptcy. Unless you're
careful, you're likely never to be paid for your work!"

Verdi, gratefully acting on Cammarano's tip, informed the
management that he would not hand over his score until the
sum he was to receive had been deposited with a third party,
to be turned over to him after the first performance.

This shrewd move caused consternation since (as Verdi
suspected) no such sum was available. Himself the most
scrupulous of men, he could not forgive questionable dealings
in others, and in vain the management pleaded with him.
Angrily he declared that unless the money were immediately
forthcoming he would leave Naples at once, taking his precious score with him. Everyone knew that Verdi always meant
what he said. What was to be done?

At this point the Superintendent of the Royal Theaters, a
certain Duke of Ventignano, had what he thought was a
brilliant idea. Marching to Verdi's hotel, he stood in the street
and shouted up at the composer's window, while a curious
crowd gathered.

"Maestro," cried the Duke, "you are perhaps unaware of
the Neapolitan law forbidding artists to leave the city without
my official visa on their passports. It's all very well for you
to threaten to depart, but if you try it you'll find that you
can't pass the border without my express permission!"

The spectators stood open-mouthed. None of them had ever
heard of this century-old law dating from a time when among
traveling actors, singers, and mountebanks there had been
all sorts of disreputable thieves and scoundrels. To apply it
to a man of Verdi's stature now, years after it had become
obsolete, was an insult, an outrage. The crowd muttered indignantly.

Verdi controlled his fury and thought fast. From his window he looked over the rooftops of the hillside city to the glittering bay below, where a French warship rode at anchor. "Very well," he called down; "but if you want me or my score you will have to look for me on board that frigate, where I shall be under the protection of the French government! Unless, of course, you agree to my conditions."

The Duke could make no answer. He learned, as so many others had done, that to argue with the iron-willed Maestro, even to threaten him, was sheer waste of time. Mumbling that Verdi would hear from him, he uncomfortably withdrew, much to the glee of the onlookers. And shortly thereafter the opera management notified the composer that the sum of 12,750 francs had been deposited as he required. Rehearsals began.

But Verdi's troubles were not over. Naples to this day is an extremely superstitious city. Its people believe, really believe, that certain persons called *jettatori* have "the Evil Eye" and, intentionally or otherwise, bring harm to anyone whom they approach. One of Verdi's most ardent admirers in Naples was an amateur musician named Capecelatro, and it was common knowledge that this poor fellow had the Evil Eye. He, the *jettatore*, had caused the failure of *Alzira*, Verdi's Neapolitan friends insisted. This time, therefore, he must be prevented at all costs from coming near the Maestro. Suppose *Luisa Miller*, too, should fail, or worse still, suppose some disaster should befall Verdi himself!

To protect the adored composer from this menace his well-meaning friends organized a guard of honor. If Verdi retired to his hotel they took turns standing watch outside his door. When he came out of his room they immediately gathered in a circle about him and accompanied him wherever he went. If he entered a café they surrounded him while he ate, and during rehearsals they posted themselves at all entrances to the theater. Not for one moment was Verdi, who so loved privacy, permitted to be alone. And poor Capecelatro, longing to pay his respects to the composer he revered, never even caught sight of his idol from a distance, though he tried again and again. If he appeared at the theater someone was sure to tell him that Verdi was at the hotel, and vice versa, or else the Maestro could not be disturbed. It was bewildering.

Verdi had other annoyances to put up with. A few days before the performance a prominent critic approached him with two reviews already prepared, though the opera was still unheard. The first was fulsome in its praise, the second scurrilous. Undoubtedly, remarked the critic, the first would be printed—*if* the Maestro could find it in his heart to make him a little present . . . Otherwise . . . He pointed to the second one, so venomous and damaging.

Verdi's face hardened. "Print whichever you like," he snapped, and turned on his heel with loathing and disgust.

The rehearsals went smoothly. At the première the first act brought tremendous applause, and there was still greater enthusiasm after the second. But the last act—as so often with Verdi's operas, it was the best of all—surely it would produce an ovation! During the intermission before it the happy and excited bodyguard relaxed its vigilance, feeling that all danger had passed. Verdi was on the stage, giving last-minute instructions to the singers, when suddenly there was a cry: "Maestro! At last I've found you!" Capecelatro, beaming with delight, rushed from the wings and flung his arms round Verdi's neck!

*Crash!* Verdi sprang to one side hauling the *jettatore* with him just as a huge, heavy piece of scenery toppled forward and fell exactly where they had been standing!

It was a narrow escape, but the set was soon righted and the curtain rose on that final act which should have been the most triumphant of all. Strangely, that night it received only a scattering of lukewarm applause, and the composer's friends cursed their own carelessness and shook their heads over the power of the Evil Eye!

Not even Capecelatro, however, could long prevent the success of the new opera. It was customary for every opera composer to hover over the first three performances of each of his works, and after that to leave them to their fate. Even before Verdi returned to Busseto he had the satisfaction of seeing *Luisa Miller* appreciated as it deserved to be.

# CHAPTER TEN

# *"If Rigoletto Lives"*

### 1850-1851

ALMOST daily Peppina, looking very smart under her little French parasol, drove through Busseto in Verdi's carriage, yet no one smiled at her or admired her as she passed. On the contrary, the street-corner gossips glanced at each other with raised eyebrows and exchanged disparaging whispers. This Strepponi had been an opera singer, and opera singers were not always respectable—that was common knowledge. Not that Peppina was flashy, but her simple, lovely Parisian clothes set her apart from the good ladies of Busseto. To their provincial eyes she had a fashionable, worldly air; one could see that she was at home in great cities and addressed celebrated persons by their nicknames. The townspeople, remembering Margherita Barezzi, were jealous of this fine lady, this outsider who rode about in Verdi's carriage as though it belonged to her. Wherever the great man was, there was Strepponi also. What did it mean? Were they married? No one knew, and the possessive little town resented this secrecy. Verdi had put Busseto on the map, for which it not only worshipped him but wanted to own him. Nobody paused to think how much privacy might mean to a man so constantly in the spotlight of fame, or to learn what kind of woman Peppina really was, or to consider how her devotion might brighten his lonely, hectic days.

Papà Barezzi, loyal both to his fellow-citizens and to Verdi,

was troubled as he saw the old rift between them widen. Not even with him, however, would Verdi discuss his private affairs. Courteously, but firmly, the composer pointed out that what he did, what Signora Strepponi did, was no one else's business; whether they were married, or whether they even intended to marry, was a matter that concerned only their two selves. This worried good Papà Barezzi. Obviously the singer's influence over his Giuseppe was very strong. Could it be a beneficial influence? At first he doubted it, but later, as he came to know Peppina well, he grew to love her dearly. The warmth, the gentle gaiety of her spirit were irresistible. She was wise, too, and utterly selfless. Papà Barezzi, seeing all that she meant to, all that she did for this genius whom he loved as his own son, learned to bless her for it.

Verdi himself looked forward to the time when he could leave Busseto for good and settle in his "desert" as he called Sant' Agata. And dreary the place must have seemed to the romantic minds of those days that found beauty only in mountains, forests, waterfalls—scenery tinged with mystery and grandeur. To them the acres of vineyard, fields of rippling grain, the few stark trees and empty, tranquil skies looked merely practical, bleak, and monotonous. Even Verdi all his life spoke of the spot as "ugly"—and loved it with his whole heart. Now, before the remodeling of the old house was finished, he could already picture what he would some day make of this property of his. Here he would build up-to-date stables to raise thoroughbreds, there he must have kennels (Peppina so loved dogs!), and over there barns for the cattle with pasture land beyond. The soil was fertile, thanks to the river near by. He would farm seriously, scientifically, not just for fun. He would employ the local peasants' sons (but for a twist of fate he himself might have been such as they) and teach them newer, better agricultural ways. And he would create beauty. The little stream that murmured through his fields—why not dam it to form a tiny artificial lake where waterfowl might make their home? On the sheltered, sun-warmed terrace before the house, semitropical plants would surely thrive. There must be a kitchen garden, too, and greenhouses so that Peppina should have flowers all the year round. The tumbledown dwelling itself was being transformed into a spacious villa, severely simple, but wonderfully comfortable and pleasing. Down by the river the wrought-iron gateway set between weeping willows would be forever open to his friends, but closed to the curious crowds that peered at him as though he were some freak of nature instead of a man like other men. Within that gate would be his refuge of serenity and peace.

Characteristically, Verdi designed and supervised every detail of the construction himself, and this in spite of the fact that he was all the while composing as busily as ever. *Stiffelio*, his next opera, produced at Trieste late in 1850, was a failure partly because the music was uninspired, partly because the story had no appeal for Italians. It concerned a Protestant German clergyman and his erring wife, and Catholic audiences, never having heard of a married priest, were confused. Moreover, for musical reasons, Verdi had scored the clergyman's part for tenor—the voice reserved for soldiers, lovers, heroes; this was a break with tradition that people found almost absurd. It was the old paradox of the public clamoring for novelty yet unable to accept it when it came.

Verdi had chosen this drama because its human side appealed to him, especially the climax in the church when Stiffelio, as he forgives his wife her sin, quotes the words of Jesus. This scene, however, was looked upon as blasphemous. Yet the poor reception of the opera did not greatly disturb Verdi. It was not his way to brood over past mistakes which might or might not be of his own making. Long before the curtain rose for the first time on *Stiffelio* his mind, soaring as usual into the future, was engrossed with new ideas. With his friend Cammarano he was already deep in correspondence about a libretto for *King Lear*, the haunting tragedy which Verdi considered Shakespeare's greatest. Though he longed to set it to music, he approached the task with reverence. Casting and staging such a work presented problems, and he himself was not yet free to give to the score the best that was in him. He was booked for a new opera shortly to be produced in Venice and he had found for it just the subject he wanted: Victor Hugo's *Le roi s'amuse*, a fine but dangerous play.

Dangerous, because everywhere that new, unfamiliar, but growing force called "democracy" was challenging the divine right of kings. To Europe's crowned heads, and to those whose power depended upon the established order, the mere word "revolution" was the sum of all evil. For their own sakes they must preserve the tottering belief that "the king can do no wrong." Yet in Hugo's play no less a monarch than Francis I of France appears as a dissolute and heartless libertine whose murder is plotted by one of his lowly subjects—shocking ideas to put into people's heads! In Paris the drama had caused a near riot and had long since been banned. What would the Venetian censor have to say about it as an opera?

Verdi wrote to Piave, and the librettist, always optimistic, hastened to assure him that all would be well. Living in Venice as official poet of the great Fenice theater, Piave had (so he said) inside information. The Maestro need not hesitate—the censor's coöperation could be counted upon. Immediately and enthusiastically Piave set to work on the libretto that was to be the finest of his career.

Verdi was intensely busy with *Stiffelio* and revivals of earlier works which he directed in various cities. There was the building at Sant' Agata besides, and of course his vast correspondence to attend to. Yet he managed to give much thought to Hugo's drama; indeed, he could not help it. The story took hold of that inner life of the imagination which, in him, was often more vivid, more absorbing than his so-called real life.

At times as he tramped over his property he saw neither fields nor stream, and the familiar wind tugged at him unnoticed. Living the parts like an actor, he was conscious only of the people in Hugo's play, people whose portraits Verdi must paint with notes. The central figure, a limping, hunchbacked court jester, he understood and pitied rather than despised. This poor creature, mocked and humiliated all his life, has turned in bitterness to evil ways, goading his wild young king to heartless pranks and cruel pleasures. Knowing himself safe in the royal favor, he even glories in the hatred he incurs, until an aged nobleman pronounces a grim curse upon him. The misshapen jester, with his tormented heart and twisted soul, loves but one thing in all the world—his daughter, and jealously he hides her from the wicked court, keeping her very existence secret. Yet, despite all his care, she is stolen away; the curse has begun its work. Thirsting for revenge, he hires a cutthroat to lure the King to a remote, disreputable inn and there murder him. At midnight, through a raging storm, the hunchback goes exultantly to claim his victim—he, the poor fool, the plaything, has brought the mighty low! The body, wrapped in a sack, is given to him. Gloating, he drags it toward the riverbank when suddenly, from the inn, he hears the King's mocking, devil-may-care voice raised in song! In that spine-chilling moment the jester realizes that his plot has miscarried. But someone is dead . . . In terror he rips open the sack and by a flash of lightning sees—his daughter!

What a scene! What a story! Verdi was determined that the

libretto should be perfect, with no superfluous word, no line that should fail to intensify the tightly woven, swiftly moving plot. Again and again he summoned docile Piave to Busseto to confer with him, and as they worked the two men grew ever more enthusiastic. Verdi, to be sure, sometimes had qualms about the censorship, but Piave cheerfully insisted that there was no need to worry. Not even when word came from La Fenice that the authorities were beginning to protest was the poet disturbed. He had ways of knowing, he said, that all would yet be well.

Suddenly from the Venetian police came an appalling letter signed by one Martello, Superintendent of Public Order, absolutely forbidding the performance and scolding both composer and poet like bad little boys! By this time the libretto was practically finished; and Verdi, though he had put scarcely a note on paper, had already found in his mind the music that he wanted. His score was clear to him and therefore, as he said himself, the major part of his task was done. He took pride in living up to his obligations, and now the date for which the completed work had been promised was rapidly approaching. In the time that remained he could compose another opera if need be, certainly—but not without a libretto, without even a subject for one, at hand. In desperation he offered *Stiffelio* instead; Venice had not yet heard it. To pacify their exasperating censor, he was even willing to rewrite the whole last act. Better than this he could not do. But La Fenice refused *Stiffelio*. The famous theater, entitled by contract to a brand-new opera, would accept no stale substitute.

Verdi was angry, very angry! Carefully he pointed out that he himself was not to blame; the whole thing was Piave's fault for repeatedly reassuring him. Now Piave was in disgrace—a state of affairs that the well-meaning fellow could not endure. He hastened to send the Maestro peace offerings: delicious sweetmeats, and fish fresh from the nets of the Venetian fishermen. But this hopeful gesture was worse than useless. Between the lines of a coldly formal letter of thanks, poor Piave could read Verdi's irritation and scorn.

If Venice was to have its opera a compromise must somehow be reached. Negotiations began, and as they dragged along Verdi composed at a furious pace, almost as though he were taking dictation. In forty days he completed the score; this was the way he liked best to work, catching the torrent of his inspiration while it was fresh and live and true.

Meantime letters and conferences, more conferences and more letters. Since Maestro Verdi was so far advanced, said the authorities, let him use his music as it was for an acceptable version of *Le roi s'amuse;* Piave was quite willing to adapt the libretto as they suggested, sweetening and purifying it beyond recognition. But Verdi would not hear of such a thing. To him, opera was not music for music's sake, however beautiful. It must be music to heighten drama, unthinkable apart from the particular situation it was created to enhance. As his genius ripened, this goal became more and more clear to him, just as his understanding of human beings steadily deepened. Ten years ago he would not have dared to tackle so unorthodox a subject as this brutal tale. Now the monotonously grandiose themes, the conventional heroes and villains of his early works, merely bored him.

Wearily he struggled to convince the authorities that the King, reformed into a noble youth, would not sing the gay and heartless music of a libertine. Nor would a fine upstanding fellow such as they tried to substitute for the jester pour out his soul to the same tune as an ugly and embittered hunchback. There were minor difficulties, too, which tried Verdi's patience. For instance, the authorities would not have the body in a sack—too horrible, they said. Why, protested Verdi, should a corpse inside a sack be worse than just a corpse? Did they suppose that the father would drag it halfway across the stage without discovering it to be his own daughter? Ridiculous! These people wanted to reduce the well-constructed plot, moving so inevitably to its tragic end, to nonsense.

Deadlock, while Verdi fumed and the days slipped by, till the performance was only three weeks off. Then came a jubilant letter from Piave: Martello, none other, had come to the rescue! The Superintendent of Public Order was, it appeared, a music lover and much distressed to think that a work of Maestro Verdi's might never see the light. If, said Martello, the scene of the opera were laid not in troubled France but in some little, unimportant state, if the conscienceless King were to become instead of a historical personage an imaginary duke of, say, Mantua—if the names of all the characters were changed and also the title (Verdi's choice, *The Malediction*, was considered blasphemous), then there would be no further objection. It was as simple as that.

And thus the masterpiece that was so nearly doomed became *Rigoletto*. With immense relief Verdi agreed to a few trifling alterations; he had won on all the counts that mattered. Arriving in Venice, he greeted Piave with a smile—all was forgiven. Once again the poet was his "good Piave," "dear Piave." Chuckling, Verdi said to him: "If *Rigoletto* lives, as I hope, think how staggered the public will be to find out that a policeman collaborated with us!"

As rehearsals progressed, Verdi regularly skipped one song which, in the last act, the Duke sings gaily over a glass of wine—a flippant ditty, such as he might have picked up in some tavern, about the fickleness of womankind. (It is this same air that Rigoletto, believing the Duke dead, hears later with such horror.) Not only was this never rehearsed but, to the distress of the tenor, Mirate, the music appeared to be missing. Again and again he approached the composer—after all, the song must be learned, practised—only to be put off with some excuse. It was not ready, it had not been copied, Verdi had forgotten to bring it. Forgotten? That was not like the Maestro. Mirate, thoroughly puzzled, looked his dismay. Verdi patted his shoulder calmly. "You shall have it, my friend, all in good time." The miserable tenor worried all the more.

Only two days before the performance Mirate in desperation appealed to Verdi again. The Maestro grinned. "Here it is," he said. "I've held it back on purpose, and before I let you have it you must make me a promise. Give me your word of honor that you won't sing it aloud, not even once, where anyone can possibly hear you. I tell you that if this tune leaks out it will be all over Venice in twenty-four hours. People will swear they've always known it—and unless it comes as a complete surprise I might even be accused of stealing a familiar song!"

Mirate eagerly agreed, and Verdi handed over "La donna è mobile" ("Woman is fickle"). At a glance the tenor saw with relief that it was easy. He hummed it under his breath—what a melody! Once heard, it simply *could not* be forgotten.

Verdi had been wise. This song was inescapable—one sang it, whistled it, whether one wanted to or not. Over night the air of Venice grew vibrant with it, and from there it traveled forth as though on the wind, to become one of the most remarkable song hits on record. And, unlike other song hits, it has lasted a hundred years—even today it is known to half the world.

"La donna è mobile," so lilting, so singable, is by no means great music, nor was it intended to be. Hearing the supremely catchy tune uprooted from its setting, we are apt to forget that Verdi's purpose was to paint a portrait of the man who sings it. And the melody is indeed the Duke himself: gay, heartless, tawdry, and irresistible.

*Rigoletto*, however, is one of the great operas, and from the first performance, on March 11, 1851, was recognized as such. Its popularity was immediate and immense, soon spreading to every corner of the globe wherever opera was known at all. Music has the power to intensify drama much as a pair of opera glasses enlarges figures on the stage; and Hugo's play, good though it was, came to be remembered only as the source of Verdi's *Rigoletto*. Hugo himself, always prejudiced against any tampering with his work, tried in vain to keep the new opera out of France. But having heard it, he handsomely admitted that Verdi's version was stronger than his own. Listening to the famous last-act quartet, he even envied the composer, confessing that, as a dramatist, he would give a good deal to be able to show simultaneously, as Verdi had done, what four different people were doing, thinking, feeling. Other operatic ensembles had been written (though not many) as beautiful musically and as perfect technically. But separate these voices, and each part expresses the character's individual reaction to the situation, so that the drama does not halt for a purely musical interlude where heroine and villain might sing the same melodic phrase, as in set pieces hitherto. Instead, the conflict continues heightened and the tremendous climax is brought nearer. Never had anything quite like this been heard, nor has the musical feat often been successfully repeated.

A composer has another advantage over a playwright: the orchestra. More and more Verdi was coming to realize its possibilities, using the instruments to set a mood, create background and weather, and reveal emotions hidden too deep for speech. Simply but brilliantly he achieved his effects. There was the thunderstorm in the last act, for instance. How much more than a storm he made of it!—with the shuddering drums and the cruel, stabbing flashes of the piccolo. But no instrument could give to the moaning wind just the vague sense of terror and desolation Verdi wanted. For that he was inspired to use human voices humming behind the scenes.

A magnificent score, the critics agreed. Yet they regretted that Maestro Verdi should squander his great gifts on a theme so rude and violent, so shocking and vulgar. It was not in good taste, they declared, to show a twisted cripple on the stage and expect one to pity a creature so hideous. Verdi, however, in advance of his time, did not confuse ugliness with vulgarity. He knew that life is not always either sweet or splendid, and he took his inspiration not from stale operatic models, but from life itself. This buffoon might be deformed, ugly, and wicked, but he was a man, a living man who breathed and suffered. Truth, rather than beauty or refinement, had attracted Verdi to the story—the very truth that at first offended his elegant audiences.

Especially in Victorian England people shook their heads. Even Verdi's music was too much for one British critic, who announced that he had always suspected that nothing of the

Italian composer's would last, and after hearing *Rigoletto* he was sure of it—as neat a piece of mistaken prophecy as one is likely to find anywhere.

"If *Rigoletto* lives," Verdi had said, and added "as I hope . . ." He did not guess how indestructible it was to prove. Could it die, its very popularity would long since have killed it. In every generation the greatest artists are proud to sing the parts, while countless third-, sixth-, tenth-rate companies give it their shabby best. Its arias, torn from their context and made meaningless, are worn threadbare on the concert stage and by the shrill, monotonous twanging of all the hurdy-gurdies in the world. The score has been imitated, even parodied, without mercy. No matter—*Rigoletto* survives. By and by fashion turned its back on the too familiar work, calling it stale, obvious, and outmoded. But no opera company could afford to omit *Rigoletto* from the repertory since, fashionable or not, it filled the house year in, year out. Today, as always, the standees wait in a long, patient line to hear it, and fashion takes the aged, ageless score again to its heart.

Most of the operas written never reach the stage at all, and of those that do the merest handful last beyond a few seasons. Why then should *Rigoletto* approach its hundredth anniversary with its vitality undimmed? The power that creates enduring music remains forever mysterious.

Verdi was thirty-seven years old. From the beginning he had known what he was capable of achieving, and though his road was long and hard he could not be lured aside to easier ways. He had learned how to write operas by writing them. He was still learning—he would always be learning—but with *Rigoletto* he had at last produced a timeless masterpiece.

# CHAPTER ELEVEN

# Time Will Tell

## 1851-1854

JANUARY, even in Rome, can be a wretched month, and it was never worse than in 1853. The yellow Tiber, swollen with continual rains, swirled over its banks and flooded the near-by streets. Cellars were submerged, and round the opera house, only a stone's throw from the river, the muddy water stood in pools ankle-deep. Nevertheless, by eight o'clock on the morning of the 19th an immense, damp, uncomfortable crowd had already queued up outside the ticket office. Some munched a dismal breakfast of soggy bread and cheese, or scraps of cold sausage. Others patiently, miserably, shifted their weight from one soaking foot to the other. But no one left the line. In those days tickets were not sold long in advance as they are now; it was first come, first served. And for this particular night the posters announced *Il Trovatore* by Giuseppe Verdi, the Maestro's first new work since *Rigoletto* had started on its triumphant and unending march around the world. By noon the house was sold out, and that evening not another human being could have squeezed inside the doors, while hundreds of disappointed late-comers lingered outside for hours in the cold and wet, hoping to catch some overflow of the excitement, the glory, within. This was Italy, where opera must go on through war and peace, famine and flood, since without it the people's spirit starves.

Even next day the glow had not faded. A dense crowd still

cluttered the streets for blocks, spreading clear across the Bridge of Sant' Angelo. Those nearest the theater simply stared at its familiar walls as though a miracle had taken place there. Those farther back tried to draw closer, like thirsty creatures round a desert water-hole. These were the little people, the starved and cramped of soul, whom Verdi's music lifted beyond their own humdrum lives, letting them share in the dignity and greatness of mankind.

Long before the final curtain came down on *Trovatore* it had been obvious that here was another success of the magnitude of *Rigoletto;* and, like *Rigoletto,* the new opera was to prove indestructible. Not all the organ-grinders in the world can wear down this heroic music—music like a huge mural painting, its figures larger than life-size. From this score the much admired romantic aura of *Ernani* shone again, but strengthened by all that the composer had taught himself in the nine intervening years. And *Il Trovatore* (*The Troubadour*) survives in spite of a story that might well have doomed a lesser work, a story in which horror is piled on horror till it becomes incredible, even absurd. One does not, after all, burn babies alive, and especially one does not throw one's own child to the flames, mistaking it for someone else's! Yet the entire plot hangs on this fantastic incident. Inevitably, as the fame of the opera grew and spread, it was mocked and parodied without mercy; Gilbert and Sullivan, especially, found in it a wealth of fun. But Verdi's score! It flows like a full river of melody, and audiences the world over, their hearts expanding to the large, simple beauty of the music, came and still come year after year after year to hear it.

Actually, the far-fetched tale is not impossible. In the witch-haunted, feud-darkened Spain of the fourteenth century, bloodthirsty doings such as these could, and indeed did, take place. Besides, the central figure in the drama, the gypsy woman Azucena, is supposed to be half-crazed. A hundred years ago, moreover, the story seemed less improbable than it does today. Many, in fact, found it almost too convincing and were appalled by the situations: Leonora, the heroine, taking poison, and Manrico, the hero, executed by his own brother while Azucena is about to be burned at the stake! Some complained that it was all too grim, too violent, too many people died. To which Verdi, unable to shake off a mood of lingering sadness, replied wearily, "What is there in life but death?"

For the Maestro the twenty-one months between *Rigoletto* and *Trovatore* had been a time of sorrow, anxiety, and petty annoyances. In June 1851 his mother died—brave, intelligent Luigia whose love had warmed his joyless growing years. She, first of all, had realized that her solemn little Giuseppe might have a destiny beyond the village—in a world she did not know and to which she could not follow. Close to her as a child, and deeply loyal as a man, he felt her loss keenly. To him the humble such as she, who earned their daily bread and led their children in honorable ways, would always be the true nobility.

Verdi settled at Sant' Agata as soon as the place was livable, although the work of building and improving the property would still be carried on for years to come. It was good to be at home on these peaceful acres at last, instead of having to drive out from his temporary quarters in Busseto to visit them, and the quiet was a blessing. Gates and watchdogs kept beggars, prowling strangers, and uninvited guests away from the Villa Verdi, as the house came to be called. Yet there was one tattered old scarecrow of a man who from time to time appeared boldly at the door, sure of his welcome. This was the fiddler, Bagasset. "Ah, Maestro," he would mumble, his weathered eyes wide with sentimental wonder, "it seems like yesterday. You were only so high, trying to scramble onto my knee, reaching for the fiddle . . . To think you first heard music from me!" He would shake his head and amble off to the kitchen, knowing that he could count on a good hot meal and a glass of wine there—the dining-room would have embarrassed him.

Not even in the "desert" of Sant' Agata, however, could Verdi find relief from business worries. Of his seventeen operas some had now been forgotten, but others were repeatedly staged in cities scattered throughout many lands, and this involved much tedious correspondence. Moreover, Verdi was often angered by reports of distant performances for which some unscrupulous conductor had cut or altered the score to suit himself. There were frequent irritations, and now as always an insistent pack of managers hounded him for new works. This pressure, this demand for more and more and more, was the price he paid for his success.

At least beneath Sant' Agata's wide, empty sky his imagination could find space in which to stretch and grow. For a time he became absorbed in *King Lear*, brilliantly outlining a libretto for his friend Cammarano to versify, and thinking with eagerness of the music. But the actual composing—he needed a long interlude of freedom in order to give to it the best that he had in him. How else do justice to his beloved Shakespeare's mightiest tragedy? Moreover, the opera, when written, could not be put on at just any theater any time. Such was his reverence for this play that he would insist on a perfect cast, a perfect production, or none at all. As yet, therefore, *King Lear* remained but a cherished dream.

During the winter following Luigia's death there had been dull, homesick weeks in Paris while negotiations for a new work for the Opéra dragged on, and gossip, back in Busseto, spread and flourished, at last reaching even Verdi's ears. The Maestro was becoming Frenchified—he, who was Italian to his very bones! He was giving himself airs with his refusal to have anything to do with his neighbors! The little town could neither understand him nor leave him alone, and its hostility nettled him more than he cared to admit; on his return to Sant' Agata he was likely to go out of his way to drive round Busseto instead of through it. Always, too, beneath surface vexations the plight of his beloved Italy oppressed his heart. If only France would help . . . But he knew well that nothing more than empty gestures could be expected from the French just now. In the summer of 1852 Louis Napoleon bestowed on him the Legion of Honor, even sending Escudier, the distinguished publisher, all the way to the Maestro's retreat to make the presentation. Practical Verdi was not in the least cheered or impressed. Medals to him were useless hunks of metal.

At home he had hoped to find peace of mind, but his father, left in charge at Sant' Agata during his absence, became gravely ill, and until the old man's recovery was assured Verdi's anxiety was a heavy burden. Then word arrived from Naples that Cammarano too had been taken ill—Cammarano who was at work not only on *King Lear* but (and this was urgent) on *Trovatore* also. Verdi, much concerned, wrote repeatedly for news. Receiving no reply, he assumed that the poet was well again, and waited impatiently for the libretto. But one July day, leafing at random through a theatrical magazine, he read that Cammarano was dead! This was a real shock. So admirable a man, so fine a poet—his was a loss that Italy could scarce afford, for the Italians are a proud people who, through these years of political humiliation, looked to their writers, artists, and musicians for comfort and glory. And why had no one thought to send Verdi word of his good friend's death? It only sharpened his sense of bereavement to learn the news thus from a printed page. What would become of Cammarano's widow? How was she to live now? He sent her not merely sympathy, but the full amount the poet was to have received for *Trovatore* and a substantial sum besides.

But time was shrinking, and in all haste someone must be found to finish the libretto. Verdi called to the rescue an obscure writer named Bardare who, thrilled at the opportunity to work with the illustrious Maestro, completed, patched, and polished the verses as best he could.

This libretto could not in any case have been a good one. The story, based on a long, complicated Spanish drama that was highly thought of at the time, inevitably became confusing when compressed into opera form. Verdi, however, had been attracted by its rugged violence (the very quality that makes us smile) and by the character of the mad gypsy Azucena. She, like Rigoletto, is an "underdog," and her suffering, like Rigoletto's, touched his imagination. In the prison scene when Azucena and her son, condemned to die,

[ 137 ]

dream with such longing of the mountains of their homeland it may be that something of Verdi's own heartache at his mother's death overflowed into the score. Yet in his music he never attempted to express *himself*. Opera, unlike a sonata or a symphony, must be impersonal. It must reveal the people of the story rather than the composer. Verdi's experience of life deepened his understanding, his unfailing sincerity gave to whatever he wrote the ring of truth; but he would not, could not, pour out his own soul in his art. Moreover, it never occurred to him that Giuseppe Verdi might be an interesting man. His was a rare nature, especially among artists—too modest, too reticent to suppose that what he thought and felt could be significant for others.

The triumph of *Trovatore* on that wet night in Rome quite failed to lift his spirits, so depressed was he. Fortunately, however, he had no leisure for brooding. Though nearly the entire score of *Trovatore* had been put down on paper in twenty-nine arduous days it had first ripened slowly in his mind, and along with it another opera, *La Traviata* (*The Erring One*), which was due to make its bow in Venice only seven weeks later. Because of doubt as to when and where certain singers would be available, Verdi had not known until almost the last minute which of these twin operas would be first produced, and so the two works were pondered simultaneously, each to take final shape at breakneck speed. Even while directing the *Trovatore* rehearsals Verdi worked on *Traviata;* and now, back at Sant' Agata, as the days raced by, the pressure increased. He could scarcely take time to eat or sleep, so intense was his concentration. A hasty note to a friend closed with the words: "I have to leave you now. I must go back to my sharps and flats, which are a real torture to me." And this was true. Not that his inspiration failed him. Rather, the difficulty was to hold the music fast before it faded, to mold it while the warm life was still there. Sometimes, dissatisfied, he worked over a passage again and again. Sometimes, as in the marvelous prelude to the last act, he wrote "all in one breath"—literally without pause, and (even more remarkable) without revision.

[ 138 ]

Peppina, longing to see him rest if only for a moment, knew
that he could not while the fury of creation was upon him,
and she was far too wise to urge him. Patiently she effaced
herself, but she was always there, ready to listen to a newly
finished scene, or to sing an aria so that he might hear whether
in the black pattern of notes still wet upon the page he had
indeed captured the effect he sought. Occasionally, though
not with her, Verdi grew short-tempered and irritable under
the strain. It made no difference: Peppina understood, and
did her best to protect him from distraction and annoyance.
Now and again, to be sure, in her letters a cry escaped her,
and once, watching him suffer, she wrote: "O God, grant
that Verdi compose no more operas!" It was the man himself,
not his fame, that she loved.

Soon Verdi was ordering a high desk to be ready in his
hotel room in Venice so that he could get on with the orchestration the very night of his arrival; Piave must attend
to it. As the première approached, the familiar excitement
took strong hold of the Maestro, and for once in his career he
dared feel confident of success in advance. *Traviata* was "sure-
fire"—he knew it! Ever since he had seen young Dumas' play,
*The Lady of the Camellias*, in Paris he had been convinced that
he could make of it another *Luisa Miller*, but infinitely finer,
more moving; and Piave had provided him with an excellent
libretto. Yet this undertaking required courage, for the scene
was laid not in the remote past but in contemporary Paris.
Here were no murders and thunderstorms, no swords and
banners, no heroics at all—only the pathetic love of Violetta,
a beautiful courtesan, and Alfredo, a young Frenchman of
good family. In a little house in the country they are idylli-
cally happy until Germont, Alfredo's father, interferes. He
disapproves of Violetta; since she is not respectable he fears
the affair will ruin his son's reputation and future. He therefore begs her for Alfredo's own sake to give him up, and she
makes the sacrifice, returning to the feverish gaiety of Paris
and her old life of champagne, diamonds, and heartache.
Later Alfredo meets her at a party. Tortured with jealousy and
despair he publicly insults her, and she faints. Thereafter her

[ 139 ]

glittering days are ended; she is ill, heartbroken, alone. In time Alfredo learns why she left him, and the lovers are re-united; but too late—Violetta, in the last stages of consumption, dies in his arms.

This sentimental tale first appeared as a novel which Dumas had based on the life of an actual woman of Paris. Then, as a play, it became a favorite with the most glamorous actresses of every land. Still later a galaxy of stars from Sarah Bernhardt to Greta Garbo interpreted the part of Violetta (in the drama called "Camille") on the screen. Again and again the story turns up in one form or another; yet only the opera, thanks to Verdi's music, remains more than a period piece today.

Back in 1853 contemporary life was not considered operatic material, and Verdi had misgivings about the cast, to whom his score, so intimate, so pathetic, so tender, did not seem like opera at all. The usual grand gestures were not called for, and the singers—who wore, instead of exotic costumes, "modern" dress such as they themselves might wear in private life—did not know how to act. This opera was so unlike anything they had done before that it robbed them of their self-confidence, and, ill at ease, they wondered how audiences would take all these disturbing innovations.

Soon enough they found out. At the première the audience was nonplussed. The music—somehow there seemed to be nothing to it, and to make matters worse the tenor was extremely hoarse. Nor did Varesi (the original Macbeth) understand the fine part of Germont. Shamelessly, he made it plain that he was bored and disgruntled because he, the great baritone, did not appear until the second act! Neither principals nor chorus seemed to grasp the frivolous, bitter-sweet Parisian atmosphere that pervades the score. How then could the public feel it? Worst of all was the Violetta. She had a fine voice, certainly, but alas, her figure! The Italians were not yet hardened, as we have since become, by huge German sopranos. Their singers, if plump, were also trim and graceful, and this mountainous woman as the fragile, exquisite, poetically dying Violetta was more than they could bear.

Until the third act there had been some bewildered, perfunctory applause. Then came the prelude—music so hushed that the composer-poet Boito later called it "a silence made of sounds"; music so touching that the aged Verdi himself, hearing it after an interval of many years, was moved to remark: "There are tears in the old man yet!" By a stroke of genius he had directed that this prelude be played with the curtain raised on the shadowy sickroom where Violetta lies as wan and still as death itself. Even at that ill-starred first performance the music cast its spell, but briefly. The sight of the soprano's healthy bulk extended in massive discomfort on the deathbed was too much for the audience. Furtive, contagious giggles soon swelled to gales of laughter and "wisecracks" which, as the act went on, nearly drowned out the miserable singers' voices. The only tears that night were tears of mirth.

As the tragedy came thus to an uproarious end Verdi, backstage, paced to and fro, his head bowed forward, his pale eyes under the heavy brow glowing painfully. He had had failures before, many of them, but not since the never-forgotten horror of *King for a Day* had he known the lash of ridicule. And this was *La Traviata*, the opera in which he had such faith—music so touching, so deeply felt it could not fail!

"Maestro . . . such a misfortune . . ." The few people who spoke to him when it was over had pity in their voices. Others, acutely embarrassed, avoided him entirely. There were no cheering crowds that evening, no torchlit celebrations. Verdi went quietly back to his hotel.

Next morning he wrote to Muzio:

Dear Emanuele: *Traviata* last night—a fiasco. Was it my fault or the singers'? Time will tell.

That was all. No excuses, no futile "ifs," no anger, no self-pity. Did ever man of genius accept a major disappointment with such fairness and dignity? Facing the public with a new opera nineteen times in the last fourteen years, Verdi had taught himself that a first audience can never pass final

[ 141 ]

judgment. Some triumphs fade, some failures come to life, and only time will tell.

Though he uttered no word of accusation or complaint, Verdi admitted, back at Sant' Agata, that he felt "out of love with work." It was spring—for a farmer the busiest time of year—and, forgetting music, he gave all his attention to his growing farm and garden. Then he became absorbed once more in *King Lear*, occupying himself with the libretto which a Venetian friend, the lawyer-poet Antonio Somma, had undertaken to prepare for him since Cammarano's death. He had no notion when or where *Lear* might be given, yet the idea haunted him. He would have liked to begin composing in earnest, but found time only for a few tentative passages. Paris was about to hold a much-heralded Universal Exposition, a sort of World's Fair, for which Verdi had agreed to supply a gala new opera. Accordingly to Paris late in 1853 he went.

He found it a tedious business, this launching of a new work at the Opéra where months of pompous preparation were required to accomplish what, in Italy, could have been done in weeks. Verdi was accustomed to writing and directing under pressure, among zealous Italians to whom his word was law. Here in Paris he found too many bosses to suit him and not enough enthusiasm. The renowned Scribe, king of French librettists, kept him waiting interminably for machine-made verses and was too bored to heed suggestions from the composer, or even to attend rehearsals. (At first Verdi did not realize that the great man, hiring collaborators for his tasks, did little more than lend his name.) Though he spoke fluent French, Verdi found that he could set a French text to music less freely than one in his native tongue, and it was trying, since he loved brevity almost to a fault, to have to spin his opera out to the traditional five long acts. Besides, he missed the serenity of Sant' Agata which had become the only spot where his imagination was not cramped. The installments of *Lear* that Somma forwarded from time to time were tantalizing and Verdi would gladly have given them all his attention. Nevertheless he worked conscientiously, though slowly and

with reluctance, to finish his new opera, *The Sicilian Vespers*.

One afternoon, while Verdi was thus worrying the months away in Paris, three of his friends sat round a small iron table at one of the outdoor cafés on the Piazza San Marco in

Venice. They were Antonio Somma, Dr. Vigna, a psychologist, and the violinist Gallo, who owned a music shop farther along the Piazza. This trio were in the habit of meeting almost daily to spend an hour over a cup of coffee or a glass of wine, sipping and talking as they gazed across at the ancient domes of St. Mark's Cathedral that shimmered tranquilly in the late sunlight. Since they were men of taste, intellectuals, and of course music lovers, the conversation was apt to turn to Verdi, who as a man was their friend, as a composer their idol. On this particular occasion they were discussing *Traviata*.

"What a score that is!" murmured Gallo. "Marvelous! And to think that it should be unheard, ignored, wasted, just because of that ghastly performance . . . Criminal—absolutely criminal!"

"A fine work, an extraordinary work—we're all agreed on that," said Vigna. "But what can be done about it?"

"Surely our judgment must be worth something. We three can't be entirely wrong," remarked Somma. "Why, you remember, one of the critics even pointed out that the production, not the music, was to blame. Still, such a disaster . . . I shudder whenever I think of it!"

"If it had been an ordinary failure," said Vigna, "there might yet be a chance. But there's nothing so fatal, so deadly, as laughter. *Traviata* will never be revived."

"Not at La Fenice, certainly," said Gallo thoughtfully. Suddenly he leaned forward. "Gentlemen, I have an idea. Why wouldn't it be possible to . . ." The three friends drew closer round the table, talking with animation until the light faded and the wheeling flocks of pigeons fluttered down to roost.

Shortly thereafter Verdi received a letter from Gallo asking permission to put on *Traviata* at his own expense—not at the great Fenice of course, but at a smaller Venetian theater which he planned to hire for the purpose. Verdi was delighted. In the back of his mind had been the hope that somewhere, some day, this opera that he loved and had such faith in might be heard again. Vaguely he had thought of Rome, where he was especially admired, but Venice as a possibility had never occurred to him. And truly, in the face of what had happened there, the attempt took courage. At once, however, he gave his consent, only warning Gallo in all fairness of the risk involved. He would not want his friend to suffer for his sake. Did Gallo really appreciate how serious the financial loss might be? Was he prepared to accept failure, even ridicule?

Gallo in his enthusiasm was prepared for anything, and his good friends, Somma and Vigna, stood staunchly behind him. Determined that there should be no mistakes this time, he engaged the best possible conductor and singers, including a Violetta who could look and act her part as well as sing it. To be on the safe side he even moved the story back a hundred years—a less appropriate era, but at least neither cast nor audience would be distracted by the novelty of contemporary dress. And to make sure that the absent Maestro's intentions should be carried out to the last detail, he put the rehearsals in Piave's faithful, willing hands. Verdi himself, informed of all the preparations, eagerly touched up the score, tightening it here and there and even adding a passage or two.

Meantime, as word of the coming event got about, Venice was set agog. "He must be out of his mind, that Gallo!" people muttered. It was an anxious time for Verdi's friends: suppose nobody came to hear the revival? But the public, whether out of curiosity, or in search of a good laugh, or simply intrigued by Gallo's daring, quickly bought up every ticket.

On May 6th, 1854, the performance took place. As soon thereafter as the mails could carry them, letters from Venice began to reach Verdi in Paris—letters that glowed with pleasure and excitement and affection. Never in the history of the sea-built city had an opera created such a sensation! Not *Ernani* in its heyday, nor even *Rigoletto* could be compared to this! It was the most beautiful, the most touching, the most exquisite . . . superlatives sparkled on every page. And, wonderful to relate, not in all Venice could a soul be found who would admit to having laughed at the fiasco fourteen months before! "Personally I liked *Traviata* from the beginning—never could understand why it failed," everybody solemnly assured everybody else, for it was not in human nature to confess to such an error of judgment. Verdi with quiet satisfaction wrote his friends that he was profoundly happy—"*contentissimo!*"

In no time a *Traviata* craze flourished all over Europe. This was the opera that everyone felt he *must* hear, and having heard it he went back for more. One elderly titled lady even made a business of rushing from city to city in a hopeless attempt not to miss a single performance anywhere, and this in spite of being so overcome with emotion that she generally had to leave the theater before the final curtain! Verdi himself, when asked at this time which of his operas he considered the finest, answered without hesitation, "As a musician I should choose *Rigoletto*, but as a layman *Traviata*."

The "Big Three"—*Rigoletto*, *Trovatore*, *Traviata*—soon became part of the national heritage, and, like the Colosseum in Rome or the frescoes of Michelangelo, a source of pride to every Italian schoolboy. This is music that in Italy belongs to everyone, heard, sung, and loved by rich and poor, humble and mighty, learned and ignorant alike. And for the rest of the world these three are still mainstays of operatic repertory.

In 1943, just ninety years after Verdi said "Time will tell," American and British soldiers, entering Naples on the heels of the Germans, found a chaotic, war-scarred city, grim with famine and disease. Reëstablishing normal living was a difficult task; not for a long time could the Neapolitans hope even for enough to eat. Yet among the first institutions to function again was the historic San Carlo opera house, one of the few in Italy to escape serious damage. There, audiences made up entirely of men in uniform heard, not *The Battle of Legnano* (which had been revived as an inspiration to Italians during the First World War), nor any other blood-and-thunder work, but *La Traviata*. Inevitably, performances were below standard. Years of strain had told on singers and musicians; costumes and scenery were frankly makeshift. Many a curious G.I., attending opera perhaps for the first time, must have come away disappointed. Yet he went back for more, and by the spring of 1946 the venerable theater was in full stride again, playing to its regular public. *Traviata* was often repeated, for to Italians this opera especially was like a homecoming. The magic of the familiar music lifted them to a gentler, not too real world, where, sharing the sorrows of Alfredo and Violetta, they could for a blessed breathing space forget their own.

# CHAPTER TWELVE

# *Viva Verdi!*

## 1854-1859

SENSATION! Scandal! It was incredible but it was true: on October 9, 1854, the day the Ópéra was to open for the season, Sophie Cruvelli, most glamorous, most popular of the current stars, could not be found! That very night she was to have sung Valentine in Meyerbeer's *The Huguenots*, and she had vanished without a trace. Nowadays every first-class company has several singers ready to step into a role at a moment's notice, but a century ago this system had not yet been evolved. Without Cruvelli there could be no performance. Worse still, since she was the prime attraction, unless she appeared soon there could be no opera season at all. Recently at the Italian Theater (a smaller Paris opera house) she had created a furore in *Ernani* and *Luisa Miller*, and Verdi had insisted that she head the cast of his forthcoming *Sicilian Vespers*, now about to go into rehearsal. The Opéra had therefore engaged her for the season, and at a record-breaking salary. But she was gone, without a word of warning, no one knew whither. Apparently the much-heralded, gala première of *The Sicilian Vespers* might not take place! The affair was disastrous, especially this year of the Universal Exposition when curious throngs flowed into Paris by the thousand to see the sights, not least of which was the venerable Opéra, most renowned, most impressive theater in the world.

Behind the scenes on that unforgettable day, preparations

[ 148 ]

for the rise of the curtain came to an abrupt halt. In a nightmare of confusion managers, staff, stage crew, singers, dancers, musicians, artists, dressers, wig-makers, wardrobe mistresses, ushers, and hangers-on shouted and shrugged, waved
their hands, argued and swore. Nor was the excitement con-
fined to the theater. The opening of the opera season was a
social event of the first importance, especially now that Louis
Napoleon, elected President of France in 1848, had managed
to have himself proclaimed Emperor, and the aristocracy was
once more riding high. Gone forever were the courtiers'
powdered wigs, silk brocades, and diamond buckles; but Paris
was still the "city of light," and this era of the Second Empire,
though far more "democratic" than the eighteenth century,
had a gay, prosperous glitter all its own. Fine ladies attended
the opera to be admired, and to see who else was there with
whom and especially what everyone was wearing. For weeks
the great dressmaking establishments had been busy with
exquisite creations for Madame la Marquise and Madame la
Duchesse to appear in. Trade in gloves, slippers, fans, jewels,
and perfumes for my lady boomed. Gallants bought tall silk
hats and swinging cloaks with satin linings for themselves, and
for their sweethearts tiny opera glasses of gold inlaid with
mother-of-pearl. When the great day arrived, florists, hair-
dressers, valets, and ladies' maids were rushed to distraction.

And then in the midst of all this activity—"Haven't you
heard? There'll be no performance! Cruvelli's disappeared!"
As everyone hurried to share the astounding news with his
neighbor, the city crackled with excitement and curiosity.
What had happened? Had the prima donna been kidnapped?
Murdered? Paris shivered and forgot international politics
while awaiting developments in the Cruvelli mystery.

At the star's locked and deserted home the police found all
in order, but Mademoiselle's traveling things were conspicu-
ously missing. Clearly she had gone away of her own free
will. But where? Why? If there was anyone who knew, he
kept the secret well.

She was bound to turn up tomorrow, the gossips said, but
the tomorrows came and went without a clue. All over the

Continent strange women of Cruvelli's approximate age and size were stared at as people wondered: "Could that be she? If I should be the one to find her . . . !" She was reported to have crossed the Swiss frontier; she had been seen in disguise boarding a ship for South America; she was recognized in a dozen places at once. In London, music-hall audiences roared at a hastily staged skit called *Where's Cruvelli?* But in Paris there was mounting anger. Such behavior was an affront to the Emperor—was not the Opéra supported by the Crown and everyone employed there directly answerable to His Majesty? And Monsieur Verdi, whom all the world knew to be the soul of honor—what a shabby way to treat him! Let her come back if she dared! She'd soon find out just how much the public would stand for!

And Verdi? Cruvelli's action seemed to him beneath contempt. Heartily sick of everything connected with *The Sicilian Vespers*, he now saw a way to be rid of the whole business and go home, for surely, under the circumstances, he could hardly be held to his contract. When he asked to be released, however, the harassed management refused to consider such a calamity. Monsieur Verdi must be patient—undoubtedly the prima donna herself, or some solution of the difficulty, would soon be found . . . He waited, fuming, and meantime a letter from Genoa heightened his restlessness. Would the illustrious Maestro care to compose an opera to inaugurate the city's magnificent new theater, then in process of building? He could have anything he wanted, anything, in the way of singers, orchestra, scenery, costumes, etc. And would he grant permission to call the splendid edifice Teatro Verdi in his honor? This last request was the bait on the hook, and Verdi promptly rejected it: the theater would have to find some worthier name. But the opera—yes, provided that he could free himself of his obligation in Paris, he would gladly supply it. Here was the chance, the longed-for chance, to do *King Lear!*

Just at that point came a report, authentic this time, that Mademoiselle Cruvelli had been seen in Strassburg attending a play, and with her was one Baron Vigier, to whom her engagement had for some time been rumored. An affair of the

heart! How romantic! It was for love that she had run away—
Paris heaved a sentimental sigh. Artists, after all, could
hardly be expected to behave like ordinary humdrum folk.
Perhaps, in spite of everything, the fascinating singer should
be forgiven . . .

A few days later Cruvelli quietly slipped home and, with as
much dignity as she could muster, reported for duty. At once
placards appeared announcing *The Huguenots.* What matter
if the season opened a month late? The Opéra was saved. But
—was it? Suppose Cruvelli had lost her following? The public,
clamoring to buy tickets, was divided. Some felt that all is
fair in love, and longed to warm themselves in the bewitching
creature's radiance. Others could hardly wait to boo the
sinner off the stage.

By the time the curtain finally rose the atmosphere had
grown electric with suspense. Riots in theaters were not un-
common in those days, and as Cruvelli made her entrance the
anxious managers braced themselves for whatever might
occur. No applause, no hisses—so far so good. On stage the
Queen turned to give Valentine her cue. "Tell me," sang the
Queen, "tell me the result of your adventurous journey?"
There was a gasp out front—no one had remembered this
line—then a vast wave of laughter flooded the auditorium,
the orchestra pit, even the stage itself. The conductor, con-
vulsed, lost control of his shaking musicians. The stage hands
guffawed and the singers, even Cruvelli, giggled unashamed.
Someone began to clap and, as the merriment merged into
applause, all danger passed. The prima donna, saved by a
lucky joke, was still the darling of Paris!

There was nothing to interfere with Verdi's *Sicilian Vespers*
now. He must stay on and finish his dreary task. Regretfully
he saw *King Lear* fade once again into the uncertain future.

All through the gray and clammy northern winter Verdi
struggled against cold, recurring illness, and what he called
his "mania to go home." Though Cruvelli (soon to retire
from the stage as Baroness Vigier) was meekness itself, rehearsals went badly and there were delays, disagreements,
quarrels, and annoyances of all sorts. Verdi, never blessed

with patience, needed all he could summon. Paris, he admitted, was the most wonderful city in the world, but it did not become for him, as for so many celebrated foreigners, a second home. It was his nature to hold himself aloof from the merry-go-round of gossip and intrigue, and from the busybodies who theorized on art, music, and politics in all the fashionable drawing-rooms.

Yet even Verdi was glad to attend Rossini's famous "Saturday nights," when the great Italian kept open house for everybody who was anybody anywhere. Rossini, long the unchallenged idol of Europe, had retired at thirty-seven with thirty-eight operas to his credit; and, settling in Paris, had become one of the brilliant city's brightest ornaments. At his house the most exquisite food and wine, the most scintillating talk, and the finest music were to be enjoyed, for he was a renowned wit and gourmet as well as musician. Immensely stout and genial, he left a wake of good-natured laughter behind him as he passed among the guests—notables all— who thronged his rooms.

Toward his compatriot Verdi felt that special reverence with which truly great men appreciate greatness in others, but this admiration was far from mutual. From his eminence the worldly Rossini had watched the rise of the younger man with skepticism, considering his music crude and inelegant, which of course it often was. When *Rigoletto* appeared, however, Rossini changed his mind: unquestionably this farmer from Busseto was a true genius. One Saturday, Verdi being present, the guests were treated to the *Rigoletto* quartet in the composer's honor, magnificently sung and (a rare compliment) accompanied by Rossini himself at the piano. For the young and comparatively unknown soprano Verdi delightedly prophesied a dazzling future. Her name was Adelina Patti, and she was to become one of the best-loved singers of all time. He was pleased too because he, and everyone, understood that with this gracious gesture the King of Italian Music officially proclaimed Verdi his heir.

It was not Rossini, however, who ruled the Opéra in those days, but the Prussian Meyerbeer, whose music, though it had not found its way to people's hearts as Verdi's had, was rated the last word in beauty and grandeur. For the Parisian public Verdi deliberately patterned his *Sicilian Vespers* on the ponderous Meyerbeerian model, and challenging the champion thus did not lighten his task. He had to contend with prejudice as well; some Frenchmen grumbled at a foreigner's being chosen to celebrate their Universal Exposition—France had her own composers after all; Auber and Halévy and the far greater but neglected Berlioz. Nevertheless Verdi came through the ordeal of the première triumphantly. Critics and public raved; he was the man of the hour. To his countrymen —half Italy seemed to have traveled north to bask in his glory—he appeared an ambassador of good will, living proof that the days of Italian greatness were not over. The opera, in due course translated and produced in his own land, was well enough received there too. But "time will tell." Of this score, written without enthusiasm in a style that was not Verdi's own, only the overture and an occasional aria have survived.

Worn and weary now that the strain was over, Verdi wondered if he would ever be willing to undertake another of "these most accursed operas." He had counted on going home at once, but a new problem arose to plague him, keeping him on in Paris until the end of the year.

It was a question of copyright. Recently the larger European nations had signed an international agreement, establishing ownership of books and music, and thus insuring to authors and composers a financial return on the use of their works. But Verdi, being a citizen of tiny Parma, did not benefit thereby—his operas had no legal protection outside of Italy. Though an authorized orchestral score could be obtained only from the publisher for a set fee, there was nothing to prevent unscrupulous managers from acquiring piano scores, cutting, altering, and orchestrating them to suit their own convenience and fancy, and producing the results without paying any royalties whatever. This practice, called "piracy," was very prevalent, and Verdi's operas especially, because of their popularity, were much abused. Even the Italian Theater in Paris threatened to put on "pirated" versions of his best-loved works. Bad enough that neither he nor his publisher should receive a penny while managers raked in profits; to such a stubborn perfectionist as Verdi the mutilation of his operas without so much as a "by your leave" was still more infuriating. He determined to put up a fight.

Friends advised him to become a French or British subject—either country would be proud to claim him, and his case would then be covered by the new international law. Verdi stiffened. Without hesitation he replied, "I will always remain what I am, a peasant of Le Roncole." There was a principle at stake—all citizens of Parma must be protected from injustice, and he undertook to persuade his native state to join the pact of great nations. He interviewed diplomats, wrote petitions, and struggled with a mass of red tape that irritated his direct common sense. Meantime he became involved in a tedious lawsuit, and was obliged also to go to England to look after his interests there. Not until December did he arrive at Sant' Agata, to stretch his soul in his own "sky and desert" after an absence of more than two years.

Still there was no rest. Naples demanded a new opera. *King Lear?* No, a perfect cast was not available. And first Verdi must write *Simon Boccanegra* to be produced in Venice the following season. *Stiffelio*, too—he had never been satisfied with it. It must be revised. Piave, cheerful as ever, and bringing a pet dog for Peppina, came to Sant' Agata to rewrite the libretto under the Maestro's critical eye.

All too soon the lawsuit and copyright troubles called Verdi back to Paris, on to London, and to Paris again, where he stayed for a sumptuous production of *Trovatore* at the Opéra—in French of course, and with the required ballet added. The enthusiasm was overwhelming, while simultaneously at the Italian Theater Parisians wept ecstatically over *Traviata*. From all sides flowed such torrents of praise for the composer that Peppina worried. Things were going *too* well, she felt—this dazzling good fortune could not last. And she was right.

For *Simon Boccanegra*, as for *Macbeth*, Verdi had a special affection. Fascinated by Boccanegra himself, the tragic Doge of medieval Genoa who dominates the story, he had composed the subtlest, richest, deepest of his scores so far. But he had failed to see the weakness of Piave's libretto—though the poor poet had done his best with an incomprehensible tangle of false names, intrigue, political and private feuds, and murder. When, in March 1857, after the usual tussle with the censor, the curtain rose, the Maestro's hopes were high. This monotonously gloomy opera, however, lacked popular appeal, and the Venetian public, confused and bored, listened with a stolid indifference almost as disastrous as the laughter that had greeted *Traviata*.

Verdi accepted his failure with a philosophic shrug. "I believed I had written something passable," he said, "but now it seems I was mistaken."

Burying his disappointment, he threw all his energy for a time into the management of his estate. Daily at sunrise he was off on his favorite saddle horse, a superb animal, to make the rounds of the property. All day long he inspected planting and livestock, conferred with his superintendent, or directed the springtime labors. It was a vast and growing enterprise, this farm of his, and absent though he often was, no detail escaped his attention. He studied the sky, seeking to read tomorrow's weather, and took intense delight in the swelling buds and each pale, waxy shoot that pushed through the moist earth. His animals, too, gave him the keenest pleasure, especially the horses. To Verdi each was an individual; this one, he told the head groom, was a bit above himself and needed a firm hand; this other was nervous and shy, and must be reassured with gentleness. There were no finer thoroughbreds in Italy than those raised at Sant' Agata. Still more famed in the neighborhood was a certain rooster that, uninvited, paraded at Verdi's heels from house to barn and barn to stable, shadowing his every step. When the Maestro went driving, children dropped their games and ran to stare, not at the renowned composer, but at the big, glossy bird perched in the carriage by his side and glaring defiantly at all the world as if to say, "You see this man? He belongs to me!"

Watching Verdi so busy, so contentedly absorbed, Peppina

smiled to remember how years ago he had protested that he loathed the country. It had been hard to persuade him to move from the center of Paris to the little house in Passy. And now no one would guess that he had ever been anything but a farmer. Indeed, he was writing no music at all. How could he—out of doors all day, returning at dusk burned by the sun and wind and, as she said, "harassed with weariness"?

But in July music called him away to lovely, ancient Rimini, nestling between two rivers on the shore of the Adriatic Sea. The little city had built itself a new theater, to be opened with a performance of *Aroldo* (*Stiffelio* revised—the Lutheran minister was now a Crusader) which the composer had promised to direct. Banners with flowery greetings spanned the streets on the day of his arrival, and his own picture looked at him from every window.

For the excited townspeople all that the great man did was news. "Did you hear about the village bell they're using in the opera? It was flat, and with his own hands the Maestro filed it away to bring it up to pitch—wouldn't let anyone else touch it!"

"He sees to everything himself—even looks over all the costume sketches and makes suggestions."

"He's so intent, so concentrated. That Piave—what an entertaining fellow—is always telling lively stories and making everybody laugh, but the Maestro only smiles and keeps on working."

"Have you seen him down by the shore? Early every morning he walks alone there and gazes at the sea. The rougher the waves, the better he seems to enjoy it."

Verdi took an immediate liking to handsome, magnetic, musically brilliant young Angelo Mariani who came to Rimini to conduct—a liking that ripened into close friendship, only to end years later in enmity and bitterness. One day at rehearsal Mariani could not induce the orchestra to play a certain passage with the right effect. He repeated it over and over, he coaxed, he scolded, in vain. Verdi, roaming about silently as usual, suddenly stalked from the back of the auditorium and leaned over the young conductor's shoulder.

[ 156 ]

"Never mind this," he said quickly. "Let it go, and get on with the rehearsal."

Mariani, though plainly annoyed, had to obey. But later, as they left the theater, he asked Verdi irritably, "Whatever got into you to stop me like that? Did you think I couldn't get it right?"

Verdi laughed. "Of course you could, my dear fellow, if

anybody could. But didn't it occur to you that the trouble is in the music? The instrumentation's all wrong—it's got to be rewritten. By tomorrow I promise you a new version that will give you no difficulty at all." Fair-minded Verdi, who would never alter a note against his convictions, was willing enough to admit a real error.

For the performance hundreds of "foreigners" from the neighboring towns flocked to Rimini, and during intermissions the ecstatic audience tossed tinkling showers of gold coins onto the stage. From the balconies floated a snowstorm of printed mottoes that read: "All honor to the most exalted intellect!"—"Your genius gives the lie to the insulting strangers who call Italy the land of the dead!"—and so on. Yet, in spite of twenty-seven curtain calls for the composer, *Aroldo* itself was not much liked. "*Stiffelio* warmed over," people said of it, and indeed they were right. Both versions of this unfortunate opera were soon to be forgotten.

Verdi stayed on in Rimini most of the summer to produce others of his works. After the sessions at the theater he loved to go for walks, especially to an enchanting spot where the town's two rivers meet. There a certain fisherman used to while away the slow, sunny hours on the river bank in true Italian fashion—by singing arias. One afternoon as his clear tenor rang out on the last note of "La donna è mobile," a voice behind him exclaimed "Bravo!" The man started, turned, and blushed; he was looikng straight into the eyes of Maestro Verdi!

Cordially Verdi clasped his shoulders. "Bravo!" he repeated. "You have a good voice and an exceptionally fine ear. Too bad you never studied—you would have made a splendid singer. Come now," he motioned to the leading soprano, who with her husband and Peppina had strolled out with him, "let's have a duet!" And there under the sky, with the rushing stream at their feet, prima donna and fisherman sang for the beaming audience of three until the sun dropped down behind the western hills.

This incident, which surely could have occurred nowhere but in Italy, was far more to Verdi's liking than the efforts of his admirers to crown him one evening with a wreath of golden laurel. Ungraciously, indignantly, he dodged away. On another occasion he got wind of a surprise demonstration to be held at the theater and, to avoid it, slipped out early by a side door. No use—the throng followed to his hotel and would not be quieted until he appeared on his balcony. But the climax came at the end of the season with an elaborate banquet in his honor held at a pavilion by the moonlit sea. The guests bathed in the surf, feasted, and listened to festive music, including a special serenade to Verdi sung by the opera chorus. Toasts and speeches in praise of the composer followed, but it was Piave who thanked the good citizens of Rimini in Verdi's name—the hero of the hour was not present! Brave though he was, he could not face such glorification as this.

Next on his crowded schedule was the opera for Naples. For lack of something better, Verdi chose a play of Scribe's about the murder of King Gustave III of Sweden—a dangerous story of conspirators, treachery, and forbidden love. Would it pass the censors? He had misgivings, and again the dream of *Lear*, carried so long in his mind and heart, returned to haunt him. If only there were more time . . . Naples had not yet heard *Legnano*, *Aroldo*, or *Boccanegra*. Hopefully he wrote offering all three and promising, during the precious months thus saved, to complete *King Lear* for the following season. But fate still thwarted him. The San Carlo, clinging to the letter of its contract, refused to accept three old operas and a promise as a substitute for one new opera right away.

Well, Somma's libretto for *The Masked Ball*, as the Swedish story was eventually called, had turned out better than Verdi dared expect. He went to work, and was soon cheered by a surprising piece of news: the prose outline submitted in advance was approved by the Neapolitan censor!

By January 1858 Verdi had completed his score, when an event occurred that rocked the world. An Italian-born assassin hurled two bombs at Napoleon III of France, and though the Emperor escaped unhurt a number of persons near him were killed by the explosion. Europe shuddered, and panicky police everywhere redoubled their vigilance. Especially in Italy, where embers of revolt now glowed again, the nerves of people in high places were on edge.

Verdi arrived in Naples the day after the crime, shocked, but foreseeing no trouble since he had already been assured of the censor's backing. Confidently he presented the complete libretto to the authorities—a mere formality, he thought— and requested permission to start rehearsals. No reply. A full week lost. Ten days. Verdi's patience ran out and he demanded an explanation. At that point the manager of the San Carlo was forced to confess that the censor, far from approving the outline of the new opera, had made furious objections!

"Then why not admit it?" Verdi thundered.

The wretched manager shifted uneasily. "It was thought that Maestro Verdi might not come to Naples if he knew . . . But now that the Maestro is on the spot matters can doubtless be adjusted . . . Certain concessions, certain changes, will of course have to be made . . ."

Verdi blazed. From the beginning he had expected trouble with the censor, but this was plain deception—intolerable, inexcusable!

Thus began a feud even more bitter than that waged over *Rigoletto,* and it lasted all winter long. Verdi was ordered to make alterations in his opera—ridiculous alterations. He refused. Very well then, the opera could not be produced, and the composer must pay a large fine—50,000 lire—for breaking his contract. He would do nothing of the sort! He had completed his score in good faith, he pointed out, and was therefore in no way to blame. Moreover, in the emergency Naples was welcome to *Boccanegra* as a substitute. But the San Carlo would have none of *Boccanegra,* insisting that it was entitled to an entirely new work. *The Masked Ball* must be altered to meet the censor's wishes. Still Verdi obstinately declined to change a note. Round and round went the arguments, and—like the Battle of Busseto long ago—the squabble soon ceased to be a private affair. It was Verdi and the people against the Government, and when at length a rumor arose that the Maestro was about to be arrested, the crowd turned ugly.

These days the words "Viva Verdi!" ("Long live Verdi!") constantly appeared chalked up on walls and doorways, or boldly displayed in windows. Placards of the forbidden tricolor—red, white, and green—with the large letters V E R D I were brazenly paraded through the streets. Whenever the Maestro left his hotel, clusters of angry-looking men swept after him fiercely cheering "Viva Verdi!" These demonstrations were no simple tributes to a popular composer. There was more to all this than met the eye—much more: Verdi's name had become a symbol of liberty.

Downtrodden peoples, no matter how harshly ruled, always find a way to speak their minds. During the Second World War the opening notes of Beethoven's Fifth Symphony (the $\cdots -$ rhythm spelling "V" for Victory in Morse Code) were used throughout the Nazi-conquered lands to torment the oppressors and inspire the oppressed with faith in the day of liberation. Just so, eighty years earlier, the word "Verdi" was blazoned and shouted everywhere, while patriots, Austrian rulers, and petty princes knew that it stood not only for the beloved composer but for "**V**ittorio **E**manuele **R**e **d**'Italia" (Victor Emanuel King of Italy) as well.

This Victor Emanuel, under whom lovers of freedom now longed to see all Italy united, was actually King of the northernmost Italian states, independent Piedmont and Savoy. A brave, energetic young man, incapable of breaking a promise, he sincerely cared more for his subjects than for his throne. To guide him he had his prime minister—the great statesman Camille Benso, Count Cavour. Wise, patient, and realistic, Cavour knew that heroism alone is never enough; one must have strength also. By setting France against Austria, he strove to win the mighty French Empire over to the Italian cause, and meantime, like the exiled Mazzini, did all in his power to enlist the sympathy of the rest of Europe, especially England. While Cavour in Turin (the Piedmontese capital) quietly and craftily played his tremendous game, Italy seethed with new hope. "*Vittorio Emanuele Re d'Italia!*"—the slogan

[ 161 ]

echoed in every patriot's heart, but to breathe it aloud was to risk imprisonment. No one, however, could be arrested for cheering a composer, so again and again, ever louder, the cry went up—"Viva Verdi!"

Most infamous, most hated of all Italy's rulers was Ferdinand of Naples, nicknamed Bomba. Now, wherever he looked, the words "Viva Verdi!" blazed before his eyes, and as he heard the hoarse and angry voices rising from the city he seemed to feel his throne rocking beneath him. While Verdi's dispute with the Government dragged on, these furious crowds, these street corner demonstrations, grew increasingly dangerous. The slightest incident might at any moment touch off a riot—even a revolution! This composer whose very name was now symbolic, whose music spoke for every man and set the faintest heart aflame with courage, had become a menace that must be removed. Quite suddenly Bomba ordered the San Carlo to accept *Simon Boccanegra* for the following year—the current season had been bickered away—and let Verdi go about his business.

Thankfully Verdi packed his unused score and turned homeward. His winter had been wasted, but no matter: he had reason to believe that *The Masked Ball* might yet be heard in Rome. Since Scribe's play on which the opera was based had been permitted there, the Roman censor could scarcely object. Verdi always liked Rome, and vividly remembered the night of *Trovatore*, when the waterlogged city forgot its discomfort in a delirium of joy. And then it was so near to Naples. He was too human not to relish the thought of staging his forbidden opera right on the Neapolitan doorstep.

But the affair was not to be as simple as he expected. To Sant'Agata came word that the Roman censor also decreed certain changes in the libretto. Apparently it was permissible in Rome to murder a king on the stage only if there were no music. "Very singular!" commented Verdi acidly, pointing out that in all fairness he could not allow revisions for one city which he had refused for another. The plain fact was, of course, that in Rome also the authorities feared Verdi himself. They knew the magic of his name, and how his music,

[ 162 ]

once heard, spread irresistibly like a prairie fire, kindling the people.

If the new score should never see the light—what of it? Weary of the struggle, Verdi gazed out across his tranquil, fertile fields and was at peace. No managers, no censors, plagued him as he ran his hands over a newborn colt, taking an expert's pride in the shaggy little creature's sturdiness and fine proportions. At ease in his own spacious study, he picked up his neglected correspondence. "Since *Nabucco*," he wrote, "I have had scarcely an hour's complete rest." And it was true. In sixteen years he had composed nineteen operas, two of them twice over, not to mention the innumerable revivals he had directed. Now, with every attempt to produce his latest work thwarted, he had had enough. He would relax, at least till autumn, when he must return to Naples to put on *Boccanegra*. Was he, at forty-five, thinking of retiring for good, Peppina wondered? Let him, if that was what he wished. She did not foresee that the greatest years were yet to come.

That summer Verdi would have enjoyed a few weeks in Venice for the sea bathing, but he got word that the Venetian managers were lying in wait, hoping to tease him into promising a new score. Rather than fight them off he remained at home, imprisoned by his own popularity.

Meantime, while the Maestro rested, the manager in Rome, loath to let a Verdi opera slip through his fingers, hammered at the authorities until at last he won a concession. *The Masked Ball* might be produced intact provided that, like *Rigoletto*, the setting were changed and the victim of the conspiracy no longer a royal personage. To be quite safe the scene was shifted clear out of Europe to Colonial Boston, where Sweden's Gustave III became an imaginary British governor called the Earl of Warwick. Nothing could be more ludicrous than an early New England background for this melodramatic episode of Renaissance court life, but neither Verdi nor his audiences thought so. In those days European notions of America were hazy at best. It was even considered correct to dress the singers in Puritan costume instead of the Georgian wigs, brocades, and laces that would actually have been worn. (Some years later this led to further trouble—in Paris a famous tenor refused to appear in such drab and unbecoming attire, and to humor him the scene had to be shifted once more, this time to—of all places—the ancient kingdom of Naples!) Fortunately, modern performances return the opera's locale to Sweden.

Since the essentials of plot and character were not to be tampered with and his music remained valid as written, Verdi consented with relief to the new setting for *The Masked Ball* for Rome. Meanwhile he reached Naples in high spirits to produce *Boccanegra;* and for once his stay in this most troublesome of cities was completely pleasant. On earlier visits he had made a number of good friends among the Neapolitans, and with them, after working hours, he delighted to drive up into the hills to dine on some open terrace whence he could look down past the steep vineyards and olive groves to the bright bay below. There, surrounded by friendly laughter, the Maestro would serenely smoke his long cigars and sip old wine until the stars appeared over Vesuvius.

Verdi had brought with him to Naples not only Peppina but also Lulu, a Maltese spaniel, small, white, and absurd. Strolling to the theater the three of them made quite a picture—the gaunt Maestro in his tall hat and high-buttoned frock coat, Peppina, her face almost hidden beneath a coal-scuttle bonnet, her vast hoop skirt of plaid silk rippling fashionably as she walked, and before them the proud and solemn Lulu with silky fur well brushed and a pert bow bouncing on her tiny forehead. Lulu attended rehearsals faithfully. While her master, chair tipped perilously forward, lanky legs stretched straight, elbows on the stage manager's table, opened his mouth wide to show some singer how to produce the tone he wanted, Lulu, inert as a white muff, curled on his knees placid and self-assured. When from the piano he vigorously led the chorus, Lulu teetered on her hind legs beside him, her front paws waving daintily and her bright black eyes fixed on him with patient attention. She was always there, as though she too played an important part in the proceedings. Perhaps she did; for Verdi, though he ignored

[ 164 ]

her utterly when working, wanted the devoted little creature near him none the less.

The *Boccanegra* rehearsals went well, and in Naples Verdi had the satisfaction of hearing this opera that he loved, and that the Venetians had merely yawned at, produce storms of resounding applause. Cheerfully he went on to Rome and further triumphs. The beloved City of the Seven Hills simmered with patriotism like a cauldron about to boil, and the throng that gathered in and around the theater for the première of *The Masked Ball* gave him such an ovation as even he had seldom known. At this point in his career Verdi the symbol of Italian liberty overshadowed Verdi the composer, but the new opera won an immense and deserved success in its own right. Here were greater flexibility, richer orchestration, characters more deeply and subtly portrayed than before. And here was something new from Verdi—humor. One heard it in the sardonic laughter of the courtiers, and in the music of Oscar, a sparkling page boy whose irrepressible frivolity, like a firefly in the dusk, intensifies by contrast the drama's dark and tragic course. No one had suspected the Maestro to be capable of so flippant, so feathery a creation as this Oscar. One could almost imagine the composer of blood-and-thunder and heartbreak writing a comedy!

Verdi, in mellow holiday mood, stayed on in Rome purely for pleasure. He had a comfortable apartment, a fine piano, and an excellent cook, all found for him in advance by his "dear lunatic," the sculptor Luccardi, a lively fellow whose high good humor was as refreshing as a breeze. Rome would have liked to fête the adored Maestro, but he avoided social functions, preferring to spend his evenings cozily at home. In his own pleasant quarters he could linger over his favorite dishes and the exquisite wines he loved and, at some irresistible nonsense of Luccardi's, let his big, rare laugh fill the whole room, while at his feet Lulu fluttered her foolish tail in rapture.

Sometimes in the caressing spring sunshine Peppina, Luccardi, and of course Lulu drove with Verdi about this city whose monuments and ancient buildings were like a panorama of civilization itself. Everywhere they pointed out to each other the steadily multiplying scrawls of "Viva Verdi!" —"Look, there it is on the corner of that house, and see, again, across the way on the garden gate!" Never had Italy's cause seemed so bright.

In truth, for all Verdi's serenity, the atmosphere was growing heavy with suspense and hope. Recently Victor Emanuel had made a speech which all patriots took as forewarning of inevitable war with Austria. But where, when, how would it break out?

Meantime in Turin Cavour waited, quiet and cunning as a spider. His web was now well spun. The labors of the dark years had at last borne fruit—in his pocket he had a secret alliance with France whereby that mighty Empire pledged itself to come to his aid should Piedmont be attacked. It remained only for Cavour to maneuver the Austrians into making the first hostile move. Carefully, skillfully, he laid his traps, while the small Piedmontese army, well trained and well equipped (he had seen to that) camped taut and watchful along the Austrian border.

Suddenly the tension snapped: Austria made the fatal blunder. From Vienna Victor Emanuel received an ultimatum ordering him to demobilize his troops or be conquered. Victor Emanuel of course did not reply, leaving Austria no choice but to invade. Just as Cavour had hoped and planned, the fight was on, and the first enemy that crossed the line released a torrent of French soldiers that poured swiftly southward to the rescue.

On that day, April 29, 1859, as the first shots rang out and rumors radiated forth, anxious thousands gathered beneath Cavour's balcony in Turin, waiting for some official word. The time had come at last, he told them. Now or never must they free their mother country from her long bondage. And as he looked down at the upturned faces of young men who were perhaps about to die, and of their fathers and mothers, their sweethearts and their wives, he sought to share with them what he himself felt in this fateful hour, to inspire in them courage and devotion with which to meet the enemy. But, statesman and orator though he was, in the magnitude of the moment he could find no words at all. The crowd stared up at him, silent, expectant, doubtful. Suddenly he leaned out to them and in his cracked and tuneless voice began to sing "Di quella pira" from *Trovatore*. With an exultant roar thousands of throats picked up the well-known air—the air Manrico sings as he rushes to save his gypsy mother from the stake—and to those stirring strains the new, free Italy was born.

# CHAPTER THIRTEEN

# Hymn of the Nations

## 1859-1862

ALONG the Austrian frontier the first sounds of gunfire cracked and rumbled. Back in Turin Cavour sang "Di quella pira" from his balcony. On that same day, miles away at Collange, a village in Savoy near the Swiss border, Giuseppe Verdi, composer, and Giuseppina Strepponi, retired singer, were married. A distinguished priest who was a friend of theirs lived at remote Collange, and in order to avoid the fuss and comment, the crowds and congratulations inevitable in a big city, they had slipped off to have the ceremony performed by him. Here the middle-aged couple—prosperous city folk by the look of them—aroused no local curiosity. Only the necessary witnesses were present at the simple service; no celebration followed and no announcement was made. This was a very different affair from the wedding twenty-three years earlier when, with bands and flowers, feasting and dancing, all Busseto had made merry.

There was something mysterious about this second marriage in that it had not taken place long before. Both Verdi and Peppina were free. They loved each other deeply and completely. They had grown dependent on each other, they were inseparable. So constantly had Peppina been at his side that some people, assuming they were married, even addressed her as Signora Verdi. Why then did Verdi wait ten long years to make her his wife? Being the most reserved of men, he never told even his closest friends what the reason might be. Was the sorrow of his youth to blame—the sorrow that had so nearly broken his spirit, and permanently scarred his soul? Did he believe that wife and family were not for him, and that to thwart his destiny would only invite fresh disaster? Perhaps an unfading reverence for the memory of his Ghitta held him back, even though that memory had long since been shut out of his consciousness—like the three strands of golden hair and the trinkets she had once pawned for him, locked in a

box that was never to be reopened. One can only guess. In any case the threat of war changed everything: he and Peppina must unite their lives before some unforeseen catastrophe should separate them. It was a decision he was never to regret. Surely no great man was ever more blessed in his love than Verdi in tender, wise, humorous, self-effacing Peppina.

Immediately after the wedding they hastened home to Sant' Agata. War, so long a probability, was now a fact that must be faced. It was hard, Verdi found, to be too old to fight; and the suspense, too, was difficult to bear. With radios still undreamed of, one could only wait and wonder, sifting the rumors for authentic news and forcing oneself to keep calm and hopeful. The struggling armies, it was said, might swing toward Busseto. Must these beloved acres be turned into a battlefield? What if the enemy appeared? No patriot could expect mercy from the ruthless Austrians. Verdi had never hesitated to express himself on the subject of Italian freedom— among his papers were there incriminating statements? All one night until sunrise he and Peppina sat by the fire sorting old letters and documents and burning everything which they thought, falling into enemy hands, might lead to imprison- ment or worse.

Anxiety throughout the neighborhood became intense. Only too vividly the older inhabitants remembered the swirl of hostile armies over helpless villages and farms—the terror, the destruction. If every peasant had a gun he could at least protect his own home, he would not feel so utterly defenseless. But there were no guns, nor any money to buy them. In the emergency Busseto appealed to Maestro Verdi.

Verdi knew that English sympathizers were smuggling weapons through the seaports. "Buy me 172 rifles, the best, and send them quickly, quickly. I will take care of the bill." Thus urgently he wrote to his dear Mariani in Genoa, quite forgetting his dislike of Busseto now that he could be of use. Fortunately the fighting swerved away, but every day until all danger passed farmers drilled earnestly in the town's public square, holding themselves proudly erect and feeling brave and free because of Verdi's fine new rifles in their hands.

War in those days was by no means the highly organized business it is now and, incredibly, little or no provision was made for the care of the wounded. A fallen soldier could not even count on his comrades' clumsy help, since they might well be forced to abandon him. He must stumble to a farm- house, or crawl into a ditch, or stay where he fell until some priest or peasant chanced to find him. Most likely he would be carried to the nearest church to lie with others in close rows on the stone floor. Barns, too, were filled, and haylofts, while distracted villagers did their pitiful, ignorant best to ease the suffering.

Came the bloody battle of Solferino, a small and indecisive affair according to the history books, but with unusually high casualties. A young Swiss named Henri Dunant, traveling in Italy at the time, happened to be on the spot shortly after the battle, and he soon found himself carrying water to the thirsty —Austrians, French, and Italians alike—cutting away blood-stiffened uniforms, applying makeshift bandages, and writing last messages to far-off families. He watched men endure need-less pain because he had no way to help them. He saw men die who might have been saved, because there was nothing that he could do. And all the while there burned in him an enor-mous indignation that such things could be. He left that grim battlefield with a new purpose in life, and at home in Geneva founded the organization that in 1863 became the Inter-national Red Cross (its symbol is the Swiss flag with the colors reversed).

There were volunteers from all over Italy in the army of Piedmont, and now, after Solferino, news came filtering even to Busseto of men who would not return, men who would come home crippled, and men who must have help to re-cover their strength. The list was long; and Verdi, like Dunant, felt that something must be done. Knowing what sorrow meant, and poverty, he created a fund for the care of the injured and the families of the dead, and to his own generous gift added more in the names of all the members of his household.

At least it appeared that the suffering, the sacrifices, and the heroism were not to be in vain. As in 1848, the Austrians retreated to the famous Quadrilateral, while from the north Italian states the foreign rulers fled in panic. Temporary gov-ernments were set up, and one delirious day the French Emperor, who had followed the fighting at a safe distance, and Victor Emanuel, who had fought bravely in the front ranks with his men, rode side by side through the streets of Milan in triumph.

Then, suddenly, after six victorious weeks, the war was over! Napoleon III, finding the cost in men and money higher than he expected, abruptly decided that he had had enough. Without so much as a word to Victor Emanuel he met secretly with Emperor Francis Joseph of Austria and agreed to an armistice. For Victor Emanuel to stand alone against Austria with her immense resources would have been but a waste of brave men's lives, thus he was forced to accept peace with the battle only half-won. Overnight Italian joy and gratitude to the French turned to disgust. Verdi had once said of Napoleon III: "If he is indeed willing to fight for the freedom of a sister nation then I shall worship him as I worship George Washington." But he always mistrusted this man who, elected President, soon had himself proclaimed Emperor. And Cavour, stunned by the French betrayal, saw his life's work in ruins. Bitterly he retired to his country estate, vowing that he was through with public office forever.

Yet the Italian cause was by no means lost. On the contrary, there had been great gains. By the terms of the peace treaty the northern states were now privileged to vote whether to recall their former rulers or to become part of Victor Emanuel's kingdom, and there could be no doubt of the result. But what of Venice? Was it not Italian too? And what of Rome, Naples, Sicily? How could the new nation hope to prosper with the peninsula still torn and disunited?

Italians had hitherto expressed an opinion only at risk of their lives. On the day of the balloting they could for the first time choose their fate themselves; and we who for generations have taken for granted the precious right to vote can scarcely realize how deep and solemn was the rejoicing. Every house showed the tricolor—that long-forbidden flag of the new Italy—and all hearts lifted at the sight of the red, white, and green flying so bravely and openly under the bright, free sky. In Busseto crowds jammed the streets round the Cathedral, where the balloting took place, waiting to see their own Verdi come to cast his vote. And when the carriage drawn by his magnificent, satiny horses came in sight, a mighty cheer went up: "Italia! Italia! Vittorio Emanuele Re d'Italia! Viva Verdi! Viva Verdi!" So overwhelming was the emotion that many in the throng watched through a blur of tears as the tall, dignified Maestro entered the Cathedral.

The voting over, a group of distinguished citizens carried the outcome to Turin and formally placed Victor Emanuel's new subjects in their sovereign's hands. Most illustrious of these delegates was Verdi, and, notwithstanding his democratic principles, the occasion moved him deeply. Life had taught him that integrity is worth more than political formulas, and he saw Victor Emanuel as something better than a king: an honorable man who government, moreover, was no tyranny but a liberal monarchy based on that of England. And Cavour believed in him, had guided him—Cavour who could do no wrong. Humbly, reverently, Verdi paid his respects to the ex-Prime Minister in his retirement. The greatest men, in the Maestro's judgment, were not artists like himself but statesmen, men like Washington, whose vision of a juster world had benefited all mankind.

The King's newly acquired territories must of course be represented in the Chamber of Deputies, an institution similar to the British House of Commons. Elections were to be held, and Verdi was being more and more frequently mentioned as a possibly Deputy. Would he allow himself to be nominated? Would he agree to serve if elected?

He would not. The very idea appalled him. Only recently his life had begun to take on the pattern of his choice; and now, in middle age, he was discovering simple pleasures he had not dreamed of in his youth. There were the solitary hours in a rowboat puttering placidly round his "mud-puddle"—the little artificial lake he had lately had built. And he delighted to poke among his flower-beds and tend the shrubs that Mariani, at his request sent up from Genoa and that he, Verdi, planted with his own hands. Best of all he enjoyed shooting quail at dawn along the marshy River Po, especially when Mariani, now almost a member of the family, went with him. Verdi, learning at last to have fun, had no desire to take on an uncongenial task that would keep him for months in dreary Turin.

Though Verdi was content in his "desert" all year round, Peppina found the winter months too bleak and lonely there. "Man of iron," she called him, drawing the curtains to shut out dull skies, brown, withered garden, and stark branches bending in the wind. But she could not shut out the monotony, the isolation that depressed her, so in Genoa, where Mariani lived, they found themselves pleasant winter quarters with a view. Verdi loved the harbor city beneath its fortress-crowned hills. The endless sunshine, the soft Mediterranean air, the wide sweep of the sea, always lifted his spirits and restored his energy. And then—immeasurable blessing—the Genoese never gaped at the celebrated composer but let him go about his business unmolested, like an ordinary human being. Prosaic Turin had no such attraction as ancient, beautiful, congenial Genoa.

But these were selfish reasons. Verdi sincerely felt himself unfitted for a political career and unworthy of the responsibility. He had no knowledge of laws and government; his business, after all, was writing music. Lately a letter had come from St. Petersburg with a request for a new opera. St. Petersburg! Perhaps . . . if he could find a subject . . . No, it was unthinkable that he should become a politician, yet the pressure to accept the nomination was increasing every day. Even Cavour himself wrote urging him to make the sacrifice. In a sort of panic Verdi decided that his only hope lay in explaining himself to Cavour in person. Accordingly he hastened to Turin.

This was in January 1861—a year and a half since the signing of the peace. Cavour's retirement had been brief. Seeing his country's need, he had smothered his bitterness, left his estate (like Verdi he was a scientific farmer), and once more taken the helm of government to steer young Italy through these first critical years. His keen mind and firm will were all-important now, for the new nation was growing fast.

During the spring of 1860 the incredible hero-adventurer Garibaldi, whose very name seemed to work magic, had gathered his band of volunteers—the famous Thousand—in Genoa and prepared to invade Sicily. Although for international reasons Cavour had closed his official eyes to Garibaldi's doings, it was whispered that the expedition had the Prime Minister's secret blessing. Certainly the Genoese police had helpfully ignored the wagonloads of supplies streaming out to the little fleet berthed in the Quarto, just outside the city limits. And they had turned their backs, too, on the husky young men calling themselves "tourists" who suddenly swarmed into town. With no more legal standing than so many pirates, but with the hopes and prayers of all Italian patriots, the tiny army embarked. By way of uniforms these adventurers had only the red shirts that Garibaldi had made famous, and their own haphazard clothes; for weapons, little more than courage and their leader's indomitable genius. Yet they swept across Sicily swelling like a scarlet snowball as sympathizers from every town and village joined their ranks.

Verdi, in Genoa at the time, had watched the semi-secret bustle of departure; and, as news of the miraculous campaign was rushed home in the breathless days that followed, his pulse had quickened with true Italian pride. For in spite of the King of Naples' hundred thousand men, the Red Shirts had taken Palermo, crossed to the mainland, and soon set Naples and all southern Italy free. The liberated people of course voted to place themselves under Victor Emanuel, and thus the dream of a united nation was all but realized. Cavour had had to cede the border provinces of Nice and Savoy to France forever (this being the prearranged price of French help in the war); Venice was still in the Austrian grip; and the Pope, with the power of France behind him, still ruled Rome. Nevertheless Italy had become a real and sizable nation at last, and the eyes of the whole world would focus on the first congress soon to be elected.

During these exciting days the Prime Minister, always a busy man, was busier than ever, and Verdi's appointment with him was for six o'clock of a January morning. Verdi, accustomed to getting his own way without resort to argument or persuasion, had no skill for such an interview as this, and along the chill, quiet streets that led to Cavour's house in Turin he rehearsed his plea to himself like a timid schoolboy. By the time he arrived he had spun his reluctance to be a Deputy into what he called a "*speak*" which impressed him as quite a masterpiece.

Cavour—compact, shrewd, energetic, with gray-white hair and a lined, thoughtful face—greeted him warmly. The great statesman's friendly handclasp, his easy, cordial manner, his sincere esteem, at once thawed Verdi's shyness. Confidently the Maestro spoke the formal phrases he had prepared. Then, warming to his subject, he went on: "Not that I don't appreciate the honor, Your Excellency. If elected, I should of course be proud and grateful that my fellow-citizens considered me a man of judgment and integrity. But frankly, what could I do in Parliament? I'm a musician, Your Excellency, a simple musician. I know nothing, nothing at all about politics. What's more, I haven't the slightest aptitude for such things. Why, I'd be worse than useless—keeping some better man out. . . . And then, surely Your Excellency realizes that I haven't the right temperament for this sort of life. I am, I admit, a very impatient fellow. How could I bear to sit, and sit, and sit, through all that talk? Ah, no . . . I can't do it . . . I can't!" Verdi shook his head, shrugged his shoulders, waved his hands, unconsciously comic in his extreme dismay.

Cavour's solemn attention broke into uncontrollable laughter. "I've won!" thought Verdi, elated, laughing too. "He sees the absurdity—"

"Maestro, forgive me!" A final chuckle, and the Prime Minister was suddenly serious and intent. "Indeed I understand your reluctance. But Italy's future depends upon the beginning that we make now. To this first Congress will come our most distinguished men from every field of endeavor: poets, artists, architects, scientists, engineers, and so on. Our foremost literary genius—Manzoni himself—is to become a Senator. We want the entire world to see that this young nation's most illustrious citizens are proud to sacrifice their personal interests if need be. We want a list of Deputies that shall be the envy of all Europe. And must your name be missing, Maestro?—your name that is to us a symbol and a battle cry, and that beyond our borders is more widely known and loved than that of any other son of Italy? I beg you to reconsider, not for your own sake, nor for mine, but for the land that we both love and try to serve!"

There could be no answer to such an argument. Verdi had met his match at last. Before he parted from Cavour he had given his promise not to refuse the nomination and, if elected, to fulfill his duties as best he could. He insisted, however, on two conditions: he would not lift a finger to influence the voters, and if he became Deputy he must be permitted to resign as soon as decently possible—after a few months at the most.

In due time, and much to his disgust, Verdi was elected, and he and Peppina moved to Turin. The opening of Parliament was of course a full-dress affair of the sort he heartily detested, and he arrived some days in advance in order, as he wrote Mariani, "to let my anger cool before I have to put on my white tie!" During the four months of that first session he was conscientious in his attendance, patiently enduring the floods of high-flown oratory day after day. "What beautiful things they say—and what a waste of time!" he sighed. Once, in his boredom, he sketched with music the shouting of his fellow deputies over a much debated question, just as an artist might amuse himself by drawing a caricature. Whenever some bit of legislation was to be voted on, he followed Cavour's lead, sure that he could not thus go wrong. At Cavour's instigation he worked out a sound plan for free musical education on a national scale, but he was too modest to admit the excellence of this committee work, always maintaining that "as a Deputy, Verdi does not exist!"

Meantime he corresponded with St. Petersburg about a new opera and read innumerable plays, but all in vain. This one was unsuitable in theme, that one lacked variety and contrast, another was not dramatic, and still another was (as he put it) not "musicable." At length he offered to do Victor Hugo's *Ruy Blas*, but Russia had a censorship of its own to which *Ruy Blas* was not acceptable. Verdi thereupon lost interest and let the matter drop.

By and by there appeared in Turin a charming young man named Achille Tamberlik, son of St. Petersburg's leading tenor. Of course he called on Verdi and soon became a daily visitor, dining, or driving, or dropping in to chat of opera and friends. Peppina shrewdly guessed that this attractive fellow was not the casual traveler he pretended to be, but an ambassador sent from St. Petersburg to induce the Maestro to commit himself to a new score. Young Tamberlik went

[ 177 ]

about his mission with patience and tact, never bringing up the subject unless Peppina, who loved to see the world and was in favor of an opera for Russia, signaled him that the moment was auspicious.

One day Verdi remarked that there was a Spanish play called *Don Alvaro, or the Force of Destiny*—he had thought of it a good deal lately. But it was twenty-five years old, he had not read it in a long time, and he could find no copy anywhere.

Young Tamberlik wasted not a moment. He was out frantically combing Turin almost before Verdi had finished speaking. But nowhere in the city was the old Spanish drama to be found. Delay might be fatal—suppose the Maestro's mood should change? There was a famous bookstore in Milan —it was at least worth trying. And sure enough, within twenty-four hours Verdi held a copy in his hands. Eagerly he read it through. Yes, it would do—Piave must set to work at once. At once!

In due course the parliamentary session came to an end and Verdi, bound for Sant' Agata, went to take leave of Cavour.

"Your Excellency, what about my resignation? I feel so useless, especially as I must be in Russia most of next winter. Surely it's time a better man took my place?"

Cavour was a good showman and he still had use for Verdi's glorious name. "Not quite yet, Maestro, I beg of you. Take leave of absence if you must—in your profession that's unavoidable. Carry Italian music, Italian fame, abroad, and more power to you. But wait a little longer to resign. Who knows? Perhaps one of these days we'll be moving to Rome!"

Verdi could refuse Cavour nothing. They shook hands warmly and parted, never to meet again; only a few weeks later Italy was stunned by news of her great statesman's sudden death. What was to become of the young nation now, without that clear head and strong, devoted hand to guide it? Verdi did not attend the pompous funeral in Turin—he was too deeply shaken. And at the memorial service held at his expense in Busseto's Cathedral he cried openly, like a lost child. Nor did he resign from the Chamber of Deputies. Instead he served his full term òf four more years out of respect for Cavour's memory.

All that summer, while Verdi composed, Peppina, half eager and half fearful, prepared for the long Russian journey. If only they could store in themselves the sunshine that baked their peaceful, flower-bright terrace! It seemed incredible that human beings could exist in what she called "the land of perpetual sherbets, the inferno of ice." Quantities of warm, bulky clothing must be bought and packed. And who could tell what barbaric foods they might be expected to eat? Better take a few essentials: olive oil, cheese, macaroni, and rice for the "divine *risotto*" Verdi liked to make himself, hovering happy and absorbed over the stove, adding a pinch of this and that and tasting thoughtfully, like a true gourmet. Painstakingly Peppina listed the supplies to be sent in advance, including fine French wines, long, fragrant cigars, and champagne for the parties they would be expected to give. She was distractingly busy. It fell to her, of course, to make arrangements with an Italian friend in Russia for procuring a suitable house, a good piano, an interpreter, etc., etc., all to be ready on arrival.

It was dreary November when they set out with two servants and mountains of baggage, prepared (they hoped) for every hardship, every emergency in what was then, as always, the land of mystery. But to their surprise they found life in St. Petersburg wonderfully comfortable, exotic, and luxurious. The rooms, warmed by huge stoves of shining, colored tiles, were far pleasanter than Italy's summery villas during a cold, damp spell, and out of doors one wore furs, magnificent furs! Verdi's new fur-lined Russian coat came to his ankles, its immense collar covered his shoulders like a shawl, and the long, wide sleeves served as a muff. Peppina, driving about this sparkling white world beside him in a sleigh cozy with bear skins, thought that with his fur hat, his thick hair, and dark, full beard, he looked exactly like one of the Czar's own noblemen. Never had they dreamed of such wealth, such gaiety, such lavish, barbaric, devil-may-care splendor! The Russians, moreover, were as warm as their climate was cold—so friendly, so polite, with the politeness of the heart, Verdi said, not the "insolent politeness" of sophisticated Paris.

And yet, what if one were poor? There was another side to all this gorgeousness, so grim that it made Peppina shudder. Time and again she saw the lines of sleighs waiting in numbing darkness while their masters caroused at some fantastic all-night banquet. The patient, velvet ponies shifted miserably from foot to foot, their noses hoary with the frost of their breathing, while on the seats the coachmen huddled stiffly in their wraps. Peppina even heard—oh, it was horrible!—that sometimes when the revelry was over a young lord starting home at dawn might find his coachman frozen dead where he sat! The shocking thing was that no one seemed to care; coachmen were plentiful, so what did it matter? Peppina could not bear to think of it. Had these rich, gay, warmhearted Russians no imagination? Did they not know that the poor and powerless are human too?

Lists and luggage, packing, unpacking, packing again. Fortunately Peppina was a good traveler, for the prima donna of Verdi's choice was taken ill and by February it became clear that *The Force of Destiny* would have to be postponed until the following season. The long, elaborate journey had been in vain and must be repeated. There was little respite these days from stations, tickets, trains, trunks, and the familiar rumble of iron wheels on iron rails.

At home Verdi hastily inspected his farm, then pushed on to Turin to drop in briefly at the Chamber of Deputies. But he could not remain in Italy. By April he and Peppina were settled in a small house near Regent's Park, London, and he was there on business he disliked.

This was 1862, the year that England had chosen to hold an International Exposition of her own. Among the events scheduled was a gala concert in the vast new Crystal Palace, with music specially contributed by the leading composers of England, France, Germany, and Italy. Sterndale Bennett (popular then, almost forgotten now), Auber, and Meyerbeer were to represent England, France, and Germany respectively. For Italy the ageing demigod Rossini was the obvious choice, but he declined, pleading infirmity. If Italy were not to default, Verdi must take Rossini's place, there being no one else of comparable stature. Now Verdi had again and again refused to write "occasion pieces" such as this; he did not "feel" them and was therefore convinced that music of the sort could never be inspired. But this was different. Italy's musical honor was at stake. Reluctantly, and with misgivings, he consented.

Characteristically, Verdi composed neither a march nor an overture as the others had done, but a short cantata for solo voice, chorus, and orchestra. It was called *Hymn of the Nations*, and the words were by Arrigo Boito, a twenty-year-old poet and musician who whimsically signed his writings "Tobia Gorrio." Verdi had met this gifted youngster at Rossini's— sooner or later one met everybody there—and besides had heard him well spoken of by friends. Son of an Italian painter and a Polish countess, Boito was everything Verdi himself was not: intellectual, refined, subtle, aristocratic. He had zealous, youthful theories about reforming art—the past must be ignored and a fresh start made. Verdi on the other hand believed that newer, better music could be built only on the old foundations. The two men had little use for each other, and would have found it hard to believe that they would some day form the closest, most perfect team of collaborators in the whole history of opera.

For the much-heralded performance an audience of five thousand gathered in the Crystal Palace, but to everyone's dismay the *Hymn of the Nations* was not on the program! Various excuses were offered: Verdi had not submitted his score in time (this was of course untrue, and he indignantly denied it in a letter to the London *Times*); he should have written for orchestra alone; the authorities were scandalized because he had made use of the shocking and revolutionary *Marseillaise!* Actually it appeared that the jealousy of London's foremost conductor, the Italian Michael Costa, was at the bottom of the matter; his ill-will dated back to the old rivalry between Her Majesty's Theatre and Covent Garden at the time of Verdi's *The Robbers*.

Whatever the reason, Verdi himself would have been thankful to escape without a performance. His cantata was, he knew, no masterpiece, and he had no sooner reached England than he regretted having broken his rule to write it. As for the honor of Italian music, it was quite plain that his latest effort was hardly needed. Then, as now, every hurdy-gurdy churned out the best-loved airs from Verdi's own Big Three, and in those radioless days men, women, and children came running through the streets to listen, their bodies swaying to the rhythm, their faces alight with pleasure. True, the English critics had often expressed a rather low opinion of him. But what of that? Everywhere London's springtime strollers whistled his melodies—his own ears told him that his music was alive in people's hearts. He was content to let the *Hymn of the Nations* go.

Not so the public, from whom there rose a tremendous outcry. Articles appeared in the papers protesting this insult to "Europe's most illustrious composer." "What boors he must think us!" Londoners exclaimed, insisting on their right to hear the promised work. To satisfy the demand a performance was finally scheduled for the end of May, not in the colossal Crystal Palace, but at Her Majesty's Theatre.

While this was being arranged, Verdi took his insatiable sightseer, Peppina, on a quick tour of Scotland and the Lake Country. She had not visited the British Isles before, and, as always, she was intensely curious about new places, new people, and new ways. To improve her command of the language she studied zealously, and it was she who translated the stacks of "fan mail" that the postman brought to Regent's Park. Verdi found the letters astonishing—all from total strangers, and all asking for autographs. At home his friends sometimes begged his autograph as a great favor, for friends of theirs. But these requests came from every corner of England, and many enclosed precious albums for him to write in, complete with return envelope. He signed and signed, muttering: "But who *are* these people? I never even heard of them!" That strangers should whistle his arias was understandable, fine, but that they should want his signature—what for? It was extraordinary, and disagreeable.

With the *Hymn of the Nations* he became even more popular. Four performances, instead of the one planned, had to be given, and each produced such thunderous applause that the entire cantata had to be repeated from beginning to end. For once the English critics raved but, as usual where Verdi was concerned, they were wrong. The music was not especially remarkable, certainly not immortal.

Yet, of the works composed for the International Exposition, Verdi's alone, because of its significance, achieved a kind of immortality. In his finale he ingeniously wove together *God Save the Queen*, *The Marseillaise*, and an Italian national air. It was as though he were saying: "Listen to these tunes, so utterly different—they can nevertheless be fitted together. In the same way the different nations can live and work together harmoniously, in freedom and brotherhood." This being the most important message in the world, the finale is still revived at appropriate times.

The most recent occasion was in 1943, when Mussolini's fall and Fascist Italy's surrender to the Allies brought the first ray of light in history's darkest years. A round-the-globe broadcast of music under the baton of the greatest living conductor, Arturo Toscanini—himself a voluntary exile from Fascism—solemnized the event. Millions that night tuned in their radios to Verdi's *Hymn of the Nations*, through which Toscanini had woven still another national anthem: *The Star-Spangled Banner*. The score performed still another war service. At the request of the U. S. Army, Maestro Toscanini, breaking his rule never to appear in a motion picture, conducted the *Hymn of the Nations* before the cameras. The film, though it showed merely an orchestra, singers, and conductor in action, was extraordinarily thrilling and proved an inspiration to the Allied forces. Moreover, shortly before D Day a recording of the superb sound track was secretly radioed to the Underground fighters of Nazi-occupied Europe, along with their instructions for the long-awaited landing of Allied troops on German-held soil. So electrifying was the effect that this magnificent rendering of the *Hymn* was used again and again, and it has been called "the most potent single musical weapon of World War II." For Verdi's music, unsuited to the concert stage under ordinary conditions, yet has a quality of heroic excitement that routs despair and calls forth the last impossible ounce of effort. It is an expression of faith—the faith on which hope, happiness, even life itself will always depend: faith in the freedom of mankind and in the brotherhood of nations.

# CHAPTER FOURTEEN

# The Giant of the North and
# the Giant of the South
### 1862-1868

IN the Great Square of Moscow, Verdi and Peppina stared about them feeling very far away from home. This four-day excursion from St. Petersburg (it would have been a pity not to see the ancient capital since they were so near) had brought them beyond the range of the civilization they had always taken for granted. Here nothing bore the stately stamp of Rome; no imitations of Italian architecture gave the scene a familiar and accustomed look. Instead, the fortress of the Kremlin, heart of Holy Russia, sprawled before them in gloomy and exotic splendor. Within its walls that had known centuries of revelry and bloodshed they saw the Crown Jewels —the fabulous, incalculable treasure of the Czar. Before such wealth one could not help thinking of Italy, so poverty-stricken after the long years of oppression. But Italy had riches of the spirit—art, culture, courage—and even her humblest peasant was blessed with dignity and pride. No coachmen there were simply left to die . . . Gazing at the soft luster of antique gold, the mysterious gleam and flash of precious stones, Peppina shuddered. A strange land this, barbaric, alien.

And yet, was it so alien? At Moscow's opera house the posters announced *Il Trovatore.* "You see, Peppina? It's just

[ 185 ]

as I said—even if you went to the wilds of Africa you'd be sure to find *Trovatore* there ahead of you!" There was truth in Verdi's joke. To whatever remote spot Europeans penetrated they took the beloved *Troubadour* with them—if not the whole opera, at least a melody or two. Verdi could not resist dropping in for a look at the performance.

To his astonishment he was recognized; someone in the audience must have seen him on his former visit to St. Petersburg. "Verdi is here!" "Where? Where?" "Standing at the back, the tall man with dark hair, that's Verdi!" Everyone turned to look and clap and cheer. As the tumult grew deafening the Maestro, forced before the curtain, bowed and bowed and bowed again. Backstage the singers buzzed about him in a flurry of pleasure, eager to speak to him, to shake his hand. Why had he not let them know he was coming? Ah, but it was not too late—the company insisted on giving a banquet in his honor the very next day!

For once Verdi was graciousness itself, even seeming to enjoy the fuss that was made over him. But then he had been taken completely by surprise, and these Russians were so genuine, so spontaneous in their enthusiasm. Truly this proof that music is a universal language warmed the heart!

Yet in St. Petersburg *The Force of Destiny*, finally produced in November 1862, was coolly received. Some people came to the performance already prejudiced: Why, they grumbled, should any foreigner, even Verdi, be paid twenty-two thousand rubles for-an opera, when their own Russian composers had to be content with five hundred? Besides, *La Forza del Destino* (known as *Forza* for short) turned out not to be exactly like the Big Three. Had Verdi continued to write as he did ten years earlier, everyone would have been satisfied—everyone, that is, except Verdi himself. He was advancing steadily, faster than the public could follow, breaking down the rigid operatic patterns into ever more flexible forms, enriching his orchestration, feeling his way toward a new musical freedom.

Not that *Forza* could be called a failure. St. Petersburg, although less than enthusiastic over it, nevertheless fêted the composer with a round of parties which, charmed by Russian friendliness, he attended willingly enough. And at the fourth performance of his opera the Czar Alexander II, who had been ill until then, appeared in all his glitter. Verdi was summoned to the huge, richly draped Imperial box to receive the Imperial congratulations. Nor was that all: he was made Commander of the Order of St. Stanislas, a distinction seldom bestowed on civilians and the more remarkable in that a favor done a friend at court, or some such intrigue, was generally necessary to obtain it. In Verdi's case the honor was not only unsought but unexpected, yet he made light of it. Peppina, however, could not keep her happy pride from overflowing into her letters home.

Then, after a hasty journey clear across Europe, Verdi presented *Forza* in Madrid, where it was brilliantly successful. The Spaniards, familiar with the play from which it was drawn, had no difficulty understanding the unwieldy, over-compressed libretto. They recognized background and atmosphere; the colorful, shifting crowds of students, soldiers, peasants, gypsies, priests, and monks—never had Verdi given his choruses so much life and character—delighted them. They were enchanted with the fat and rascally Fra Melitone, a creature straight out of comic opera. Verdi's laughter, first heard in *The Masked Ball*, was richer and heartier now, and in this tale of woe and disaster came as a welcome relief.

Had Verdi been a man of wide culture instead of a self-educated peasant, this narrative of well-intentioned people misused by cruel fate might not have appealed to him so strongly. But because it had the one quality needed to kindle his imagination—emotional intensity—he was blind to its faults. He did not see that the rambling plot was built on too many accidents and coincidences, or that the characters (before he gave them music) were no more human than so many costumes hanging on a wall. He "felt" the situations in which they found themselves, and with his special magic warmed the puppet hearts, making them really beat and break.

Now, and later when *The Force of Destiny* reached Italy, the critics were somewhat hesitant in their praise, and indeed the

[ 187 ]

score has uninspired passages. But there are also pages as
fine as any Verdi had yet written—magnificent moments,
and melodies that, stripped of all superfluous ornament, soar
hauntingly in bare, essential beauty. *Forza*, therefore, though
it never attained the steady popularity of the Big Three, has

refused to die, and crowds still wait thirstily in line to hear it and drink of the clear, sweeping glory that was peculiarly Verdi's own.

Not even after the triumph in Madrid could the much-traveled Verdis go home. There was time only for a little sight-seeing in Spain before they were due in Paris for a revival of *The Sicilian Vespers*. As luck would have it, the city, in July 1863, sweltered under a heat wave. The people dragged themselves listlessly along the baked and dusty streets, and crowded the parks seeking relief from the shimmering torment of the sun. Even inside the cavernous Opéra the air was stale and suffocating. Verdi, to whom rehearsals here were always hateful, had to drive himself to maintain his usual standard of perfection. From his prowling place at the back of the dim auditorium he glared past the musicians to the vast stage beyond, empty now but for some odds and ends of scenery and two or three apathetic workmen. For scenic effects, of course, no theater in the world could equal this, with its marvelous mechanical devices and precision-trained crews. There was no denying that the staff was expert at everything—except music. Verdi, listening to the orchestra and fighting the sense of frustration that always plagued him here, would gladly have scrapped all the machinery the French were so proud of for a little musical understanding. But there was none; these Parisians seemed to squeeze the breath of life out of his score.

Take that piece they were just ending now, for instance—too fast, much too fast. At that tempo the whole effect, the point, was lost. He strode down the aisle and in exasperation spoke to Dietsch, the conductor.

"No, no, no—impossible! It can't be played like that. You'll have to take it slower. So—" Verdi beat out the time. "Let me hear it once more."

The hot and weary musicians, assuming that the rehearsal was over, had already begun to put up their instruments. Dietsch glanced at Verdi sullenly, then tapped on the conductor's desk. "The Maestro says that was too fast. He wants to hear it slower—like this. You will repeat it, from the beginning."

The men took out their instruments again, exchanging angry looks. They played, but holding back on every note, deliberately dragging, slower . . . slower . . . until the piece became a grotesque dirge, a mockery. This was worse than insolence—it was mutiny!

Verdi's fatal temper boiled. "Rather a poor joke," he said to Dietsch, and his voice was deadly.

Dietsch shrugged, avoiding the Maestro's eyes. "Good heavens! These gentlemen think they have rehearsed enough."

"Indeed?"

"Surely you realize that they have other things to attend to."

"Ah, they have other things to attend to—more important than the opera. Very well then." Verdi turned on his heel, stalked out of the theater and went home—all the way home to Sant' Agata. *The Sicilian Vespers* had to be produced without him, and without the miserable Dietsch whom the management promptly fired. The revival, however, was a decided success.

During Meyerbeer's long reign at the Opéra, Verdi was not the only composer who found that famous institution uncoöperative, and there were those who claimed that Meyerbeer himself was to blame. Certainly the Prussian, a master of advance publicity, was not above courting favor with everyone who could enhance his reputation. There were, for instance, such matters as the handsome presents from his wife for the members of the orchestra. Verdi, abhorring artificially stimulated enthusiasm, believed that music must stand on its own merits; no liking or gratitude for the man who wrote it should cloud the hearers' judgment. Characteristically, however, he made no complaints, no accusations. Instead, he scornfully washed his hands of the whole intrigue-ridden mess and went his way. This was a very different reaction from that of Richard Wagner, whose *Tannhäuser* had failed disastrously at the Opéra only two years before.

[ 190 ]

Wagner, like Verdi born in the year 1813, had as yet won little recognition for his music, which the public still found incomprehensible. He had struggled in vain to be rid of Dietsch, and he had openly accused Meyerbeer of deliberately obstructing the careers of other men. Whereas Verdi accepted his failures in silence, Wagner, when *Tannhäuser* crashed, had defended himself and his new theories with the zeal of a prophet.

These two towering geniuses of opera, who, though they never met, were to cast long shadows on each other's lives, could not have been more unlike. Wagner, man of wide learning and brilliant intellect, was a theorizing reformer who discarded the past and evolved a new art form of his own, the "music-drama." Verdi, revering the great traditions, sought to improve upon them, to modernize them, not do away with them entirely. He had no use for theories: for him, there was no right and wrong in music—there was only good and bad. Wagner was contemptuous of whatever did not conform to his own ideas, but Verdi could admire and enjoy anything— old or new, big or little, gay or somber, serious or trivial— provided only that it was *good of its kind*. And while Wagner wrote literally volumes in his own defense, Verdi quietly "let public opinion take its course."

Even in their choice of subjects, the two men differed widely. Wagner turned to fairy tales, myths, cloaking the deeper meaning of his operas in allegory. Verdi's direct mind was not drawn to symbols and abstractions. A magical world of gods and goddesses, or Power, Greed, Purity, and so on with capital letters, meant nothing to him. He cared only about flesh-and-blood human beings, their loves and hates, their sorrow and rejoicing. Moreover—and this was the most fundamental difference of all—for German Wagner the orchestra was always paramount, whereas Italian Verdi thought and felt in terms of song. Wagner's music, therefore, seemed to Verdi (when he eventually heard it) scarcely opera at all, but rather "symphony with voice."

Not only as musicians but as men these two were poles apart. Wagner throve on praise; Verdi, when paid a fatuous compliment, retorted in real fury: "I will allow no flattery to my face!" Wagner considered himself a superior being to whom the ordinary rules of conduct did not apply; Verdi insisted that he did not differ from his fellowmen, and was incapable of a dishonorable thought. Wagner often spoke maliciously of other composers, living and dead; Verdi's appraisal of other men's music, including Wagner's, was always fair, and, respecting all honest effort, he never stooped to sneer. Wagner, however, so resented his Italian rival's popularity that he reserved for him the supreme insult: never once did he give any public sign, in either his writings or his talk, that he knew such a man existed! This was childish, of course, and merely revealed the depth of his bitterness. Inevitably between the two, so utterly unlike, there arose a strange and lasting warfare, whose echoes still have not quite died away. But Verdi, returning thankfully home in 1863 after his wearying journeys, did not as yet foresee this conflict, nor could he guess how profoundly the German composer was soon to shake the whole musical world.

The previous summer, what with the trips to Russia and to England, the Maestro had paused only briefly at Sant' Agata. Now he settled down, resolved to be the country squire again. As usual, requests for new scores followed him—from St. Petersburg, from the Opéra, from where not. He turned a deaf ear to them all. The dust and turmoil and frustration of Paris were soon forgotten in the dawn hours along the river Po where, crouching alert and motionless among the reeds, he waited for the sudden, thrilling whir of wings. It was good to feel the gun in his hands, so delicately, so precisely made, so exquisitely balanced. He had bought this one and another equally fine in London, was as proud of them as a boy, and could hardly wait till his friend Mariani, who shared his enthusiasm for duck-shooting, should try them out.

Verdi found plenty of work to do: the farm accounts to be checked over with his superintendent, the whole estate to be inspected, the final alterations to be made on the house. For these last he was his own architect, drawing up plans, giving orders, and even taking a hand at mixing cement and laying bricks. Meanwhile poor Peppina, patiently dodging scaffolding, paint pots, and carpenters' tools, supervised the "perpetual waltz of furniture" from room to room, and was obliged to sleep anywhere—everywhere, except the kitchen and the cellar! There was a day when dignitaries from Turin arrived for lunch; the table had to be set in a hallway and all through the meal, while she played the gracious hostess, swallows swooped in and out through an open space under the roof. Peppina, who always met trials and discomfort with humor, laughed to think of it. But she was thankful when the building was done and she could rearrange her household with a feeling of peace and permanence.

What with the remodeling at Sant' Agata, a session of Parliament in Turin, and a well-earned rest in Genoa, more than a year slipped away with no thought of opera. Finally, however, a suggestion that he revise *Macbeth* for the Théâtre Lyrique in Paris lured Verdi back to music. *Macbeth!* He still felt the old warmth, the special affection for this score that had gone deeper than any other of his early works. Yes, surely this one was well worth revising. But on going over it he found much that he would rather not have found—stilted, lifeless passages that he could scarcely believe had once satisfied him. It was hard to pick up the thread again after so many years, especially for Verdi who wrote best "all in one breath." Nevertheless he worked eagerly and, though he refused to go to Paris himself, sent page after page of detailed instructions as to staging. *Macbeth,* he felt, ought to succeed; the public must respond to the great drama even as he himself had responded when setting it to music.

But *Macbeth* failed—too serious, no doubt, and not spectacular enough for the Parisian taste. "Amen," said Verdi quietly, admitting that he was both surprised and disappointed. One critic accused him of not knowing Shakespeare —Shakespeare who, though he lived so long ago, had been his friend, companion, teacher, since early youth, and whose *King Lear* was still his dearest dream! The injustice of the comment pierced even Verdi's armor of indifference.

In April 1865, only a week after the performance of *Mac-*

*beth*, Meyerbeer's last work, *L'Africaine*, was produced at the Opéra, and the sensation that it caused quite snuffed out any remaining spark of interest in Verdi's opera. But Meyerbeer himself had been dead almost a year, and it was Verdi who was chosen to succeed him as foreign member of the *Académie des Beaux Arts*—an extraordinary honor. Who would take the Prussian's place in the operatic world that he had ruled so long? Who could produce the vast eye- and ear-filling works, the true "grand" operas that the French people loved? One of their own composers perhaps—Berlioz, Gounod, Auber, Halévy, Thomas? Or Wagner? He was not seriously in the running. Or Verdi? Now, when the Opéra asked him for a new score, he agreed; here was a challenge to himself, to Italy, that he could not refuse.

Should he attempt *King Lear* at last? No. With the fate of *Macbeth* still fresh in his mind he felt more than ever convinced that Paris could not understand or do justice to it. Besides, all the fancy stage machinery at "the Big Store" (thus, because of its commercialism and lack of soul, he branded the Opéra) would lie idle. Better some huge spectacle with pageantry as well as drama. From Spain, Verdi had drawn *Ernani*, *Trovatore*, *Forza;* once again he turned to that vivid land whose turbulent history attracted him the more since he had traveled there. He chose Schiller's fine play, *Don Carlos*, set in the sixteenth century when the tyrannical zealot, Philip II, seemed to rule half the globe, and persecuted peoples struggled for freedom, as in our own time and Verdi's. In those days the Inquisition, bloodthirsty and terrible as the Nazi Gestapo, tortured or put to death whoever dared think for himself or plead for justice. Schiller's drama was built around the rebellion of Philip's son, Don Carlos, in history a weakling, but here portrayed as a noble and tragic figure. It was the sort of story, with its thwarted lovers, its dramatic incidents, and its strong plea for liberty, that Verdi was sure to "feel," and the characters were no automata into whom life must be instilled, but subtle, complex human beings.

Yet the music cost him an immense effort of will. The special requirements of "the Big Store"—the five long acts, the grandiose manner, the high-lighted ballet—hampered him, as did the libretto, which for once he himself took no part in shaping. His librettists, the elderly Méry (who used to speak of Italy as "God's Conservatory of Music") and young Camille du Locle, were Frenchmen and would know best how to capture the Parisian fancy. But their verses were too long-winded to suit Verdi, who in his love of brevity and swiftly flowing action was again Wagner's opposite. As so often happened when he composed under a strain, the old enemy, sore throat, fastened on him, bringing with it headaches, indigestion, and leaden fatigue.

World events, too, weighed his spirit down. In this year of 1866 Italy again went to war, this time as Prussia's ally when Bismarck, the aggressive Prussian chancellor, launched an attack on Austria. There came days when a cannon ball crashing through the walls of Verdi's beloved home, so recently perfected, would hardly have surprised him. For safety's sake his friends urged him to leave the country. Leave now? When there was danger? Unthinkable—this was the very moment when he could least endure to be away! The unrest, the anxiety must be borne, and also the bad news: news of disastrous defeats suffered by Italy's armies and her fleet. Though the brief Seven Weeks' War, as it was called, soon ended with Prussia victorious, the Italians, thirsting for glory, had to swallow bitter humiliation instead. For Austria, forced to surrender Venice at last but unable to resist a final sneer, turned the passionately Italian city over, not to Italy, but to France! Of course France then held a plebiscite in Venice, and the Venetians voted to become Victor Emanuel's subjects; yet Italian pride smarted under the Austrian slap, and hatred of both Austria and France reached fever heat.

Verdi, puttering listlessly in his garden and working at *Don Carlo* whenever he felt well enough, was saddened by thoughts of a darkening future in which bigger and still bigger wars would forge an endless chain of suffering for mankind. In his depression he tried to be released from his contract with Paris, but in vain. "This opera," he said, "written in the midst of fire and flame, will be either better than the others or else a horrible thing." And he added that the score would never have been finished without his new "collaborator," a dog named Black.

Black had succeeded Lulu, the unforgettable, whose portrait now hung in Peppina's bedroom, and over whose grave in the garden stood a small marble column touchingly inscribed "To the memory of one of my most faithful friends." But at Sant' Agata a household pet was a necessity, and Black, who had no worries aside from the intoxicating scent of rabbit in the fields, was a refreshing creature in an anxious world. While the Maestro bent frowning over his music paper it was good to have the dog there with him in the study, drowsing serenely at his feet. The least word, even a glance, from his master never failed to set Black's tail to thumping, and Verdi, who loved and understood all animals, drew strength and reassurance from this simple contentment.

Occasionally Black dictated letters addressed to his brother, who lived with one of Verdi's distinguished friends in Turin. This correspondence is full of the delights of Sant'Agata: the punctual bowl of soup, the large, luscious bones from the kitchen, the macaroons that rain from Verdi's hand into Black's waiting mouth. He mentions a young kitten whom he has undertaken to educate, and refers often to his "secretary," of whose intelligence he has a low opinion. "I've read in some newspaper that he's on the verge of a new blunder!" Thus did Verdi inform his friend that *Don Carlo* had been announced by the press.

In due course the Maestro went to Paris to supervise the production. He had already begun to coach the singers in their parts when word came that his father, who had long been ailing, was dead. Of late the simple villager and his world-famous son had had little in common, but the bond of loyal affection between them remained strong, and Verdi was deeply shaken by the news. For a while his grief made him incapable of working, and the preparations for *Don Carlo* came to a halt. The rehearsals, when they were eventually resumed, made but slow progress—Verdi had learned to expect annoying delays at the Opéra, where, as Peppina tartly commented, "they argue twenty-four hours whether a singer should raise a finger or the whole hand!" Not until March 1867 did the eagerly awaited première take place.

*Don Carlo*, commissioned to celebrate Paris' new Universal Exposition, was of course the gala event of a gala season. The audience, even more glittering and cosmopolitan than usual, included many Italians, among them Mariani, who had come to witness Verdi's triumph in this, his most prodigious undertaking. But the performance was a poor one. Unfortunately, too, when certain heresies were expressed on the stage, the Empress Eugénie, who was an ardent Catholic, turned her back to show her disapproval, and naturally no one at court dare admire what had displeased Her Majesty! So, although the final curtain came down to the customary applause, congratulations, compliments, the enthusiasm did not quite ring true, and Verdi, who knew the real thing when he heard it, was not deceived. This evening, which had cost him such weary months of work and strain, should have been the climax of his career. Now it was over, and he felt curiously flat, empty and tired. But Mariani, as they left the Opéra together, turned to him and whispered: "Wait, Maestro, just wait till I conduct *Don Carlo* in Bologna next autumn. Then, ah, *then* we shall see!"

This huge opera, not exactly a failure and yet by no means the success Verdi had hoped, baffled the critics. They spoke of its orchestral richness and eloquence, and the loosening of the old patterns to create ever stronger unity of words, action, and music, as the Maestro's "new style," and could not quite make up their minds to like it. But as though from Mount Olympus, "Jupiter Rossini" (Meyerbeer's name for him) made a pronouncement. He had already pointed out that Verdi was the only composer whose operas were beloved in every country. Now he declared that Verdi was the only man alive capable of writing true "grand opera."

Verdi went home, busied himself with settling a splendid apartment he had newly taken in Genoa, and, at Sant' Agata, energetically studied books on agriculture. From England he had imported the latest machinery to irrigate his fields, and he spent long hours in a deep pit dug in the earth, encouraging, scolding, and helping his workmen as they installed it. To a friend he wrote: "Tell me if you like that *Don Carlo* is worthless and I shan't care a fig, but if anyone dare say that I'm not a good mason I shall take offense!" Thus, humorously, he covered the painful wound of disappointment.

In midsummer there came a keen new sorrow. Good Signor Barezzi, who for some time past had made his home at Sant' Agata, grew desperately ill—was, in fact, dying. With his last strength he motioned his Giuseppe to the piano, and Verdi, guessing what he wanted, softly played "Go, thought, on golden wings." It was Barezzi's favorite, this air. To him it meant the fulfilment of his belief in the gruff, shy, smouldering youth of long ago to whom he had given his daughter and whom he had loved as his own son. In Verdi's and Peppina's arms the old man died, and his last words were "Oh—my Verdi—"

With his unwavering faith, and by the simple nobility of his soul, Barezzi had done more than any other human being to set a groping young genius on the right path, the path of destiny. Verdi's love and gratitude had never faded, and in his bedroom at Sant' Agata—now a museum—the old man's portrait hangs to this day. Inevitably his death flooded Verdi's mind with memories of 1840, the terrible year that he had tried so hard to forget; and the months of discouragement, illness, war, and grief that he had recently been through seemed to him almost as crushing.

The shadows were lightened, however, by the presence of a new member of the household—the child Maria Verdi, an orphaned cousin for whose upbringing Carlo Verdi had made himself responsible. At his father's death the Maestro became her guardian. Childless Peppina lavished affection on "the little one," undertook her education, and, as they studied together, often laughed to discover how much of her own learning had slipped away with the years.

That September in Bologna, Mariani conducted *Don Carlo* as only he could. Cast and orchestra were also superb, and the performance was greeted with an ovation such as no Verdi opera had won in the eight years since Rome cheered *The Masked Ball.* Verdi, though he had assisted at a few rehearsals, was not present, and actually the torrents of applause were for Mariani and the performers rather than for the opera itself. *Don Carlo* never attained the sure and easy popularity of *Rigoletto, Trovatore,* or *Traviata.* Yet, in spite of the difficulties of production, it is occasionally revived today, for in this score, uneven and overlong though it is, Verdi was feeling his way into the future, and with it he made his greatest advance thus far. But at that time in Italy, as earlier in France, the critics were puzzled. What "system" had Verdi now adopted, they asked themselves? Undoubtedly, they said, he must have been influenced by Wagner!

About the time that Paris turned a cold shoulder on the revised *Macbeth,* Richard Wagner had come into his own. Until then, though he shouted forth his revolutionary ideas in a stream of books and articles, he had been unable to impress the public at large or even to get a hearing for his major works. Hounded by debts, worries, and lack of appreciation, he seemed doomed to obscurity, when abruptly the picture changed. Ludwig, the "mad" King of Bavaria, discovered him, hailed him as a prophet, and with almost religious fervor not only provided a salary and a home for him but even built him a theater in which to give the Wagnerian operas to the world. From Bayreuth, temple of this Wagner cult, as one after another of the great works were staged tidings of the new art form, the "music drama," spread over Europe like ripples widening on a pond. Wagner was now a force to be reckoned with—the most challenging, the most disturbing musical force of the century.

When Verdi finished writing *Don Carlo* he had never heard nor even seen a note of Wagner's music. While rehearsing it in Paris he had gone to a concert at which the Overture from *Tannhäuser* was played. "Crazy!" was his only comment. So strong was his conviction that music, to be alive, must come entirely from within oneself that he purposely took little interest in the work of other men lest, even unconsciously, he should be affected by it. Moreover, he was sure that what was natural and right for a German could only be false and unreal for an Italian; to create more than empty sounds one must be true to one's heritage, one's blood, one's self. Wagner's influence, therefore, as he watched it grow, seemed to him a destructive power threatening to lure even Italians into betraying their great traditions and their artistic selves. He had a theory, a creed, of his own: true art could never be superimposed from without—it must come from within.

Sadly Verdi read what the learned had to say about his latest work, his "new style." "It seems I'm a perfect Wagnerian!" he murmured wearily, and there was a world of bitterness in the remark. Ah, the public, the incomprehensible public! Had no one listened closely enough to realize that *Don Carlo* was only *Ernani*, only *Nabucco*, vastly improved? Those crowds, pouring into theaters all over the globe to applaud his operas year after year, did not really hear, did not really understand. And the critics apparently must always be searching for systems, methods, theories of art, instead of answering the simple question: Is it good or bad? Had he no right to grow and learn, as he constantly did and as every artist must? Verdi advanced with his times—he too was drawing away from opera as it had been, was coming closer to the perfect blend of music and drama. But this had been his goal from the beginning; he was approaching it in his own way and by a path of his own making.

Watching Wagner's ideas rising like a flood tide, Verdi knew that there was only one man strong enough to confront the German genius as Italy's champion—himself. Yet years ago, when the ponderous works of Meyerbeer had first eclipsed Rossini's sparkling scores, Rossini had simply withdrawn before the dark wind from the north. Now the foe was much more formidable. Ought Verdi to follow Rossini's example and retire? Already his achievement was more than enough for any one man's lifetime, and glory and riches were abundantly his. Surely he had earned the right to give up the grueling labor of creation . . . But he *could not* give up, not until he had brought forth the best that was in him. He would stand firm against the northern spellbinder.

And so these two giants, Wagner and Verdi, though they were never actually to meet, faced each other across the Alps like knights chosen to defend their faiths in single combat.

It was as though Wagner said: "My way is the right way, the only way. I shall destroy you and all that you stand for."

And as though Verdi answered: "As long as our music is good music, no matter how different, there is room in the world for us both. I have no wish to destroy you. But you shall not destroy me. I stand for the immortals whom no one can destroy. I stand for Italy, where song was born, and I will prove to you that Italy is stronger than you know!"

# CHAPTER FIFTEEN

# Aida

## 1868-1872

AUGUST 15, 1868, was Busseto's great day—the day on which the town's ten-year-old dream of having a theater of its own, a Verdi Theater, came true. For the gala opening, flags draped the façade of the fine new building, and the park surrounding it was gay with lantern light. Only green evening gowns were worn that night, and even the gentlemen all sported green cravats in honor of the world-renowned composer Giuseppe Verdi, or, as we should say, Joseph Green!

Older Bussetans boasted happily before the younger ones: "I can see him still—used to pass my window every day going to the Barezzis. How lean he was, and solemn! Even then there was something about him, though. I always said he'd make his mark in the world!"

"Remember how he'd pound the big drum at the band concerts in the square? So earnest, so serious! And those strange eyes—as if he saw something far away that others didn't see."

"He was always quiet and shy—never seemed to be quite at ease with people like the other young folks his age."

"It's odd that he's never outgrown that shyness. Do you know, only the other day he had his right arm in a sling? There was nothing wrong with it at all, but he had to appear in a crowded place and couldn't bear to be pestered for autographs!"

[ 202 ]

The performance opened, sentimentally, with *La Capricciosa*, one of Verdi's unremarkable efforts at the age of twelve. The ever-beloved *Rigoletto* followed, but the climax came during an intermission when, before the dense, jubilant throng, amid flowers and speeches, cheers and even tears, a bust of the Maestro was unveiled. It was a memorable, a heartwarming event in spite of the fact that Giuseppe Verdi himself was not present. Deliberately, he had chosen this moment to take a "vacation" at a near-by resort.

More lay behind this absence than his habitual shrinking from vapid compliments and curious, glory-hungry eyes. Time had not softened his old feud with Busseto. "We made him what he is today," the Bussetans told each other, not realizing that genius finds its own path and that the memories they recalled so proudly were full of bitterness for him. He could not forgive these complacent townsfolk the hopeless, petty struggles of his youth, and still more did he resent the ugly whispers and raised eyebrows that had greeted his blessed Peppina. Jealously Margherita Barezzi's fellow-citizens wished him to be forever faithful to her ghost. . . . What right had they to punish Peppina with their disapproval? Outrageous— this pretense that they owned his heart and soul!

Nor was that all. Like celebrities the world over, Verdi at times received anonymous letters full of abuse and even threats. He recognized them of course as the work of cranks and lunatics, not worth a moment's notice. But it was annoying, and none the less so because the letters happened to come from Busseto.

Then there was the matter of the new bridge over the Ongina, the river that flowed past the Maestro's estate. A spring flood had swept the old bridge away; and since the town, as usual, was short of funds, Verdi had had it rebuilt at his own expense, with the understanding that he was to be repaid within a certain time. But the time came and went and shabby excuses were all that he received. He suspected Busseto of trying to take advantage of his wealth and good nature, and no one ever succeeded in taking advantage of Giuseppe Verdi. No matter what the circumstances, a promise was a promise. Long, long ago he too had had a debt to pay . . . Ghitta had pawned her trinkets. . . .

He sent for his superintendent. "Get a heavy iron chain," he ordered. "Have it put up across the far end of the bridge, and padlock it. Then bring me the key. I paid for this bridge; therefore it belongs to me, and no one else shall use it!"

And so, greatly to the inconvenience of the Bussetans and the local farmers who were now obliged to go a long way round, the bridge was closed. Verdi, though he had no wish to punish individuals, was determined to teach the town itself a lesson in honor.

Besides all this, he had not forgotten the distressing affair of Muzio's appointment. Asked to recommend someone to fill the vacant post of music master that he himself had once so desperately needed, he had happily suggested his dear friend and only pupil. (The "Redhead," though an insignificant composer, was both a sound musician and a gifted conductor, much more than qualified for the little job—but he had had consistently bad luck.) Solemnly the authorities thanked the Maestro, adding that Signor Muzio would of course have to submit to a contest. For a man of Emanuele's standing, especially with Verdi's recommendation, this was insult enough, but there was worse to come. Shortly thereafter someone else was appointed without any contest at all! Jealousy, intrigue, petty politics—the same old story. No wonder that Verdi's carriage was never seen on Busseto's streets unless his going there were absolutely unavoidable.

As for this notion of building a theater, Verdi thought it utter folly and said so again and again. The town was chronically poor; if it could raise a sum large enough for a theater, let the money rather be spent on schools, hospitals, highways, —bridges—on the vital needs of the community. Let the Bussetans be practical instead of seeking to bask in the glory that he, not they, had earned. His disapproval became sharp anger when he learned that the Mayor had gone about announcing that he, Verdi, had promised to write a new opera for the dream theater and to persuade the greatest singers to appear there. Ridiculous lies—he had of course done no such thing! Busseto was no Bayreuth, where the artistically-minded flocked to worship a new genius whose like had not been seen before—while a mad king footed the bills. Busseto was an average Italian town near which there happened to live a farmer who wrote operas. Yet it proposed to squander money on a theater that, because of the small population, would have to remain closed eleven months of the year. Fantastic! Senseless!

In the end, when he found that nothing he could say or do would stop the foolish project, he relented to the extent of subscribing 10,000 lire and even permitted the use of his name for the theater—thanks to the patience and tact of his Bussetan friend and lawyer, Doctor Carrara. The town thereupon gratefully presented him with a private box, to be his as long as the building should stand. This he stiffly declined; nevertheless he appreciated the intention, for soon the iron chain came off the bridge. Let them call the account square. . . . As for attending the opening or having anything to do with this "Teatro Verdi" nonsense—no, never! Quietly, but pointedly, he went away just before the event.

Verdi was depressed these days over the state of the Italian theater in general. Times were bad, the hard-pressed government had withdrawn its financial support, and henceforth opera—so costly to produce—must pay its own way or perish. At La Scala the situation was especially threatening, for recently an incompetent manager had offered performances so slipshod that audiences shouted and shook their fists in protest. The man had been replaced, but more than a change of management was needed to set the historic institution on its feet again. If anything could save La Scala, a new Verdian opera would do it. Not since *Joan of Arc*, however, had Verdi composed expressly for this theater of his first triumph. Except for one brief, recent visit he had not even been in Milan for twenty years.

To Ricordi, whose wealth and power in the musical world stemmed largely from Verdi's popularity, it was vitally important that opera should flourish and that Verdi should keep on turning out new scores. But since *Don Carlo* the Maestro had shown not the slightest inclination to undertake anything; in fact he grew ever more difficult to tempt into composing, more wary of making promises. Perhaps, thought Ricordi, if he could be induced to revise *La Forza del Destino* especially for La Scala, he might thereafter feel in the vein to write a whole opera. Some years earlier Verdi, dissatisfied with *Forza's* ending, had withdrawn it from circulation, and Milan therefore had not yet heard it. Ricordi suggested a new version, and to his delight Verdi agreed.

Since *Forza's* weakness lay in the plot, a poet must be found to recast the libretto. Poor Piave, alas, could no longer be of use. The cheerful, easy-going fellow had had a stroke and was to lie paralyzed for eight long years, waiting to die. Verdi saw to it that he got the best of care and, since Piave had saved nothing, even helped support his wife and daughter. Often during their long association the Maestro, while quietly paying his debts, had lectured him on his extravagance. Now, too late, Piave worried over his child's future, and once again Verdi came to the rescue. He wrote a song, persuaded five other composers to do likewise, and got Ricordi to publish the collection in an album from which all royalties were to go to Piave's daughter. This would provide the girl with a little income, nor was there any sting of charity about the gift: the volume was dedicated to her father as a token of affectionate esteem. Verdi's kindness was not only practical but exquisitely tactful as well.

To replace Piave, Ricordi recommended Antonio Ghislanzoni, a literary jack-of-all-trades who, before settling down to writing and editing, had been a medical student, a double-bass player, and an opera singer. An unpredictable character, this Ghislanzoni, and the source of many anecdotes. People still remembered the night he had quite unself-consciously alighted in Milan's crowded cathedral square wearing the helmet, wig, tunic, and sword of a Roman general, plus a flamboyant make-up. He had been singing in an out-of-town performance of Verdi's *Attila* and, impatient to return, had simply not bothered to change to his street clothes.

The poet, arriving at Sant' Agata to work on *Forza*, was impressed by the melancholy beauty of the place, especially the long avenues of trees which Verdi himself had planted, and the thick vegetation round the house, transforming it into an island of shade and shelter in that sun- and wind-swept plain. The life was monotonous—Verdi had warned him of that— yet refreshing after the late hours in smoky cafés to which Ghislanzoni was accustomed. Peppina—hard to think of her now as Strepponi, the glamorous opera star—ran her household, attended to little Maria's lessons, wrote her long, twinkling letters, and took charge of Verdi's enormous mail. Somehow, too, she managed to find time to read the many plays that Verdi read, discussing with him their operatic possibilities; the search for new material went on, with varying intensity, all the time. Verdi himself, off on horseback at dawn to watch the rising sun gild his wide fields, and keenly occupied with cattle and crops, weather and soil, seemed as unlike a famous opera composer as a man could be. There were no parties, no gaiety of any kind, not even music for entertainment. In this household music was not a pastime but the most serious sort of work, and the piano (Verdi apologized) was at the moment badly out of tune and even had a broken string or two. In the evenings Ghislanzoni joined the family at a card game for tiny stakes and was amused to see the Maestro as pleased as a child whenever he managed to win a handful of pennies. Verdi kept country hours, and soon after ten o'clock the house was dark.

*Forza* with its new ending was produced in February 1869. At first, remembering past difficulties at La Scala, Verdi had agreed to look in on a few rehearsals, nothing more. Once there, however, the old grudge was quickly forgotten while, as usual, he took complete command—with splendid results. Here he found the kindling imagination, the fire, feeling, and musicianship he had so missed in Paris. As for the Milanese, they felt that Verdi had at last come home. For fourteen nights they packed the theater, and the box-office receipts swelled reassuringly. Their beloved opera house was not yet doomed.

As Ricordi had hoped, Verdi was now in the composing

mood; but, for lack of a subject that suited him, he turned down all requests. In declining an offer from the Paris Opéra he felt no regret whatever—he had not forgotten the eight tedious months of work for a "worse than mediocre" performance of *Don Carlo*, or Mariani's brilliant production of the same opera in Bologna that had taken only one month to prepare. Now, fresh from the zeal and enthusiasm of La Scala, he remarked "Whenever I think of the *Don Carlo* rehearsals I get the shivers!"

Ricordi soon realized that no opera would be immediately forthcoming, for La Scala or anywhere else. All the rest of that year Verdi was distressingly preoccupied with a memorial Mass for Rossini, who had died in 1868. For once the Maestro's idealism outweighed his practical sense: he had suggested that Italy's thirteen most distinguished composers should each contribute one section of the traditional Requiem Mass, the whole to be performed under Mariani's direction in Bologna (Rossini's musical home) on the anniversary of the great man's death. To make this Mass a perfect tribute, sincere and selfless, everyone from composers to chorus must give his services gratis. Nor must anyone derive profit from the score. Unpublished, it must be kept under lock and key, to be revived only on Rossini's anniversaries.

Verdi's impulse was a noble one, but the committee formed to carry it out immediately faced difficulties. Some composers excused themselves from taking part. Others who were not invited to contribute felt that they should have been. It was argued that some financial reward would be necessary for so time-consuming a project. Verdi was adamant: the thing must be done his way, with complete selflessness, or not at all. It was pointed out that the music would lack unity. Of course, Verdi retorted. The idea was not to glorify a group of composers by creating a great work of art, but to honor Rossini, who had been the bright star of a whole epoch, and Italy's own. The quality of the music was a secondary consideration: let each man simply do his individual best. It was the fact that mattered—the historical fact of many people working together in perfect sincerity of purpose to bring this memorial into existence.

Punctually Verdi wrote the last part of the Requiem, the *Libera me*, which had been allotted to him. Of the other twelve composers (whose names, then well-known, have lost meaning now) some sent in their completed manuscripts. But the project, so dear to the Maestro's heart, foundered on the rock of Mariani's indifference, or rather, hostility. Verdi felt betrayed, as though he stood alone against a greedy and irreverent world. By the end of the year, bitterly disillusioned, he no longer spoke to the friend whom he had loved for years as a younger brother.

Even before the rift became final there had been a growing coolness between the two men. Where his operas were concerned Verdi demanded absolute obedience; but Mariani, brilliant musician though he was, did not always scrupulously respect a composer's wishes when conducting. Of late only politeness had masked the clash of their strong wills, and their affection for each other had grown strained.

There was another factor in their quarrel, too—the soprano, Teresa Stolz, a handsome blonde from Bohemia with a magnificent voice. She was engaged to Mariani, whose apartment in Genoa was in the same house as the Verdis' on the floor above. Whenever the Verdis, Mariani, and Stolz all happened to be in Genoa at the same time they made a congenial and inseparable foursome.

One day Teresa called on the Verdis alone and in great distress. Some time ago, she told them, she had given Mariani a large sum of money to invest for her. Lately his manner toward her had changed, and, suspiciously, he constantly postponed their marriage. At last, thoroughly alarmed, she asked him point-blank what had become of her money, and he was obliged to admit that he had spent it. He intended to pay it back, of course, but . . . just now he was unable to . . . Her faith in him was shattered. What was she to do?

Nothing could have shocked Verdi more profoundly, and his fondness for Mariani died then and there. Both he and

Peppina advised the distracted woman to break with her fiancé, which she did, and thereafter the closest friendship bound her to the Verdis.

This sordid story was of course kept dark, and the gossips, observing the sudden estrangement between Verdi and Mariani, murmured that Mariani must be jealous. Was not the Maestro himself showing a little too much interest in the gorgeous young soprano who sang his music so superbly? There came a time when even Peppina felt a pang of fear that she might lose his love. But her anxiety did not last long. Throughout the half-century of their life together his deep devotion to her did not waver.

Since the Mass for Rossini had been abandoned, Verdi was considering, restlessly and without eagerness, a new work not for the Opéra but for the Opéra Comique, and in the spring of 1870 he paid an unofficial visit to Paris. He found no suitable comedy, although Camille Du Locle, librettist of *Don Carlo*, was helping with the endless search. The Verdis saw a good deal of their young friend who, having lately returned from a pleasure trip, talked constantly (as travelers will) of the wonders he had seen. Verdi and Peppina listened with the keenest interest—Du Locle had been to Egypt.

All Europe, and especially France, was at that time Egypt-conscious, for the Suez Canal, after ten years of incredible difficulty, had been formally opened only a few months before. The French engineer De Lesseps had built it with French money, and the French Empress Eugénie with all her retinue was on board the first ship to pass through. In November 1869, after a day of parades, flags, speeches, and salutes, a fleet of sixty-eight vessels sailed from Port Saïd and, moving only by daylight and feeling its way cautiously through the muddy, breathlessly narrow channel, reached Suez safely three days later. A momentous journey, for a waterway linking the Eastern and the Western worlds was no new idea. Thousands of years earlier, the Pharaohs had dreamed of it and had even cut a passage, ruined long eras ago, to the Gulf of Suez from the Upper Nile. There had been later schemes and attempts, all doomed to failure. But now, at last, the Canal was a fact—a fact that altered the face of the globe and transformed Egypt itself from a dead end of civilization into a world crossroads.

The Khedive Ismaïl Pasha, ruler of Egypt, intended his country to rank among the great nations of the earth, and he embarked on a vast program of public works. Nor was he satisfied with mechanical and commercial modernization. Culturally, too, he determined that Egypt must shine, and with true Oriental love of display he built in Cairo the accepted symbol of culture—a dazzling opera house that was the last word in luxury and splendor. Furthermore the Khedive decided that, to celebrate the opening of the Suez Canal, a brand-new opera must be written and launched in his brand-new building.

Verdi knew all about this still unfinished opera house—an emissary from Ismaïl Pasha had called at Sant' Agata to sound him out about composing the work for the grand opening. The Maestro had declined, courteously but with finality. He felt no interest in so remote a project. He had no opera in mind, no subject even, and did not intend to bind himself for the Khedive of Egypt or anyone else.

It was, however, neither of this opera house nor of the marvelous new Canal that Du Locle talked to the Verdis. Instead he told them of the mystery and fascination of that ancient land in whose strange dry air nothing decays and where three thousand years ago seems no more remote than day before yesterday. He described temples and pyramids and palaces, and their vanished inhabitants—princes and slaves, warriors and priests of a great civilization that had perished. He spoke of the enchantment of the broad, languid, palm-fringed Nile and of the exquisite art that had flourished along the river bank while Greece was still a land of barbarians. Du Locle had seen and learned far more of Egypt than the average tourist, for his companion and guide had been the famous French archeologist, Auguste Mariette.

Almost twenty years earlier, the Louvre Museum in Paris had sent young Mariette to Egypt to purchase ancient manuscripts. The visit was supposed to last two weeks, but Mariette,

once there, forgot Louvre and manuscripts and everything
else. He felt like an explorer discovering an unknown continent, though his was a continent of time, not space. Thereafter, until he died, Egypt was his headquarters and his home,
and no living man knew as much about its ancient life as he.
He excavated tombs and temples and rock-cut caves, he
founded museums, he studied and wrote about the treasures
he unearthed, for which the grateful Egyptian government
gave him the title of Bey. And, in spare moments, Mariette
Bey had managed to produce a short novel of ancient Egypt,
historical in setting but pure fiction as to characters and plot.
This story, he thought, might make an appropriate subject
for the opera that was to open Cairo's beautiful new theater—
an idea with which his friend the Khedive heartily agreed.

Naturally Du Locle had a good deal to say about the celebrated Mariette Bey. He did not, however, mention the archeologist's novel, or the fact that he (Du Locle) had the
manuscript in his pocket with instructions to interest Verdi,
Wagner, or Gounod in setting it to music. Du Locle could
take his choice.

For the young poet the choice was easy, but—how was he
to obtain Verdi's consent? Once or twice he brought up the
matter of an opera for Cairo, only to be waved aside. Verdi,
not in the least interested, at once found other things to talk
about. What would tempt him? Obviously not the immense
fee the Khedive offered, nor yet the resounding glory of the
occasion. After careful pondering, Du Locle decided that only
one bait might lure the reluctant composer: a good story
would perhaps kindle the creative spark. He realized he must
proceed with caution; the Maestro said "no" too often and
too readily these days. So, hoping that fate was on his side,
Du Locle breathed not a word to the Verdis of what he had in
mind.

Peppina, sorting the mail at Sant' Agata a few weeks later,
handed Verdi a package.

"Here's something from Du Locle," she remarked.

"Oh, yes, the play I asked him to send me." Verdi tore off

the wrapping and fingered the pages without enthusiasm. "I doubt if it will do—but I'll have to read it carefully. Why, what's this? He's enclosed a little pamphlet—only four pages. It's his outline, he says, of a story by an important personage who prefers to remain unknown! Who could have written it? Let's see—it takes place in ancient Egypt. What a setting, eh, Peppina? Do you suppose the Khedive could be the author? I wonder; it seems unlikely. But who else? Who would want to make such a mystery of it?" Intrigued, Verdi skimmed the pages, explaining to Peppina as he read.

"It's about a captive Ethiopian princess named Aida, slave of the King of Egypt's daughter, Amneris. Both women are in love with Radames, a young warrior who is chosen to lead the Egyptian army against the Ethiopian invaders. *There's* a situation for poor Aida—her lover going into battle against her father!"

"What happens?" Peppina asked.

"Let me see . . . Radames returns in triumph and, as a reward for victory, is promised the hand of Amneris in marriage. But it is Aida he loves, and he meets her secretly at night by the river. Now among Radames' prisoners was Aida's father, the king. The old man has escaped . . . has found his daughter, and pleads with her to save her country . . . the war's not yet over, you see. So she induces Radames to tell her by what route the Egyptian army is about to march. Unfortunately Amneris, returning from the temple with her maidens, overhears him betray the military secret . . . She denounces him as a traitor to the priests, who seem to have been the judges in those days—she's jealous, of course, and this is her revenge. Later Amneris repents and offers him his freedom if he will renounce Aida. He refuses, and is condemned to be buried alive in a cell beneath the temple floor. There he finds Aida in hiding—waiting to die with him . . .

Verdi stood silent, rereading the story. Suddenly he said "Peppina, this is remarkable. This has possibilities—!" And Peppina, glancing up at his altered face, knew at once that there would be another Verdi opera.

Shortly thereafter Du Locle received an enthusiastic letter

from Verdi, and the jubilant poet, unwilling to trust the mails in so vital a matter, appeared unexpectedly at Sant' Agata as soon as he could get there. The wheels began to turn: Verdi and Du Locle worked out a scenario from which Du Locle would write the libretto in French prose, to be translated into Italian verse by Ghislanzoni. Meantime, while the Khedive and Ricordi rejoiced, Verdi, businesslike as ever, drew up the terms of his contract.

The world première would take place in Cairo in January 1871, to be followed in February by a performance at La Scala. Verdi's fee for Cairo alone would be 150,000 francs (about $30,000). This did not include the rights for Italy and the rest of the world. Scenery and costumes must be of the finest, designed and made in Paris; Mariette Bey himself— Verdi had learned that he was the mysterious author—should see to it that every detail was historically accurate.

Verdi, refusing to make the long journey to Cairo himself, would have liked to send Mariani in his stead. This was a question of art, not of personalities, and though he had lost all respect for the man he still insisted that as a conductor Mariani had no equal. But Mariani, when approached by a third person—the two no longer had any direct communication with each other—curtly declined.

Who, then? Muzio? Impossible. Fortune seemed at last to smile on poor Emanuele; he had been offered the post of regular conductor at the Italian Theater in Paris. Not for the world would Verdi have had him sacrifice this opportunity, although the devoted fellow would gladly have done so. In the end the task fell to Bottesini, an adequate if undistinguished musician who became Cairo's regular conductor.

Verdi was, on the whole, delighted with Ghislanzoni's libretto, but the installments no sooner arrived at Sant' Agata than he returned them with comments: "Excellent, admirable, although—you must forgive me—this scene drags, and this passage is not so strong and clear as it should be." Patiently Ghislanzoni would forward a corrected version, only to have this too come back to him. "Vastly improved, but this word is not effective—in a large theater it would carry no meaning. And this phrase is ugly—the combination of syllables would be clumsy to sing." Often Verdi wrote out whole scenes in his own words for Ghislanzoni to polish and put into the meters he required. The poet would have found it exasperating to work with anyone so particular but for the fact that the Maestro was always courteous—and always right.

Meantime the score grew scene by scene, as fast as the words were perfected. The music flowed strongly in Verdi's mind, and the hours went by uncounted. Often the lamp burned in his study-bedroom long after all the countryside was dark and still. There were nights when Peppina, roused from sleep, would find him standing by her bed. "Peppina, Peppina, come. You must come at once." And he would lead her, still dazed and dreamy, to the piano. "Listen, now listen carefully."

Often over the years it had happened that she had been the first to hear one of those magic melodies of his—melodies like no one else's, that sound so much simpler than they are, in which note follows note so unalterably, so inevitably, with such deep rightness. Sometimes at an unexpected, inspired interval she would catch her breath. Sometimes, wide awake and excited, she sang while Verdi watched her intently—did the music tell her what he meant? Had he made her "feel" it? "O terr' addio"—"Farewell, O earth,"—gently their voices rose in unison as the final duet from *Aida*, never uttered before, drifted on the night air to melt away in the hushed darkness of the garden. It was late, so late—but Peppina, seeing her Verdi's rapt, exalted face and glowing eyes, knew that he did not feel his own fatigue.

The new opera, begun in July, was practically finished by November, but the gala première did not take place the following January as planned. About the time Verdi put the first notes on paper, the Franco-Prussian War had broken out, and within a few weeks the conquering German armies were laying siege to Paris itself. For the beloved "city of light," the days that followed were perhaps the darkest in all its stormy history. Its citizens, cut off from the rest of the world—the mail went out, if at all, by balloon—starved. The Parisians, who had made cooking one of the fine arts, baked their bread with sawdust and devoured cats and dogs, while even rats sold for two francs apiece. And still they held out to the limit of human endurance, suffering famine, sickness, and misery, without hope, for honor's sake alone.

As long as the grim siege lasted there could be no *Aida* in Cairo; for scenery, properties, and costumes, crated and ready now, were trapped in the desperate city, and with them poor Mariette Bey who had supervised their making. With alarm Ismaïl Pasha realized that La Scala could build its own scenery—there was nothing to prevent Milan from staging the world première and thus stealing his thunder. He hastened to appeal to the Maestro, but too late. Verdi, hardly the man to take unfair advantage, had already arranged that the Milan performance should take place six weeks after the one in Cairo, whenever that might be.

At the beginning of the war Verdi quietly contributed a handsome sum for the relief of French wounded. He grieved for France and would have liked to see Italy fighting at her side. Who knows? An Italian army, arriving in time, might have turned the tide. . . . Yet for him and his countrymen there was a bright side to the ghastly struggle. For their own defense the French had been obliged to call home the troops that maintained the Pope's power in Rome, and the Italians had promptly seized the city, forcing the Pope to retire to the Vatican. Now, at long last, Rome became what it should be: the capital of free, united Italy.

In January 1871 Paris surrendered. The war was over. Brazenly the arrogant Prussians tramped through Napoleon's Arch of Triumph and down that fairest of avenues, the Champs Élysées, while the gaunt Parisians stared from behind drawn blinds, their haggard eyes burning with hatred. In Versailles' great Hall of Mirrors, King William of Prussia was proclaimed the first German Emperor. "Victory is ours because God is on our side," he declared. And Verdi, reflecting that conquerors have spoken thus since time began, had

Ghislanzoni put William's words into the mouth of the High Priest of Egypt.

Verdi, glad that the hunger and bloodshed had ended, nevertheless lamented the fate of Paris, the brilliant and beautiful, "capital of the world." The German victors he distrusted and despised. To a friend he wrote: "in their veins there still flows the old Goth blood; they are of a measureless pride, hard, intolerant, scorners of everything that is not Teutonic, and of a greed that knows no bounds. Men with heads but no hearts; a strong, uncivilized race." And looking into the future he added sadly: "The European War cannot be avoided, and we shall be devoured. It will not come to-morrow, but it will come."

Nearly a year still had to pass before Cairo could produce *Aida*—a trying wait for Verdi, since the opera was the more talked about in advance because of the delay. He wrote and discarded an overture, and retouched his score. Then, in November, he went to Bologna for a musical event that concerned him perhaps more closely than any other Italian: the first performance in Italy of a Wagnerian opera. It was thanks to two enemies of Verdi's that Wagner's music at last succeeded in crossing the Alps. Long ago, at the time of the forgotten failure, *Il corsaro*, the publisher Lucca had earned Verdi's contempt, and thereafter had enviously watched the rival firm of Ricordi flourish on the proceeds from Verdi's works. Finally Lucca's widow, having sought in vain an Italian composer to compete with the Maestro, turned to Germany and acquired the Italian rights to Wagner's scores. Thus she hoped for revenge; and so, in bitterness, did Mariani, without whose direction and prestige so risky an undertaking would scarcely have been possible. Now, in the same theater where *Don Carlo* had so enhanced his reputation, Mariani conducted *Lohengrin*.

Verdi, quietly attending the dress rehearsal, listened with intense curiosity—there was so much at stake! From time to time he scribbled on the margin of his score: "*Beautiful!*" "Bad, ugly!" "Too long, the interest lags," etc. Shrewdly, and

with perfect honesty, he appraised the giant who threatened
to eclipse him.

The audience responded to *Lohengrin* with a tremendous
ovation. Was the applause for Wagner or for Mariani? Impossible to be sure. But the newspapers loudly and eloquently
proclaimed a wonderful "new era in music." Verdi read them
without comment. Was Italy to be Wagnerized? No, it was
his turn now. *Aida* must be Italy's answer to Germany. If
only it would prove to be the great answer he hoped . . .

Christmas Eve in Cairo! The gleaming white and gold
opera house opened its doors to an extraordinary throng:
dark-skinned, almond-eyed Egyptians, resplendent Turkish
officers, beribboned diplomats, Greek merchants, Copts and
Jews, Persians and Arabs. Among the turbans, veils, rare
silks, and exotic jewels were Parisian toilettes and European
tail-coats too, for many in that cosmopolitan audience had
made the long journey to Egypt just for this event. Corre-
spondents from everywhere looked eagerly about them, already describing the scene in their minds for the home papers.
From three boxes discreetly curtained in white muslin the
veiled ladies of the court harem watched unseen, and in the
royal box sat the Khedive himself, gorgeous in full regalia.
Some of his retinue seemed a trifle weary. They had attended
the dress rehearsal with him from seven o'clock the night
before until half-past three in the morning—no one, of course,
could leave as long as he remained, spellbound in spite of
endless repetitions and delays.

The house lights dimmed and the babel of uncounted lan-
guages abruptly ceased. Footlights flooded the curtain and
Bottesini, silhouetted against their glow, took his place at the
conductor's desk. Up went his baton, and the curtain rose on
what may well be the best-loved opera ever written.

Since that night three-quarters of a century ago *Aida*, too
spectacular for small companies to attempt, has been the
mainstay of the major ones. Again and again it has the honor
of opening a season, although too often the scenery is faded,
the costumes are shabby from overuse, and even the perform-

ers sometimes grow stale in their parts. We hear it, or bits of
it, more frequently than any opera was ever intended to be
heard. Everyone knows "Glory to Egypt," but few perhaps
realize that this triumphant chorus, which the delighted
Egyptians adopted for their national anthem, was interpreted
by Italians as Verdi's way of celebrating the final liberation of
Rome.

From time to time a manager will decide to put away the
painted sphinxes and temples and palm trees, the plaster
statues and the tremendous trumpets—but not for long. *Aida*
always returns to the repertory by popular demand. In 1945-
46 the Metropolitan of New York, where it has had more
performances than any other opera, omitted it, and that same
year the Opera Guild undertook to poll the huge audience of
the air to determine the nation's favorites. Would *Carmen* be
the winner, as was expected, with *Faust* perhaps in second
place? Surprisingly, 150,000 people took the trouble to obtain
and mail in a ballot; and when the votes were counted, *Carmen*

was trailing, a poor second, followed not by *Faust* but by *Traviata*. Far in the lead stood the unquenchable *Aida*.

*Aida* is often called the finest specimen of true "grand" opera, but it is more than that. For it has everything: unique and splendid pageantry, excitement, heartbreak, tenderness, and the old Verdian patriotic thrill—all poured forth in beauty. There is, besides, the quality of greatness. Through the haunting score there runs a live, mysterious power that cannot be defined. *Aida* is old-fashioned. No matter—it still casts a spell.

We, the generations who have grown up with it, must stretch our imaginations to appreciate its impact on that first audience in Cairo long ago. The sheer novelty of the opera, both musically and scenically, was overwhelming; and, as is not always the case with novelties, the response was instantaneous and electric. To Bottesini it seemed as though the audience were almost more eager to applaud than to listen.

Verdi was pleased, but also humiliated. Too much publicity—all this fanfare only clouded the real issue: Is it good or bad? Art and notoriety, he believed, did not belong together. His music was no better because the whole world could read that such and such notables had traveled to Egypt to hear it. Wistfully he thought of the old days when a new opera by him had been, not an international event, but simply a score to stand or fall on its own merit as fate decreed. Well, the première had been a success, a great success. But Cairo was not Italy. He knew that the real test would come at La Scala.

Never had Verdi worked harder or been more demanding than for this performance. In Genoa he coached the singers in their parts, and commuted from there to Milan to help Boito's friend, Franco Faccio, who was to conduct, with the early rehearsals. He even had the orchestra pit sunk below the level of the audience so that the harps and double basses no longer obscured the view of the stage—an innovation for which he was careful to give Wagner credit. And as the day approached he moved to Milan and took full charge. His commands were not sweetened with flattery or coaxing, and he was at times aware of the performers' sullen glances. "They look at me as though I were a wild beast. I know I'm not very amiable in the theater—or anywhere else!" he later confessed, and often spoke of himself as "an old bear."

But, whether they liked it or not, the cast profited from his direction. Never hesitant, never in doubt, he always knew exactly the effect he wanted—and got it. For those few who dared to murmur "But, Maestro—" he had a final answer: "You will do as I say, because I am Verdi." It was not fame that gave him the right to speak thus. He had earned his authority with countless hours on bare, drafty, half-lit stages all over the continent of Europe. This was his field in which, by virtue of experience alone, no one might challenge him.

On February 8, 1872, a celebrity-studded audience, more sophisticated if less exotic than in Cairo, filled La Scala, and never had the light of glory blazed so fiercely on Verdi as that night. A committee of distinguished citizens presented him with an ivory and gold scepter topped with a star of diamonds, and on the stem AIDA spelled in rubies—precious replica of the property scepter used by the King of Egypt on the stage. And the applause! In roaring billows it swept over him while he took thirty-two curtain calls—alone. In vain he sent stage managers scurrying in search of Ghislanzoni. The devoted poet had modestly slipped away lest he intrude on the Maestro's triumph. Verdi, deeply touched, could force him to take his bow only at later performances.

Old-timers that night recalled *Oberto, Count of St. Boniface*, with which an unknown peasant youth had first faced the critical Milanese public. How far their Verdi had climbed in the thirty-two years since then! Surely no one could rise higher—surely this was the peak!

There are mountains with false summits. The top turns out to be only a ridge, a shoulder, leaving a long way still to go. Verdi's career was such a mountain. At fifty-eight he had traveled an immense distance from the rickety organ of Le Roncole; and his listeners, once a handful of peasants, now covered the globe. The journey had been steadily upward: never had he been content to turn back in his own footsteps. As he climbed out at last on the dizzy height of *Aida* no one guessed, not even he, that the true summit still loomed far above.

# CHAPTER SIXTEEN

# Requiem

## 1872-1877

PEPPINA, at her daily task of opening and sorting the mail, chuckled over a letter she was reading.

"Verdi, do look at this—it's from one Prospero Bertani of Reggio. He says all the excitement over *Aida* made him curious, so he went to Parma to hear it and, though he admired the scenery and the singers, he was not satisfied with the music. However, on the train going home he overheard the opera so highly praised that he thought he might be mistaken, so he went back and heard it again. Now he's sure that the audience sits through it only because of the magnificent scenery. He says: 'It will fill the theater a few more times and then gather dust in the archives.' And he goes on: 'Now, my dear Signor Verdi, you can imagine my regret at having spent 32 lire for these two performances. Add to this the aggravating circumstance that I am dependent on my family, and you will understand that this money preys on my mind like a terrible specter.' So, if you please, he's sending you a bill!"

Verdi grinned as he looked over the statement:

April 2, 1872
Return railway ticket............ lire 5.90
Theater...................... " 8
Detestable supper at the station... " 2
April 4, 1872      15.90
Same as above................ " 15.90
Total........................ " 31.80

"What will you do?" Peppina asked. "Ignore it?"

"Certainly not! I'll have Giulio [Giulio Ricordi, third generation of the publishing firm, acted as Verdi's banker] send him the money at once. But we'll deduct the detestable suppers—he would have had to eat anyway, *Aida* or no *Aida*. However, Signor—what's his name?—Bertani must promise never to hear another of my new operas. We can't have him pursued by any more specters, and I must be spared his traveling expenses!"

In due time came a communication from Signor Bertani agreeing to the Maestro's terms. "I, the undersigned, certify herewith—" he began, and he ended: "In confirmation whereof I have affixed my signature." Verdi had never received a more formidable document.

There was another complaint. An obscure composer named Sassaroli wrote to a musical journal declaring *Aida* worthless and its success entirely the result of publicity. To prove his claim he offered to set the libretto to music himself and let an impartially appointed group of judges choose between his score and Verdi's. For this effort, moreover, he expected to be paid! The challenge was printed in a column of humorous items—whereupon Sassaroli, enraged, returned to the attack, even getting out a pamphlet on the subject of his wrongs. No one, however, paid the slightest attention, except for a few pitying smiles. The poor fellow was half crazy.

Like Sassaroli, Verdi himself resented the deluge of publicity that followed *Aida*. Asked to appear at performances here, there, and everywhere, he refused. It was all very well to attend when he had directed rehearsals (as he had done for Parma, capital of his home state); but merely to let the gaping public stare at what he called his "beautiful snout!" Ah, no, his sense of dignity rebelled. He was neither an Apollo nor a monster; let people listen, let them look at the stage, not at him. And remembering the immense fuss, the deliberate advance publicity, over *Lohengrin* in Bologna, he muttered, "I'd rather burn my score than Lohengrinate!"

*Aida* was, of course, in great demand, bringing in torrents of applause and money. Verdi, however, would not permit it to be heard in Rome, believing that the current management there could not do it artistic justice. He insisted on quality and labored mightily to raise standards of performance. Yet the superb staging of the opera at La Scala won him no special thanks. Instead of the appreciation he had hoped for, he was given a jeweled scepter—a toy!

His disappointment went still deeper. There were even moments when he wished *Aida* had never been written. Under his armor of reserve Verdi was the most sensitive of men, and actually the public triumph was a private failure. Some critics stupidly found fault with his new opera, but far stupider, Verdi thought, were the floods of praise. *Aida* had been utterly misunderstood.

Step by step over the years Verdi had developed his orchestration, and in this score the orchestra is more important, richer, more colorful and glowing than in any of his works hitherto. Moreover, the old pattern of set pieces strung like beads on a thread of recitative is less discernible beneath the music's now unbroken dramatic flow. Verdi, the critics therefore announced, had embraced Wagnerism; they had suspected this with *Don Carlo* and now they were sure! At the time, the shadow of the mighty German seemed inescapable, though we who look back from a long distance find this incredible, as Verdi himself did. For *Aida* was no "symphony with voice" like Wagner's operas: the instruments were still supplementary to the singing. And the basic operatic structure was still there, like man's ancestral skeleton under the living flesh. Verdi once said: "Let us return to the past—it will be a step forward." By this he did not mean to encourage imitation of earlier music—as valueless as fake antiques—but rather that the new should develop from the old, like the flowering of a seed planted long ago. And this he achieved. He did not scrap the old, outworn traditions as Wagner did; he revitalized them, pruning away dead branches and proving that the roots were very much alive.

But what was the use? Of the crowds that flocked to hear opera no one, it seemed, really listened either to his music or to Wagner's; and never before had the feeling of frustration weighed on him so heavily. All this re-echoing applause was worthless; he would have preferred a single flash of understanding.

Not all the critics, bewildered as they were by the novelty of *Aida*, accused Verdi of Wagnerism. Some spoke of the influence of other composers, including forgotten tenth-raters. Originality is difficult to grasp; in fact, the more intensely original a work of art, the more avidly do the sages pick it apart seeking for sources and derivations. At first, therefore, no one seemed willing to accept *Aida* as what it was: brilliantly Verdi's own. Bitterly he remarked, "It's hard, after thirty-five years of work, to end up as an imitator!"

There were other extraordinary comments. Whence had Verdi drawn the music's strange, exotic quality, its fascinating "Egyptian" flavor? Surely, people said, for this local color he must have sought out ancient Egyptian tunes—which was ridiculous since no one has ever been able to do more than guess how the music of that vanished civilization sounded. Besides, if he *had* been able to reproduce it, it would undoubtedly have struck modern ears as a thin blowing of pipes and twanging of strings, expressing nothing. When questioned Verdi answered frankly, "I just imagined it that way." But it seemed so improbable—this simple truth!

Meantime, while *Aida's* popularity swelled like a rolling snowball, Mariani tried in Bologna to repeat the brilliant success of *Lohengrin* with Wagner's *Tannhäuser*, and failed. The audience remained cold, and later *Lohengrin* itself was a dismal fiasco in Milan. Verdi was too human not to feel relieved. It was inevitable, it was right, he knew, that people the world over should admire all that was admirable in Wagner's music. But—let Italy's young composers beware! He made no speeches, wrote no articles, yet his very silence seemed to cry out: "Study the great traditions of your *native* land, master the fundamentals of your craft, then follow your own soul. He who pursues a cult, a theory, instead of listening to his own inspiration, produces not art but its barren, empty shell."

Naples, in the spring of 1873, was agog over the prospect of hearing *Aida* for the first time. La Scala's famous Aida and Amneris, Teresa Stolz and the enchanting contralto Maria Waldmann, were to sing. Verdi himself had come to direct, and meantime delighted throngs were flocking to the opera house to hear *Don Carlo*.

Then, suddenly, Stolz was taken ill with sore throat. The remaining *Don Carlo* performances had to be canceled, and the *Aida* rehearsals came to a halt. Verdi had nothing to do and, though he growled restlessly at the delay, enjoyed this interlude of unexpected leisure. He took long drives into the surrounding hills, absorbing sunshine and the incredible view, and spent the evenings puffing luxuriously at his fine cigars among his lively, humorous, affectionate Neapolitan friends. To help an impoverished young sculptor buy his way out of military service he and Peppina sat for their portraits, with splendid results. And every day, for his own amusement, Verdi secretly put light-hearted notes on paper.

After three weeks Stolz recovered, her precious voice unimpaired, and rehearsals were resumed. On the night of the performance Naples went mad. Till dawn the celebrations lasted, while the moon shone full over the shimmering bay and on Vesuvius, smouldering in the distance. By the light of thousands of torches Verdi was escorted from the theater to his hotel, and there the orchestra serenaded him with the Grand March from *Aida*, complete even to the famous "magic" trumpets he had had made especially for this opera, chiefly because they looked so festive and triumphant. It was springtime, the air was warm and sweet, the night unbelievably beautiful. From his balcony Verdi looked down on the hundreds, thousands, of faces turned up to him in the shifting, flickering torchlight and saw only the wildest joy. Impossible at that moment to feel that he had failed. His disappointment lost some of its sting.

The next day a few of the Maestro's friends, gathered at his hotel by invitation, found that he had prepared a musical surprise for them: they were to hear a string quartet of his own composing! Except for the *Hymn of Nations*, the forgotten *Sound the Trumpet*, and poor Piave's song, Verdi had produced nothing but opera since his student days. It seemed incredible, exciting, that he should turn to chamber music—and such a charming quartet, too—so bright, melodious, and graceful!

His friends congratulated him. "But, Maestro, this is enchanting—you must publish it!"

Verdi protested, beaming. "I wouldn't think of it! I'm glad you enjoyed my little joke, but don't take it seriously. I wrote it simply for my own pleasure, to pass the time while Signora Stolz was ill. You know, I always compose a little something every day—an exercise I set myself, or just some passing fancy. One must keep one's hand in, not let the tools grow rusty."

The news spread rapidly, the music was soon in demand, and eventually Verdi relented, allowing it to be published and performed. Without any claims to greatness, this quartet is attractive and has survived. Today it often appears on Toscanini's programs enlarged for the orchestra's full string choir —an arrangement which Verdi himself highly approved. His venture into a new field surprised him as much as anyone. "I don't know," he wrote, "whether this quartet is beautiful or ugly, but I do know it's a string quartet!" What might he not do next, his friends eagerly asked each other?

He had been home from Naples less than two months when he learned that his idol, Alessandro Manzoni—Italy's greatest writer—was dead. "The Saint" he and Peppina always called this man of world renown, who was as good as he was great. Manzoni's best-loved book, *The Betrothed* (*I promessi sposi*), they had read and reread again and yet again. It was Verdi's favorite novel, appealing to him especially because its hero and heroine were little people, humble, ignorant, human, struggling in the evil web of Renaissance power and corruption.

Long ago, when Verdi first went to Turin to represent his district, he had seen from afar the great Manzoni, who was a Senator in that same Congress. Shyness and humility, however, had kept Verdi from seeking the older man's acquaintance at the time. They did not meet until many years later when a friend of both men took the Verdis to call on Manzoni in his retirement. The author, now old, received them with the utmost graciousness. Yet the Maestro, whose fame was by then more spectacular than Manzoni's own, found himself tongue-tied before the man whom he so deeply revered. Little was said—there could be no banal compliments, no vapid small talk between these two. Nevertheless the meeting was one of the high spots of Verdi's life.

Unwilling to parade his grief before a staring crowd, Verdi avoided the pompous funeral. But a few days later he stood alone in Milan's vast, deserted cemetery, bareheaded beside the fresh-turned grave. Sorrow had been his intimate companion, had left its mark forever on his face, but he felt more than sorrow now. Verdi was angry. The obituary notices, he felt, had been ungenerous; it seemed that not even "the Saint" could escape the slurs of the malicious and the condescending judgments of small men. Why must humanity always be niggardly of honest admiration? A life, a spirit such as Manzoni's should be an inspiration to all mankind, and yet—Verdi looked at the piled wreaths, now wilted, dreary, useless, and his knowledge of the world told him that already, even now, the great man's memory was growing cold. He turned and walked slowly away, burning to keep that memory alive.

Verdi was a man of action. It was not his nature to fritter his convictions away in reverie or talk. Even before paying his solitary tribute at Manzoni's grave he had come to a decision. At home he took up the manuscript of the *Libera Me*, the final part of the Requiem which had been his share of the proposed memorial to Rossini. His friends had spoken highly of it, urging him to finish the entire Mass himself—a tempting idea, especially since under the pressure of inspiration he had already set down other fragments in his daily composing. But he had shaken his head. "There are so many Masses for the dead—so very many . . . I can think of nothing more useless." Now he felt otherwise: the Requiem would have a purpose and a dedication. He wrote to the Mayor of Milan offering the still unfinished work for a memorial performance on the first anniversary of Manzoni's death. The Mayor of course accepted with profound gratitude. No thanks were due

[ 229 ]

him, Verdi protested. He was only fulfilling "an impulse—a need, rather"—of his heart.

All this while Mariani, unforgiven and unforgiving, lay incurably ill alone in Genoa, in the apartment above Verdi's own. His money had melted away, his "friends" had grown indifferent, and disease warped his mind. Just as Verdi was setting to work on the *Manzoni* Requiem, death at last released the great conductor from his suffering. The Maestro was expected to attend the funeral or at least send some tribute for the sake of their former friendship, but he did nothing of the sort. "What a misfortune for art!" he exclaimed, and that was all.

On May 22, 1874, in St. Mark's Church in Milan, Verdi himself conducted his Mass before an audience gathered at the Mayor's invitation from all over Italy and Europe. Since no one knew what sort of sacred music to expect from an opera composer, there was intense curiosity. And truly, Verdi's proved to be unlike any other Requiem Mass ever written. For inspiration he had gone not to the ancient ceremonial rites, with stiff-robed priests and chanting choirs in churches cloudy with incense, but to the magnificent old Latin text itself. He felt the drama in those austere words, and in his music the Last Judgment "happens" just as an opera happens on the stage. In the sudden, terrifying downward swirl of sound that announces the Day of Wrath, the world's very foundations seem to crumble in bottomless ruin, and the coming of the Great King, the Lord God of Hosts, in all His awesome majesty to judge the quick and the dead is like doom itself. There follows an appeal for mercy—tender, piteous, fearful—to the Lamb of God who died to save mankind; then the music swells to an ecstasy of praise and adoration. But again the terrible wrath breaks like a crashing, crumbling wave. Comes a fierce, helpless moment of rebellion against Death . . . then resignation, and the ultimate prayer of all erring mortal men, the prayer for forgiveness, life everlasting, and eternal peace.

This colossal drama of the human soul, as Verdi painted it,

was so fraught with excitement, terror, pity, and exaltation that time and again the listeners unconsciously cried out aloud. Moreover, the one memorial performance at St. Mark's was not enough. Three more had to be given at La Scala, the last two under Faccio's baton, while Verdi hastened to Paris to rehearse the Mass with a French orchestra and chorus. The original soloists—Stolz, Waldmann, and an Italian tenor and bass—joined him there; he himself conducted. And in Paris too, ovations, furor! The season was almost over, yet the Mass had to be repeated seven times—unheard of for music of this solemn character—and still so many people were turned away that Verdi agreed to return for more performances the following year.

That spring of 1874 the German musician Hans von Bülow happened to be in Milan, where he was much admired as pianist and conductor. Although some time before this, Wagner had stolen his wife, Cosima Liszt, Bülow remained one of Wagner's most ardent disciples, and he now felt called upon to attack the new Requiem with an explosion of frantic sneers. Through the newspapers he announced that he, Hans von Bülow, had not attended the first performance, nor did he wish to be numbered among the many foreigners who had come to Milan on purpose to hear this latest "opera" by the "omnipotent corrupter of Italian artistic taste." A glance at the score, he said, had cured him of any desire to be present; but he neglected to explain how he had seen it, since it was not published until the following day.

Italians love a good row, and the newspapers immediately tore into Bülow without mercy. The public was reminded that not long ago he had hoped to become conductor of La Scala and director of the Milan Conservatory, and had failed —largely because Verdi and Ricordi opposed his appointment on the ground that the positions should be held by an Italian. The squabble developed into a volley of insults, from all of which Verdi, of course, remained aloof. But up in Germany the great Johannes Brahms, who had composed his own magnificent *German* Requiem only a few years earlier, grew curious. He obtained a copy of Verdi's score, read it, and gave his verdict: "Bülow's talking nonsense. This is a work of genius!"

Eighteen years later Verdi received from Bülow an extraordinary letter. "Deign to hear the confession of a repentant sinner!" it began. Then in strangely florid sentences the German explained that he had lately heard the *Manzoni* Requiem and, even though the performance was a poor one, had found himself moved to tears! And he ended: "Illustrious Maestro, I now admire you, love you!"

Serenely, with perfect dignity, Verdi replied that there was nothing to forgive. Though Bülow's former opinions differed from his present ones, he had nevertheless done well to express them. "I should never have ventured to complain. Besides, who knows? Perhaps you were right before."

If Bülow *had* been right before, then Brahms and thousands upon thousands of others must have been wrong. In Paris in 1875 the *Manzoni* Requiem was repeated another seven times, while the enthusiasm, if anything, increased. Thence Verdi took his soloists to London for three performances in the Albert Hall with a chorus of twelve hundred voices. Then on to Vienna for a particularly fine performance there. The French pressed honors and decorations upon him, the Londoners gave him immense public acclaim, the Viennese praised the new work to the skies. And this triumph was more gratifying to the Maestro than his operatic successes. With this score he felt that he had gained in dignity and stature as an artist.

Not that Hans von Bülow's was the only dissenting opinion. Some people, especially in England, were even shocked. Sacred music, they insisted, should not be heard in theaters and concert halls. Above all, it should not be so exciting, so dramatic—surely certain passages reminded one more of the stage than of the church. And because Verdi, instead of imitating the early masters of religious music, had composed from his own heart in his own way they accused him of insincerity and even sacrilege!

In Italy, too, there were occasional murmurs. Verdi was no

church-goer—what business had he with sacred music, the gossips asked? In Genoa his carriage was seen every Sunday driving to Mass, but it was the devout Peppina, not he, who attended. Invariably he left her at the door, returning to call for her after the service. Furthermore, the little chapel at Sant' Agata had been built solely for her use; this was common knowledge. Few people, however, knew that on his morning walk he almost always slipped alone into a favorite church to spend a while in silent meditation. And as yet still fewer understood that all his life his spirit knelt before an altar. Moreover, in this score as always, Verdi remained impersonal. He had not said: "This is *my* faith, *my* creed." Instead he had quite simply, literally, and with immense imaginative power set the ancient words to music.

That autumn, 1875, Verdi went to Rome to take his oath as Senator and appear briefly in the Senate Chamber. This was a distinction somewhat like receiving an honorary degree today, for Italian senators were then not elected—they were appointed by the Crown for life. At his own request, however, "Senator Verdi" was granted immediate leave of absence from all governmental duties. Since Cavour's death he had felt no obligation to take an active part in politics; one might as well expect a politician to write operas.

For a man in his sixties the Maestro, though he had undertaken no new musical work, was certainly busy enough. It was he who held the baton when, in the spring of 1876, the curtain rose for the first time in Paris on *Aida*. The French had had to wait four years to hear the new masterpiece—Verdi refused to let the Opéra have it at all, and now permitted it, in Italian, at the smaller Lyric Theater only under his own exacting direction. Exceptionally, he had even consented to conduct the first three performances himself, leaving the capable Muzio to carry on thereafter. The result was dazzling, sensational—Paris rocked with delight, filling the theater for twenty-six successive nights and bringing the management the handsome profit of 100,000 francs. Practical Verdi was never above watching the box office. On the contrary, he took the keenest interest in it, knowing that on its receipts rather than on the critics depended the ultimate survival of opera as an art. On this occasion, however, critics and box office were in accord. The French had sometimes treated Verdi with lukewarm condescension hitherto. Now, since *Aida*, since the Requiem, all France was at his feet.

In Wagner's Germany, too, his star was riding high. Ovations had long ago become routine in the Maestro's life, but in May 1877 as guest of honor at the Lower Rhine Music Festival, an annual affair held this year in Cologne, he received a welcome of a sort that was new to his experience. In Germany the Big Three—*Rigoletto, Trovatore, Traviata*—were immensely popular. But the Festival audiences, German to the core and made up of ardent music lovers and musicians, both professional and amateur, were more sophisticated than the general public. Though minor composers often appeared on their programs, these people had been nourished chiefly on Beethoven and Brahms, Schubert and Schumann. Could Italian Verdi hold his own among such mighty names as these?

It gladdened him to hear his String Quartet superbly played and much admired, but the climax came when he himself conducted the *Manzoni* Requiem. The applause, although less frenzied than in emotional Italy, surprised him by its genuine, spontaneous fervor, its affectionate warmth. More than that, the Germans had gone to the most touching pains to do him honor. There was a fine ivory and silver baton presented by the ladies of the chorus, there was a gold and silver wreath with the names of the donors engraved on the leaves, there was a magnificent souvenir album of specially painted views of the Rhineland, with decorations illustrating *Aida*, the Requiem, and even the String Quartet. There were banquets, and serenades to welcome him and to bid him farewell, and during his stay an avalanche of invitations—far more than he had time or strength to accept. Said Muzio, who was with him, "It makes one proud to be an Italian!" Here was the living proof, had Verdi required it, of his belief that there is always room in the world for every kind of music, provided only that it be beautiful and true.

What next? There had been talk lately of a Verdian symphony, but the Maestro let the rumors die away without troubling to contradict them. Symphonies, he knew, were not for him. Purely orchestral music belonged to the Germans, to the "fortunate sons of Bach." Nor was he, son of Palestrina, tempted to forsake his heritage. To him failure would have seemed inevitable and deserved.

Actually Verdi had no intention of composing anything at all. He had spent many years in harness, and now considered himself an old man. The world, he said, had had enough notes from his pen. For the public's sake and for his own it was high time that he retired.

No one believed him. He was still so keen, active, and slender (though much more robust than the haggard and

ailing youth of long ago) that one could not possibly think of
him as either aged or idle. His energetic figure—with the
wide-brimmed black hat pulled far down on his heavy,
whitening hair—was a familiar sight at every market place
within a day's drive of Sant' Agata as he shrewdly bought and
sold cattle and horses, poultry and crops. On his ever-growing
property, which contained several villages, he still had a hand
in all that went on, from the pruning of a shrub to the digging
of an artesian well. His stride was vigorous, springy, purposeful, and in Genoa he still took his long walks in the sunshine
he so loved. His eyes, gazing far out over the serene Mediterranean, were clear and luminous as ever. Besides, the "old
bear" had begun to mellow and seemed the younger for the
change. Not only his intimates but even casual acquaintances
now felt his fundamental kindness and gracious, friendly
warmth.

Sometimes people were bold enough to question him:
"Surely, Maestro, we can hope for a new opera from you
soon?"

"Have you ever seen my birth certificate?" As Verdi answered, the small lines that fanned out from the corners of his
eyes would deepen with amusement. Yet though he smiled he
always insisted firmly that he was through. But—was there
really no more music in him?

# CHAPTER SEVENTEEN

# Otello

## 1877-1887

VERDI was sixty-five, sixty-six, sixty-seven . . . The passing days took on a gray monotony. For years he had thought of leisure as something remote and desirable, not realizing that unless he worked at full capacity he soon grew restless as a panther in a cage. Now he lived in the retirement he had so often longed for, and he was bored with it.

What was he doing with himself, people wondered? But no answer came from beyond the thick, well-trimmed hedges of his private grounds—only silence. And the old man acquired legendary nicknames: "the Sage of Sant' Agata," "the Swan of Busseto." It began to seem that the long, glorious career might indeed be over.

His friends continued to beg for a new opera, but the thought only filled the Maestro with melancholy. Why should he compose again, he growled? For whom? Futility . . . The state of opera in general depressed him, and, ever a pessimist, he prophesied that the great theaters were doomed one by one to close their doors. He had made tremendous efforts to show what could be done with devotion and skill, but "the lesson would not stay learned." All too quickly the high standards of performance he achieved were allowed to slip, and indifference again sent a composer's finest inspirations limping and crippled out into the world. He was not aware, as we are today, that this most costly of the arts always

[ 237 ]

appears to be dying, yet always lives on; and the struggle seemed to him hopeless.

"I do nothing," wrote Verdi gloomily to a friend, "and I know nothing about anything. I wander about the fields until I am tired out; then I eat and sleep." But he could not shake the lifelong habit of putting notes on paper, and two new scores appeared—an *Ave Maria* for soprano and string orchestra, and a *Pater Noster* for five-part chorus—settings of Dante's Italian versions of the old Latin prayers. Like other geniuses Verdi, retired or not, was the slave of his own need to create.

For the winter months in Genoa, Verdi left his old apartment, now obstructed by new buildings and haunted by memories of Mariani, and took a floor of the venerable Palazzo Doria, a villa with a long, glamorous history. Here both Charles V and his son, Philip II of Spain, had lodged in royal splendor; and here Napoleon had made his headquarters in the city. The Maestro had some twenty rooms at his disposal—vast, high-ceilinged rooms of an earlier, more spacious way of life. There was a terraced garden too, a poetic spot mellow and mossy with centuries of careful tending; and beyond, a soul-filling view of the sunlit sea. This was a home worthy of a great man's old age.

But the moving! In the midst of the inevitable lists, trunks, and packing cases, Verdi fondly remembered the days when he had traveled effortlessly up and down the earth—days when his only possessions were four shirts and the suit on his back. Life was too complicated now, he wistfully complained, forgetting that it was always Peppina—incessantly busy, as Verdi put it, "circling and circling through the house"—who bore the brunt of such upheavals. He was not even conscious of the minor burdens that she shouldered to protect him, grumbling gaily to her friends the while. This, she vowed, would be the last move. But then—"not everybody can write a Requiem Mass, and there must also be someone to count the laundry!" Peppina's tongue was often in her cheek, and it amused her, in her sparkling letters, to refer to her husband as "the renowned composer," or "the illustrious Maestro."

She loved him, revered him with her whole being—and sweetly laughed at him, and at herself.

In the summer of 1879, to raise funds for the victims of a flood, Verdi emerged from hiding and conducted the Requiem once more in Milan. Ricordi, not yet convinced that the Maestro's opera days were over, seized this opportunity to set a little trap. It seemed natural that Verdi, while in town, should be invited to dine with his good friends Ricordi and Faccio; natural, too, that their talk should turn to Shakespeare in general, and to *Otello* (as Italians call *Othello*) in particular. All three agreed that Rossini's opera, *Otello*, so brilliantly successful in its day, was not Shakespeare at all—the librettist, according to the fashion of the period, had even given it a happy ending! With growing eagerness they discussed the "noble Moor," Desdemona his wife, so innocent and "lovely fair," and that incarnation of Evil, "honest" Iago, whose fiendish scheming brings them all to ruin. Was ever tragedy more poignant? And what poetry! Here, said Ricordi, was material for great music . . .

Verdi agreed. But how, he asked, could anyone compress the play into an opera libretto to do Shakespeare justice?

This was Faccio's cue. There was a man, he said, who could and would do it—though for no one but Verdi. And scanning the Maestro's face for signs of interest, he mentioned his friend, Arrigo Boito. Might he bring him to call the next day?

He might. To the delight of the conspirators—Ricordi, Faccio, Peppina, Boito himself—Verdi took an immediate liking to the younger man. So far so good.

These two had not met since the poet supplied the text for the *Hymn of Nations* seventeen years before. There had been a coolness on Verdi's part, for Boito in his rebellious youth had scoffed at the old-fashioned early Verdian operas—an indiscretion he later came to regret. Admiring all that was modern—for a time Wagner especially—he had watched the Maestro's music grow, until *Aida* convinced him that of all operatic composers Verdi was the greatest. As there was hardly a composer of renown for whom Boito had not provided a libretto, his opinion carried weight. More than that, his own *Mefistofele* (for which he wrote both words and music) was truly sensational. Boito, always advanced, always in the forefront of the experimental in art, with this opera had caused a riot at La Scala in 1868. At first hearing, it seemed so outrageously strange that long before the end the curtain had had to be lowered because of actual fist-fights in the audience! The composer-poet, though temporarily crushed by this disaster, had revised his score and seven years later tried again, this time with a success that equalled some of Verdi's own.

Since the triumph of *Mefisto* (as it was always called for short) Boito no longer wrote libretti for other men to set to music. Yet for the privilege of working with Maestro Verdi he would be only too proud to make an exception. In fact, only three days after their meeting he brought Verdi his outline of *Othello* in opera form.

This was a brilliant piece of work to which much more than three days' thought had obviously been given—and Verdi at once saw through the plot to wreck his leisure and his peace of mind. He hesitated, hovering near the bait—reluctant to take it, unable to leave it alone. Certainly the "cup of chocolate" (Verdi always spoke of dark-skinned Othello as "the chocolate one") was tempting . . . Boito must finish the libretto. The effort would not be wasted, for if he, Verdi, did not set it to music surely someone else would—perhaps Boito himself.

This was not the promise for which everyone hoped, but at least it was no refusal. The seed was planted. Would it grow? Peppina, in the months that followed, could not help noticing how often Verdi spoke of Shakespeare. Most opera plots were highly artificial, he told her—just opera plots, like *Forza*, for instance. But Shakespeare—that was different, that was humanity itself! Surely this preoccupation was an encouraging sign.

That autumn Ricordi paid a visit, partly to see whether the seed had yet begun to sprout, partly for another reason. A French writer named Pougin had published a biography of the Maestro based on hearsay and such facts as he had been able to gather, and this book was about to be revised and translated into Italian. For Pougin, Ricordi had undertaken to obtain from the Sage of Sant' Agata himself the true story of those early days about which there were only legendary rumors.

On the Villa Verdi's pleasant, graveled terrace the two men sat at ease over cigars and coffee. "I can see no point in such a book," said the Maestro. "Frankly, were I one of the public it would never occur to me to read such a thing. It's not as though I were an interesting character, or had led a remarkable life."

"Maestro, if I may say so, you scarcely appreciate the vast curiosity as to what manner of man you really are. And then you yourself mentioned that Pougin's book is full of errors."

"That's so. If it must appear at all it might as well be right. Well, let me see . . . What would you like to know?"

"Maestro, there are anecdotes of your childhood—so many different versions—"

"Oh, those old tales!" Verdi waved them aside. "They have no meaning, no importance. Besides," he laughed, "I don't want to seem a miracle child! No, all that is best forgotten. But it's true that my youth was hard . . . A wretched, broken spinet . . ." The ancient bitterness saddened his strong features. Then slowly he, who never spoke about the past, about himself, told his own story up to the time when *Nabucco* had banished his obscurity forever.

A remarkable document, this statement that Ricordi wrote down while the shadows lengthened across the terrace and the blue smoke from the Maestro's cigar curled peacefully toward the darkening sky. Verdi told his tale simply, as a man speaks to a friend. He had, unconsciously, the rare power of saying always exactly what he meant, and, without a trace of vanity or distortion, the truth shone in his words. And yet, strangely, not quite the truth, for when he spoke of the death of his wife and children he became confused. The disasters, he said, had followed each other within a few weeks, instead of months, and he was wrong about which baby had died first. How could a man forget such things?

When suffering becomes unendurable the human mind shuts it away. Verdi had walled off his sorrows in the caverns of his memory, and now, after forty years, he looked once more at those grim days. What he saw was a chaos of pain, loneliness, despair—blow upon blow falling in rapid succession. The truth was actually almost more tragic, since after each disaster hope had had time to reappear, only to be cut down again and again.

Naturally, Verdi's own version was accepted as fact. Indeed the error came to light only recently when Carlo Gatti, whose biography of the composer took ten years to write, uncovered the burial records. The mistake, though strange, was understandable enough, for Verdi was not a man to live and relive his grief letting it fester and corrupt his soul. Instead he had mastered it, as a strong man must. Nor did dates ever impress him. He set no store by reminiscences, even the happiest; he took no notice of anniversaries; and all his life he was confused about his own birthday.

Not long after young Ricordi returned to Milan with his precious pages, Verdi received the first draft of the new libretto. "Look, Peppina," he exclaimed, "Boito's already sent me that chocolate fellow!" Did the Maestro set to work? No, indeed—but don't press him, Peppina urged the others; be patient, let things take their course. She knew that he was thinking these days of what Othello and Iago looked like— had even described them to an artist friend from whom he wanted their pictures.

The following March—1880—*Aida* reappeared in Paris, this time at the Opéra, which had burned down and been rebuilt. Wonder of wonders, Verdi himself was at the conductor's desk! It was the new manager, Vaucorbeil, who had persuaded him to bury the old grudge against the "Big Store." Cleverly, Vaucorbeil had not written for permission to produce *Aida;* he could imagine Verdi's letter of refusal. Instead he visited Sant' Agata, and deliberately made himself a charming guest. He seemed to enjoy the tranquil daily routine, he admired horses, dogs, gardens, fields, the whole estate. He agreed that operatic standards must be raised. He drifted to the piano and, finding there the manuscript of the new *Pater Noster*, still unpublished and unheard, played it with genuine delight. And all this subtle flattery bore fruit. Vaucorbeil went home with Verdi's promise not only to stage *Aida* at the Opéra but to conduct the first three performances himself.

For this production Verdi worked, as he said, "twenty-six hours a day." Seldom—never in France—had he met with such coöperation, the results were magnificent, and this *Aida* far outshone all his former Parisian triumphs. Furthermore, the French discovered that the "old bear" could be charming, for he submitted to the inevitable deluge of honors and gifts graciously, even happily.

Shortly thereafter, at a Milan concert of old and new Italian vocal music, the *Pater Noster* and the *Ave Maria* were presented with such success that Verdi's spirits rose still higher. Now, surely, thought the conspirators, he must be in the mood to begin his *Iago, Otello*—whatever he wanted to call it.

The Maestro, however, seemed to have no such idea, and all summer long busied himself with the construction of new dairy buildings on his farm. Not that he needed more dairies— they were only an added burden and responsibility. But times were hard and more and more Italians, out of work, hungry and hopeless, were turning to the land of promise across the Atlantic—America, where the streets were paved with gold and any man might become a millionaire. The stream of emigration grew alarmingly and the politicians, frightened by this draining away of the country's man-power, made impassioned speeches in a vain effort to stop the flow. Verdi said nothing, but no one emigrated from his neighborhood. There was no unemployment—thanks to these costly new buildings that he did not need or want.

This was excellent for Italy, but hard on Ricordi's patience. He remembered that the revision of *Forza* had succeeded in putting Verdi in the frame of mind to compose *Aida*. Why not try the same trick again? He suggested a new version of *Simon Boccanegra* for La Scala. Verdi, who always had a special fondness for *Boccanegra*, was enthusiastic—provided Boito would consent to reshape the old libretto.

A thankless task—no amount of patching and polishing could ever make the tangled story clear, plausible, and dramatic, Boito rightly declared. Nevertheless he agreed. Perhaps Verdi wanted to test him . . .

Never before had the Maestro been privileged to work with such a mind as Boito's—so cultivated, subtle, poetic, and profound. Both were perfectionists and they saw their goal as through a single pair of eyes. Though Verdi was always the dominant partner, each so admired the other's genius that there was never an inharmonious moment between them. Small wonder that from their teamwork grew the warmest, most enduring and devoted of friendships.

During the *Boccanegra* rehearsals there came a day when Boito felt obliged to point out a sizable blemish in the score.

"I know, I know," muttered Verdi impatiently, "but there's no time to change it now. A pity, but the passage will have to stand as it is. One can't do the impossible!" And, with a grin, he added, "Your standards are altogether too high, my friend. I have humbler ideas myself." This was the pot calling the kettle black. Though the première was only a few days off, Verdi of course did the impossible and rewrote the passage —as Boito knew he would.

That spring of 1881 the new *Boccanegra* was an immense success—and deservedly, for some of Verdi's finest music is to be found in this score. The opera, therefore, has survived in spite of its improved but incurable libretto, and is especially admired by serious music lovers. Moreover, many a baritone lucky enough to sing the title role (Lawrence Tibbett, for instance) has found in it his favorite part.

Two members of the cast at La Scala impressed Verdi especially: the huge tenor, Francesco Tamagno, whose ringing high tones seemed made to order for Othello, and the incomparable baritone, Victor Maurel, whose acting was no less remarkable than his voice.

In the flurry of congratulations that followed the fall of the curtain Verdi delightedly clapped Maurel on the shoulder. "Magnificent!" he exclaimed. "If God gives me health, I'll write Iago for you!"

Sensation! Was not this almost a promise? Now, now at last, the Maestro would surely reach for his music paper, dip his pen.

Nothing of the kind. For any sign that came from behind the hedges of Sant' Agata, the whole project might well have been forgotten. Verdi remained in seclusion, unheard from except in the autumn of 1881 when he refused to attend the unveiling of statues of Bellini and himself, to stand with those of Rossini and Donizetti at La Scala. It was undignified, he protested. Besides, it made him feel really old, shelved. Only the dead belonged on pedestals.

That Christmas, Muzio and Teresa Stolz, spending the

holidays at the Palazzo Doria, watched the Verdis open a big box from Ricordi. Inside was a fine specimen of the traditional Italian Christmas cake, but with an untraditional decoration in the center—a chocolate baby, pitifully small!

"The chocolate fellow!" Verdi roared with delight.

"How little he is, poor thing!" Peppina chuckled. "One would think he had only just been born—or perhaps Giulio merely hopes that he *will* be born soon!"

"Poor little Otello! He'll make good eating anyhow!" The Maestro thoroughly enjoyed the joke. But as for taking the hint . . .

The following Christmas, 1882, came another cake with another chocolate baby—alas, no larger than the first.

"Verdi, do look!" cried Peppina. "The little creature hasn't grown at all! What a pity!"

Verdi laughed heartily, but beyond amusing him Ricordi's gentle reminders seemed to have no effect. He was strangely quiet and withdrawn these days. To any question as to what he was composing he answered gruffly, nothing. Why should he? To be called a second-rate Wagner? No, he had done his share. Anyhow the theaters were all about to close. And he wished people would stop meddling in his affairs.

But Peppina still counseled patience, knowing that when he tramped the fields or strolled along the shady garden paths he was no longer alone. Three constant, invisible companions walked beside him: Othello, Iago, Desdemona. He was learning their inmost hearts, living their lives, *being* each in turn, as a great actor might. And thinking, thinking, thinking. The time for writing music was not yet. This seed must ripen slowly if at all.

Meanwhile he was creating not an opera, but a hospital. The peasants living on his estate had dangerously far to go for help in case of illness or accident, and this fact had troubled him. So he now planned, built, equipped, and endowed a fine small hospital for them, first reading books on hospital administration and visiting similar institutions with his usual thoroughness. He would have no useless extravagance or showy trimmings, but the essentials must be the best that money could buy. Characteristically he and Peppina supervised every detail, even selecting uniforms and crockery and kitchenware themselves.

"Of course it must be called the Verdi Hospital," said the grateful neighbors.

"Nonsense!" retorted Verdi. "Since we're building it in the village of Villanova it will be called what it is: the Villanova Hospital. After all, it's intended to care for the sick, not to publicize a man's name." Nor would he permit any formal opening ceremonies. Yet it was a happy day for him when the first patients were admitted, and for Peppina, who always took a keen interest in the villagers, visiting them and bringing thoughtful gifts: wine for the shoemaker who had been ill, a new dress and a toy for the second gardener's daughter, a shawl or a basket of fruit for the stableboy's crippled mother.

In February 1883 came news that shook the whole musical, artistic world: Wagner was dead! He had died suddenly, in Venice, at seventy—just Verdi's age. . . . The giant had fallen, never to write another note. Surely the Maestro might have been forgiven a momentary, secret sense of triumph. But he was too big a man for that. Wagner had been his rival— and his brother. Did not the same fire burn in both their souls?

Impulsively, he dashed off a note to Giulio Ricordi:

"Sad Sad Sad!
"Wagner is dead!
"Reading the news yesterday I was, frankly, stunned.
"Let there be no argument. It is a great personality that has vanished. A name that leaves a most mighty imprint upon the History of Art."

The words, hastily scribbled, shine with honesty. Verdi had written "mighty"; then, weighing Wagner's achievement in his mind, had added "most." Thus he wrote of the man who had pretended in public that he, Verdi, did not exist, and in private caricatured at the piano one of his weaker arias to show how low Italian art had sunk. But Verdi's heart was clean of malice. Sincerely grieved, he paid a just and gallant tribute to one of the greatest of composers.

Not yet, however, could he free himself from Wagner's ghost. During the winter of 1884 a successful revival of *Don Carlo* at La Scala, in a new, shortened version, only depressed him. Once again it was said that he followed in Wagner's footsteps. Had he then spent all his life creating music for deaf ears?

He felt discouraged, gloomy, and in such a mood it seemed unlikely that he should start a tremendous new work. Yet just as, many years ago, he had set down *Nabucco* almost against his will, so now *Otello*, ripened in his mind, was no longer to be resisted. Boito came to the Palazzo Doria to make improvements in the libretto, and suddenly Verdi, though he still made no promises, began to write. The conspirators rejoiced, but quietly lest too much advance talk nip the new opera in the bud.

The Maestro had covered no more than a few pages when he saw a newspaper account of *Mefisto* in Naples. He was glad to read that the performance had been triumphant and the author-composer much fêted. But at a dinner in his honor Boito was reported to have remarked that he had once considered Shakespeare's *Othello* unsuitable for opera. Since he had been at work on it, however, he had completely changed his mind. It was, in fact, so fine that he could almost wish to be writing the music himself!

At once Faccio received an alarming letter from Verdi. As Boito's oldest, closest friend, Faccio must "tell him by word of mouth, not in writing, when he returns to Milan, that I will return the manuscript untouched—without a shadow of resentment, with no grudge of any kind. Furthermore, the libretto being my property, I offer it to him as a gift in case he means to write the music. If he accepts I shall be delighted, hoping thus to further the art we all love."

Was it possible? Boito, aghast, hastened to explain. Rumors of his collaboration with Verdi had made everyone curious. A tactless question fired point-blank had caught him off his guard, and he had answered half in jest—never dreaming of the interpretation that might be put upon his words, nor that those words would appear, misquoted, in the newspaper.

Even if Verdi should not write another note, he, Boito, would never attempt the music for *Otello*. No one but Verdi should touch it, since no one else was equal to the task. Besides, his own next opera would be *Nerone*—if indeed he ever wrote another.

So be it then, answered the Maestro. But, as for *Otello*—

". . . There has been too much talk about it; too much time has elapsed. I have too many years on my back, and too many *years of service* behind me! Too many for the public not to tell me all too plainly that they have had enough.

"The consequence is that all this has dashed some cold water on *Otello* and stiffened the hand that had begun to sketch a few measures.

"What next? I don't know . . . I shake your hand affectionately and give you Peppina's best."

It was curious, this hesitancy. A career such as Verdi's might well have inspired self-confidence, if not conceit. Yet no beginner could have approached his task more humbly, or suffered stage-fright more acute. A whole summer passed, and Boito came to visit Sant' Agata once more before Verdi again took up the score he had begun and set aside.

Verdi worked, and the months became a year—two years. He composed swiftly as always, but more tentatively now, feeling his way in preliminary sketches. Often he summoned Boito to adjust a scene or alter a few words to fit a more expressive rhythm. And Boito, hearing each act as it approached its final form, marveled increasingly. There had been nothing quite like this before, he knew. No longer was it possible to think of poetry and music as separate elements. This music came to life through and around the words, every note breathing new intensity into the play. In shaping the libretto the Maestro himself had made invaluable suggestions. Now Boito saw his text—the finest yet written for an opera—grow luminous in Verdi's hands.

When would *Otello* be produced? When the composer was satisfied with it, if ever . . . He would not say. Yet he went all the way to Paris to hear Maurel sing once more, and by the spring of 1886 Italy's best scene designer was studying costumes and furnishings in the museums of Venice. Still Verdi refused to commit himself. He was rewriting the score, experimenting in his own study instead of on the stage as some composers do.

At last he agreed that, if all went well, the new opera might be given, and in the autumn the principal singers, already chosen, visited Sant' Agata to be coached in their parts. Verdi meantime continued to polish his music, not yet convinced of its unalterable rightness. Then one November day Boito, in Milan, received the following letter:

> Dear Boito: It is finished!
> All hail to us. . . . (and to HIM too!!)
> Farewell.
> VERDI

HIM? Not once during those interminable months had either musician or poet forgotten the third member of their team lying silent close to three hundred years in a far-off English grave: Shakespeare, the "greatest searcher of the human heart."

The manuscript, finally ready, must be sent to the printer, but Verdi felt a queer, shy reluctance to let it go. He went through it a last time "to see whether it flows—it does!" Then the precious package was in the postman's hands. "Poor Otello, poor Desdemona," murmured the Maestro, suddenly desolate; "they will never come back here any more. . . ."

January 1887. Rehearsals at La Scala were in full swing. But Verdi, still hesitant before the ordeal, reserved the right to cancel the performance even up to the last minute, should he be dissatisfied. And an ordeal this première was sure to be. Fifteen years had passed since *Aida* was first heard in Milan, thirteen since the Requiem. Now that the long, rumor-filled silence was about to be broken, public excitement and curiosity exceeded all bounds. Would this new opera prove to be the greatest of Verdi's works, as some maintained? Or— ghastly thought—suppose *Otello* were only the pathetic attempt of a tired old man who should have stopped composing long ago? Everyone wanted advance information, but no one could obtain it, not even the journalists gathered from all parts of the world to report the event. Because Verdi strictly forbade the presence of outsiders at rehearsals, these gentlemen were frankly furious. They tried intrigue and bribery, they even formally petitioned the Maestro himself—in vain. Thwarted, they haunted the most fashionable drawing-rooms, where singers and others connected with the performance might be met, and for their pains learned only that the public might expect a surprise. Obviously this opera, like *Nabucco* so long ago, was indescribable and must be heard. There was no other subject of conversation in all Milan—a city that one writer, during those feverish days, christened "Otellopolis"!

A certain young musician, to be sure, did manage to attend rehearsals. As a boy he had made solitary pilgrimages from his native Parma to Verdi's birthplace at Le Roncole. When seventeen he had served as 'cellist at La Scala and since then, though not yet twenty, had begun to make a name for himself as a conductor. But now, for the privilege of working under Verdi's direction, he asked and received permission to take his old place in the orchestra. For a rising conductor this was, of course, a downward step. No matter—to this extraordinarily gifted youngster music itself meant more than his own advancement. His name was Arturo Toscanini. Again and again, throughout an unprecedented career, his devotion was to illuminate Verdi's music; and critics, even those with long memories, would call his broadcast sixty years later of this very *Otello* the greatest operatic performance they had ever heard.

Verdi's kindness, especially toward the less experienced members of the cast, made an enduring impression on the inconspicuous and attentive young man at the second 'cellist's desk. The hard taskmaster of other days was now unfailingly considerate. It was no longer necessary to enforce his will, since his mere presence in the theater was enough to make the humblest member of the chorus sing as he had never sung before.

Rehearsals were progressing smoothly when suddenly

Tamagno, the tenor who was to play the title role, became ill. Would he recover in time? The season was already advanced—perhaps *Otello* would have to be postponed until the following year! Appalling thought, especially for the innumerable foreigners whose journey to Milan might turn out to have been in vain. Frantically the reporters scurried after every wisp of news, while ordinary people greeted each other with questions: "Have you heard how he is today? Will he be able to sing?" Outside the opera house crowds watched for an announcement to be posted. And at last it came: Tamagno had recovered. *Otello* would be heard on February 5th.

That morning hotel guests found no one to serve their breakfasts—at dawn the waiters had disappeared in the direction of La Scala. Beds were left unmade—chambermaids, too, had joined the thousands milling about La Scala to watch the comings and goings of the great. Shops were closed —no one could be bothered with customers on such a day as this. Traffic grew snarled, while between the Grand Hotel (where he always made his headquarters) and the theater Verdi's carriage crept back and forth in the center of a moving swarm of humanity like a great, buzzing clump of bees.

At last the moment came—La Scala threw wide its doors to an assembly of notables such as even that historic auditorium had never held before. Not only notables: the little people were there too, as many as were lucky enough to squeeze in; while outside, thousands more stood in the square, seeing nothing but the building's walls, hearing nothing but the shuffle of their own weary feet, waiting and waiting for a chance crumb from the feast of glory.

The houselights—electric now—dimmed. In an oppressive silence Faccio took his place, raised his baton. There came from the orchestra a quick gust of sound and then, abrupt as thunder, the first tremendous, crashing chord. Up swept the curtain on the drenched and darkened coast of Cyprus—no time for an overture—with a tempest raging at sea over battle and shipwreck. The listeners, blown and buffeted by the music, gasped for breath. Here is a storm to wrench the very soul. (The boy Giuseppe, nearly sixty years ago, had cowered in a quaking chapel while human beings were struck by lightning before his eyes.) But soon the fury of the winds is spent. Otello, great soldier, valiant general, is safely home. His figure dominates the seething crowd as, with the huge, ringing cry "Rejoice!", he proclaims victory. No opera in all the world opens in such a whirlwind of excitement.

No opera in all the world draws more inevitably to its tragic end than this familiar story of the triumph of evil. Like a slow poison, Iago's music seeps through the score as scene by scene he fans the flame of jealousy, torturing the Moor with hints and lies and manufactured evidence of Desdemona's faithlessness. Subtly, magically, Verdi's notes, welded to Shakespeare's thought, to Boito's words, intensify the pain and ruin of a noble heart, until "the pity of it, Iago, the pity of it," already overwhelming in the play, is in the music scarcely to be borne. Boito, having heard Verdi's first three acts, had almost dreaded to hear the last one, for Shakespeare's pages seemed to him "the most anguished ever written." And he was right. No opera in all the world closes more poignantly than this; there is no tragedy in music more profound and moving.

Even now, when it has long since ceased to seem new or strange, *Otello* is not to be fathomed at a single hearing; and that first audience was tense and a bit bewildered. Yet no one, then or now, could fail to be deeply stirred as Iago's unspeakable villainy is disclosed—too late. The stricken Moor turns to Desdemona—dead by his own hand. Heartbreakingly, there comes an echo of the great first-act love duet sung in the starlit hush after the storm—music never surpassed in tenderness and beauty. "Otello is no more . . . I kissed thee ere I killed thee; no way but this, killing myself to die upon a kiss." He sinks, and slowly, somberly, the long chords fade into an aching stillness.

At the fall of the curtain there was a moment of utter silence, then the applause broke like the bursting of a dam. "Verdi! Verdi! Verdi!"—the cry surged and thundered. Keeping a firm grip on Boito's arm lest the poet try to escape, the Maestro stood in the blazing light, his massive head with the thick, shining, gray-white hair bowed in the lonely humility of greatness. On this same stage forty-five years ago he had first heard the now familiar sound of glory. But this was something more—this was the roar of immortality itself.

The ecstasy of an Italian mob can be terrifying in its violence, and that night the Maestro's short trip back to his hotel became a nightmare. He had no sooner climbed into his carriage, from which the horses had been unhitched and led away, than the crowd swarmed around and over it, fighting for a chance to say to future grandchildren: "I saw his face—I was *this* close to him!" Verdi and Peppina, both looking suddenly old and frail and tired, clung to each other and to Boito, while in the midst of indescribable howling confusion the carriage was actually lifted clear of the ground and, since it was far too heavy to be held, dropped with a sickening jolt. Frightened and shaken, the three inside huddled together as, yard by perilous yard, they neared their destination.

This frenzy had deep roots. There was in Verdi something of every man, and in every man something of him. To these people he was no ordinary hero—he was their own greater selves. His was the power to release their courage and their tears, to show them the bigness of the human soul. His voice was their voice, and his language the universal language. What matter that not everyone could follow all the subtleties of this new opera? That was for educated people who had studied Shakespeare. Only a handful of this delirious throng had been inside the theater, and no new "Donna è mobile" had emerged to sweep the world. Yet all sensed that something momentous had taken place, that a new Verdi had come back to them, bigger and greater even than the old Verdi they knew and loved. And so, dragging the carriage with its precious burden, they heaved and struggled and shouted in fierce joy.

Here at last was the hotel entrance, flag-decked and carpeted in Verdi's honor. But between him and the bright safety of the flower-banked lobby, only a few steps away, seethed a hoarse, cheering mass of humanity. Would he be torn to pieces? Turning to Boito, he said in a voice half comic and half sad, "I leave my wife in your hands!" and stepped out. At once the crowd, suddenly quiet, fell reverently back to let him pass. There was nothing to fear. Peppina, following pale and shaken, did not even need Boito's shielding arm.

But the ovation was not yet over. From his balcony the Maestro, led out by Boito and Tamagno, was obliged to bow and bow, while the huge tenor sang once more Otello's great triumphant cry, "Rejoice!" For hours Verdi's rooms were thronged with friends, singers—all the comrades of opera. He sat quietly, the center of a bright confusion of congratulations, flowers, gifts, receiving homage, turning it aside.

"Poor Otello," he murmured, "poor Desdemona! They've gone out into the world now. They won't come back to Sant' Agata. . . . I shall miss them. I feel so strange, so empty—as if I had fired off my last cartridge. It's over, all over." Then, brightening, he reached for Boito's hand. "And yet, if I were thirty years younger I'd want to start another opera tomorrow, provided Boito wrote the libretto!"

For many in Milan that night there was more revelry than sleep, and for the Maestro a full week of festivities and celebrations followed. It was exhilarating, but exhausting too, and he was thankful to go home to his garden and his fields. On the last day he said, "Till midnight I'm still Maestro Verdi, but after that I'll be the peasant of Sant' Agata again."

A peasant, yes, a farmer who at seventy-three had produced his twenty-fifth and greatest opera—so far. More than that, *Otello* was and is the greatest tragic opera ever to come out of Italy—one of the towering miracles of music.

# CHAPTER EIGHTEEN

# *Falstaff*

## 1887-1893

O BERTO, *Count of St. Boniface*, first opera by an awkward, tense young nobody named Giuseppe Verdi, appeared in 1839. As the year 1889 approached, the Maestro got wind of a plan to celebrate the fiftieth anniversary of that event with a Verdi Jubilee. Immediately he took fright, protesting that "of all useless things in the world this is the most useless." So emphatic was he that the sentimental idea of reviving *Oberto* had to be abandoned. How could anyone be asked to sit through that antiquated piece nowadays? There must be no special opera performances, nor any musical program whatever, he insisted. He would not even hear of raising a fund by national subscription to help some promising composer in his name. With shrewd common sense he pointed out the pitfalls in such a scheme: a small sum would do little good; the vast amount needed to produce a first opera would be next to impossible to obtain. But supposing it could be done— the opera, through lack of merit, inadequate performance or sheer bad luck, might fail. Then time, money, effort, and hope would all have been lost. One could not force the hand of fate.

Verdi, however, was powerless to prevent some sort of celebration, and on the great day, November 17th, a torrent of messages and tributes poured in. Even the King sent a congratulatory telegram. The papers devoted columns to the

Maestro's career. A musical journal got out a special issue in which the nation's best authors praised his achievement and all that he stood for. He was "the voice of Italy's great soul," they said, and fervently recalled his patriotic songs, sacred to every man born before Italy was free. Rarely is genius destined to receive such heartfelt admiration as the whole country now expressed, and Verdi's gratitude was deeply humble and sincere.

It was, of course, *Otello* that had brought him really into his own. This triumph left no bitterness in its wake, nor did any shadow of "Germanism" or "imitation" now dim his glory. As the score, considered so new and daring at the time, grew more and more familiar, the universal wonder increased. Here was perfection which, though it stemmed from all that was finest in the Italian tradition, had been undreamed of hitherto—the culmination of three hundred years of opera.

Opera's groping founders, centuries earlier, sought to express dramatic emotion through music—to use music not for its own sake but to enhance the spoken word. Yet often, as the new art form passed through its circus-pageant phase and later became a conventional framework for vocal display, the original purpose had been all but lost sight of. Verdi returned to it, and never, as he climbed the steep road from *Oberto* to *Otello*, had he allowed himself to be sidetracked. Instead of adopting or contriving some new theory, he put his faith in mastery of the rules, inspiration, and a deep instinct for truth, and, knowing that time alone can tell, scorned to explain himself to the public. Among close friends, however, he spoke occasionally of his convictions. He tried always, he told them, to unite past and present, to build upward on the ancient foundations, using the good new ideas but discarding all that was false or faulty. And at last the world discovered for itself that he had done just that. For the first time he learned the taste of full artistic satisfaction.

Not at once, to be sure. Cautiously he waited till the hysteria due largely to his own presence at La Scala had died down, and till *Otello* found its way without him to other theaters, before admitting its complete success. And the new opera did not sweep the world as some of Verdi's earlier works had done. There was in this score no rousing tune that a man might whistle to lift and warm his heart; its gems were not to be pried loose from their golden setting. But the chorus of glowing comments grew steadily louder. Some critics praised structure and design, harmonies, orchestration, character portrayal, while others sought words to describe the opera's sheer beauty and intense emotional power. Some marveled at the magic of certain moments—that spine-tingling cascade of notes with which Desdemona, in a sudden chill of fear, bids her maid good-night, or Otello's heartbroken "And thou, how pale thou art . . . ," the simple phrase sung without orchestra as he turns to Desdemona lying lovely in death, and many, many more. Even the British, so possessive about Shakespeare, forgave the cutting of the drama's whole first act and many favorite lines. It was an English critic who wrote after the Milan performance, "This is the most important first night of modern times." And when the opera reached London, people said that Verdi had captured all of Shakespeare's overtones. No matter that Iago's terrible "Credo" ("I believe in a cruel God") and the tremendous finale of Act III were not drawn from the play at all but were introduced for musical reasons. Desdemona's haunting "Prayer," too—exquisite lines that Boito, suddenly inspired, had scribbled down leaning against a pillar in a country church. Surely Shakespeare, had he used music, might have done the same. *Otello* the opera was *Othello* the drama glorified.

And so, although no hurdy-gurdies twanged forth airs from the new score, no snatches of it lightly sung were to be heard in the streets, admiration for the composer everywhere grew and deepened. By universal admission he had produced an incomparable masterpiece. Thus Verdi the musician came at long last into his harvest years.

Verdi the farmer also was now reaping the reward of all his patient cultivation of livestock and soil. No grain so full-kerneled as from the fields of Sant' Agata, no grapes so sweet as from its vineyards, no milk and cream, butter and cheese so rich and pure as from its dairies. Nor were there finer horses anywhere than the superb animals bred in Verdi's stables. The autumn of his life was at hand, and the days glowed with bright fulfilment.

Nevertheless he could still growl and grumble. Always he had done his best, yet when he asked himself what, in the final accounting, that best was worth, the answer seemed to be: nothing. He had no self-importance to pad his soul with smugness, and, contemplating the world's political tangles and the sorrows, the stupidities and injustices of mankind, the old sense of futility and frustration occasionally closed down on him even now. But the dark moods were growing much less frequent and intense.

From childhood Verdi had carried his unwritten music like a burden. The formula, discovered long ago, that satisfied the public did not satisfy him, and, teaching himself to write operas by writing them, he had gone on and on, bearing his load. Now, after *Otello*, he could at last set it down, look about him with free, tranquil eyes, and rest. Yet he reached his goal only to find that the road wound on beyond it; and, no longer burdened, he must explore a little further, just for fun. Besides, there was an old score to be settled, an old memory to be effaced.

Verdi had never forgotten the cruel disaster of his one attempt at comedy: *King for a Day*, buried a half-century ago. For years he had hoped to redeem that failure—especially since "Jupiter Rossini" had announced that Verdi could never compose a good comic opera—but he had never found a subject that attracted him. There was Shakespeare's *Merry Wives of Windsor*, of course. It had been in the back of his mind almost as long as he could remember because of the immortal Falstaff, the fat knight so gross and awkward of body, so subtle and rapier-keen of wit. But where was Verdi to find a poet who could transform this rambling, shapeless comedy into the bright, compact, swiftly paced libretto of his dreams?

During the winter of 1889-90 Boito, then living on the outskirts of Genoa, was at the Palazzo Doria almost daily. He and Verdi were by now the most devoted of friends; but, even

so, what could they talk about hour after hour, closeted in the
Maestro's study? Was Verdi considering another opera? It
seemed unlikely at his age, and yet these days the two were
in high spirits, as though they shared some happy secret.

Not until the following autumn was the mystery explained
—by Boito himself at a small dinner party in Milan. When,
rising to his feet, he raised his glass, the others naturally assumed that he was about to drink Verdi's health.

But Boito glanced mischievously round the little group.
"Friends, I have the honor to propose a toast. Let us drink
to—the Paunch!"

The lifted wine glasses paused in midair. Verdi was slender.
No one present that evening could be called stout. What did
Boito mean?

Suddenly Ricordi brought his fist down on the table in such
excitement that the silverware jingled and danced. "Falstaff!"
he shouted. "Ah, Maestro, your old dream! At last!"

Everyone cheered and drained his glass, while Verdi, beaming, became the center of a gale of questions.

Yes, yes, it was true. For some time now he and Boito had been hard at work. The libretto would be incomparable—if possible even finer than *Otello*. Much of the best of Falstaff was to be found, not in *The Merry Wives*, but in *Henry IV*, from which Boito, with extraordinary skill, was lifting many of the old rogue's most delicious lines. Verdi talked with the enthusiasm of a youngster.

"And when are we to hear it, Maestro? When will it be produced?"

At once he was veiled in shyness. "Who knows? Never, perhaps. I'm writing, yes, but I assure you only to please myself, for my own amusement. Remember, I'm an old man now. No doubt at my age it's folly to compose at all; but then, we old men are like children."

Before agreeing to do *Falstaff*, Verdi, who was both eager and reluctant, had raised a string of obstacles for Boito to knock down. There were his many years—would he be able to withstand the strain? The creator of a tragedy suffers and is exhausted; but comedy, Boito assured him, exhilarates, refreshing body and mind. Nevertheless, suppose Verdi should not be able to finish? "Then," said Verdi, "your time and labor would have been wasted to no purpose. Not for all the wealth in the world would I have that happen!" To safeguard his friend he took a generous precaution: as always he would pay for the libretto, but it would remain Boito's property as a gift "to remember me by" in case for any reason he (Verdi) should be unable to complete the music. "You are to do with it whatever you see fit," he added; for, though he did not say so, he was quite aware that he might not live. He worried also lest Boito's own opera, *Nerone*, be delayed, but needlessly, since it was still unfinished in 1918 at the time of Boito's death. And then there was the fear of anticlimax—a real danger after *Otello*. But Boito wrote him: "There is only one way of ending your career better than with *Otello*, that is to end it with *Falstaff!*" and Verdi was at last convinced.

Once the matter was decided, he could not hold his eagerness in check, and impatiently set himself to writing fugues—practising at seventy-seven as in his student days—while waiting for the first installments of the libretto to arrive. And what a libretto it was! So carefully had the two men planned it, so brilliantly right were Boito's verses, that the final form differed by only a few words from the first draft Verdi received. Moreover, as Boito had foreseen, Verdi soon found that the actual composing, instead of the familiar, agonizing strain, was pure delight. For his health's sake he worked two hours a day, never more nor less—a schedule that required will power, so hugely was he enjoying himself.

As once Othello, Desdemona, and Iago had been constantly beside him, so now Falstaff was always vividly present to his mind. Inevitably, Verdi began to show the effect of daily contact with the eternal rogue, the lovable, fat rascal who remarked, "I am not only witty in myself but the cause that wit is in other men." The littlest, simplest things could now set the Maestro chuckling, and his big laugh rang out as never before. He was as full of fun as Peppina herself.

But there were interruptions. In 1890 word came from Paris that Muzio had died. His pitiful last letter, full of love and loyalty, brought tears to Verdi's eyes. Poor "Redhead"! Poor, good soul destined to constant misfortune! His marriage, to an American girl, had been a tragic failure. His only child Giuseppe (Verdi's godson) had died. In music, though he lacked the greatest gifts, he had deserved far more success than he attained. "Everything ends," said Verdi. "Life is sad. . . ."

Faccio, too—ill health had forced him to leave La Scala and become head of the Parma Conservatory, a less exacting position. But his malady was fatal, and work of any sort was soon out of the question. Boito, selfless as always, not only took charge of his friend's affairs but substituted for him at Parma so that Faccio's salary might be continued. This unavoidably delayed the last parts of the *Falstaff* libretto, and Verdi, grieving for the conductor who had taken Mariani's place as his favorite, restlessly returned to his fugues while waiting.

Faccio's death moved him deeply. Of late he had lost others of his close friends, most of them men much younger than he. One by one they were going, and with each new sorrow a cold fog of loneliness passed over Verdi. He was beginning to feel the pathetic isolation of great age. But he worked on, two hours a day, nor did the faintest shadow of grief darken the shimmering pages of his music.

By the autumn of 1891 *Falstaff* was finished except for the orchestration—to which Toscanini would one day point as a model for all composers of what orchestration should be— and the inevitable retouching. Verdi had been secretive about the new work, but now, at Sant' Agata, he played and sang the whole score through to Giulio Ricordi.

Peppina, coming to the study door, found the two men at the piano, both unconsciously wearing wide smiles—no one, not even the composer, could listen to this music with a solemn face. Catching Ricordi's eye, she whispered happily, "You see? He's still good—my Verdi!" Indeed he was. Richard Strauss would later call this shining wonder among operas "one of the greatest masterpieces of all time!"

What about the performance? There was still a great deal of work to be done, Verdi insisted, and he refused to be pinned down. He felt that *Falstaff*, composed for his own pleasure, really belonged to him, and even spoke of producing it just for a handful of friends in the drawing-room at Sant' Agata. There was, in fact, some danger that the subtleties of this comedy, so delicate that it was almost chamber music, might be dissolved and lost in a vast auditorium. No one, however, paid much attention to these familiar symptoms of panic. Verdi, though reluctant, was at the same time eager as a child. So Ricordi waited patiently, confident that *Falstaff* would be heard in the Maestro's own good time.

The following spring, 1892, Verdi set aside his score to conduct the "Prayer" from Rossini's *Moses* in Bologna, as part of the centenary celebration of Rossini's birth. "For no one else would I consent, and fortunately I shall never have to do such a thing again. There are not two Rossinis!" But though he disliked the task he went about it with as much zeal as if his whole career depended on this one performance. When he took his place on the stage the audience rose in tribute, and of course gave him an ovation at the end. By the austerity of his manner, however, Verdi tried to deflect the applause from himself to Rossini, whose memory he was there to honor.

*Falstaff* was also interrupted by brief illness and by visits to Montecatini, a health resort where Verdi, careful of his strength, now rested for some weeks every year. But the score was at last ready to be printed, and we now know that he parted from it wistfully. In 1923 Arturo Toscanini, having occasion to consult the manuscript (preserved among other treasures in the Ricordis' safe), found between two pages a slip of paper that, by some mysterious chance, had lain there unnoticed for thirty years. On it was written in Verdi's impulsive handwriting, "The last notes of Falstaff," and a paraphrase of a stanza from the libretto followed:

"All is finished!
"Go, go, old John – – –
"Go thy way, as long as thou canst – – – –
"Diverting specimen of a scoundrel;
"Eternally true, beneath varying masks,
"Always, everywhere!!
"Go – – – Go – – –
"Be on thy way Be on thy way –
          *Farewell!!!*"

Thus, touchingly, the old man had bestowed a final, private blessing on this last child of his brain and heart.

By January 1893 Verdi was in Milan rehearsing the new opera. Although, as with *Otello*, he reserved the right to cancel the performance at any moment if he were displeased, Verdi worked with enthusiasm, taking full responsibility. Six to eight hours a day he spent in the theater, yet he seemed neither weary nor nervous. He ate heartily and, after a tranquil evening game of cards, slept like a child. Sometimes he even returned to La Scala after dinner, but always he was punctually on hand for the morning rehearsal, fresh, rosy, and brimming with energy. Younger men watched him with amazement. He moved freely and easily, he stood erect, his hands and his voice were steady, his speech fluent and sure. His strange, pale, deep-set eyes shone luminous as ever. But for the gleaming whiteness of his hair no one would guess that he was almost eighty.

It was not as though he had only *Falstaff* to occupy him. Letters and callers descended upon him like an avalanche. People wanted to pay their respects, to bring gifts, to ask favors, to solicit contributions for charities, and above all, by hook or crook, to gain admission to the secret and closely guarded rehearsals. Even for a man in the prime of life the pace and pressure would have been hard to bear, but through it all Verdi remained serene.

As in the days before *Otello*, Milan was vibrant with excitement, but there were fewer doubts now. This old man, who dared attempt comedy after a single, historic fiasco fifty-three years before, had acquired an aura of the miraculous. For genius such as his nothing could be impossible. February 9th, the day of the performance, dawned bitter cold, yet by eight o'clock in the morning a dense crowd surrounded La Scala to stand, a shivering, impenetrable mass, until the doors opened that night.

The première! It was *Otello* all over again—the same glowing worship, the same thunderous applause, only that pride and affection for the old "Lion of Busseto" seemed to be even stronger, deeper than before. Once again, uncounted thousands lined the streets to cheer his return from the opera house, but this time there was no terrifying frenzy. Verdi wisely made his escape by an unexpected door and rode through the crowd safe and unmolested, drawn by horses instead of human beings. At the entrance to the Grand Hotel he found that a group of Milan's most distinguished citizens had formed a guard of honor to escort him inside. Upstairs, in his brightly lighted apartment, the former scene of rejoicing was repeated, with flowers, congratulations, serenades, and the throng of happy friends. For the miraculous had come to pass: the incredible Verdi had once again, as Boito put it, "climbed on his own shoulders." Quietly, modestly, he let the excitement whirl around him, yet he was radiant as any youngster first tasting success.

How did he work his miracles? What was his secret? Again and again Boito, who had known the Maestro so long and worked with him so closely, was asked the question. And Boito found the perfect answer. Said he, "It's just that he puts the right note in the right place!"

The papers next day published a rumor that Verdi was about to be created Marquis of Busseto. A title? He protested that he would feel too foolish, too undignified, and hastened to write a government official urging that whoever was responsible for the idea nip it in the bud, thus saving him the embarrassment of having to refuse.

He grumbled, too, because the public seemed to pay more attention to himself than to his opera. And this was true. *Falstaff* had left the audience breathless, and a little cool. This swift and subtle music is, in fact, a maze of enchantment through which only the most agile of mind and ear can, at first hearing, find their way. Even more than *Otello* this score, to which the passing years have merely added luster, is meat not for the crowd but for the connoisseur. And so, although the enthusiasm of the man in the street was faintly reserved, the critics chanted *Falstaff's* praises in loud unison.

Yet they were baffled, and still are. It is their custom to select the choicest measures for comment and quotation, but how choose the high spots of this opera that is all high spot from the first page to the last? One might as well try to catch soap bubbles—reach for a lovely, shimmering, rainbow globe and it is gone, but here's another, and another, and another. Take, for instance, Falstaff's tiny aria, "When I was a page," —a feather-footed moment that floats by like thistledown brushed against the cheek, a few seconds of song that at La Scala literally stopped the show. Is it any more wonderful than the harmonies beneath the twelve strokes of the village bell heard in the moonlit forest, or than the boy-and-girl love music that drifts through the score, as fresh and magical as the first spring breeze? Or take the famous tipsy trill that ripples over the whole orchestra as the fat knight consoles himself with wine. Or the little tune to which, in all his foolish finery, he sets out to woo Mistress Ford—a handful of measures that contain the very essence of human vanity. Or Verdi's ultimate joke—the great final fugue with which he brings down the curtain, proclaiming in this most formal, stiffest, most austere of musical patterns that "All the world's a jest!" Or . . . or . . . Everyone always ends by putting the whole opera in quotation marks.

And this aristocrat of scores was actually written by the people's idol, the blood-and-thunder composer whom the critics, summing up the brassy crudeness, the heavy emphasis, the banal pages that marred so many of his earlier works, had called "vulgar." In this music, so warm and wise and subtle, there were even elusive and delicious hints that Verdi was poking fun at—of all people—Verdi! Self-taught, he had worked clear of all his faults, and in his fine old age this man of tragic gloom and violence could look at the world with amused, tolerant eyes. The days of stress were over, and, forgiving mankind its weakness and its folly, he took his final bow with the most deeply, delicately humorous music ever written. He had never known the careless gaiety of untried youth, but "he laughs best who laughs last."

Which is the greater masterpiece, *Falstaff* or *Otello?* Some musicologists rate one higher, some the other. *Otello* has a stronger pull on the heartstrings; *Falstaff,* "the musicians' opera," is even more nearly perfect in form; and each, in its own field of tragedy or of comedy, stands supreme. The average listener is likely to prefer whichever he knows better, or has lately heard. But neither opera can be absorbed as casual entertainment, with a passive imagination. One's understanding must stretch up on tiptoe, for there is always something more to see. Today, however, the general public shows signs of catching up with the connoisseurs. *Otello*, ranked with Wagner's *Tristan und Isolde* as one of the two greatest tragic operas, was long considered "highbrow"; but it now fills New York's Metropolitan to the doors and stands far up in the list of favorites on the air. As for *Falstaff*, it is admittedly unique. One cannot, for instance, compare it to Wagner's great comedy masterpiece, *The Meistersingers of Nuremberg*, because each (like an elephant and a hummingbird) is wonderful in its own way.

A few weeks after the La Scala première, Verdi went to Rome to supervise the final rehearsals of *Falstaff* there, with Mascheroni (Faccio's successor) and the original cast. Unparalleled ovations were to be expected in Milan since it was the Maestro's operatic home, but the capital city now paid him equally moving tribute. So swamped with invitations was he that he had to decline them all by means of a newspaper announcement. On the night of the performance King Humbert, although no opera devotee, appeared at the theater unexpectedly, and, leading the Maestro to the front of the royal box, presented him to the cheering audience. No higher honor was possible. Italy's heroes have always been men of the arts rather than of the sword, and she has bred more than her share of the world's great men. Proudly, and with enduring love, the Romans gazed up at the simple old man whose music had become part of the nation's heritage. In the long procession of Italian immortals who have enriched and comforted the human spirit his would be an honored place, and they saw him as the living symbol of all that was most precious to his countrymen. As she looked down at all those glowing faces, white-haired Peppina, radiant between Signora Ricordi and Teresa Stolz in the box next to Queen Elena's, felt that this was the climax of her Verdi's whole career.

But there was more to come. On the following evening the Maestro was surprised to hear strains of the *Nabucco* Overture. His hotel adjoined the theater, and, going to the balcony, he saw Mascheroni and the entire orchestra assembled on the theater terrace to serenade him. Verdi, taken unawares, was pleased as a child before a Christmas tree. *Nabucco*—how long ago that seemed! As the best-loved melodies out of his past

came floating up to him he listened in delight, remembering.
The world was now a different place. But he himself had never
changed, and his music was basically what it had always
been—only, over the span of years, almost incredibly improved.

"This is wonderful!" he exclaimed. "What a charming
gesture, eh? Just like the Little Imp!"—it was his pet name
for Mascheroni. "I'm enjoying this. Quick, Boito, you must
find another subject so we can get to work on a new opera
right away!"

He was not serious, of course; he seldom was these days.
Lately there ran through all his letters and his talk a rich
chuckle, a warm, crinkling smile. He joked constantly, and
when his jokes were poor laughed at the feebleness of his own
wit. Vanished were the dark, doubting moods. "All the
world's a jest!"—a comic fugue!

Yet it caused him a pang of regret to realize that his opera
career had at last come to a close. He knew that he would
miss the comradeship of theater life and work, the tense,
ardent weeks of preparation when everything but the task in
hand must be forgotten, and especially the familiar, terrible,
wonderful suspense of a first night, which is like nothing else
in the world. All that was over now, and he could not help a
farewell nostalgic glance at this life he had loved more than
he knew.

His admirers, however, refused to be convinced that *Falstaff*
was indeed the end. There were rumors that another opera
was already in the making, and people even spoke knowingly
of *King Lear*. Ah, *Lear*—the long, long dream that never did
come true. . . . If only in those days he had had Boito to
help him as only Boito could. Too late now.

Laughingly, Verdi waved aside the queries that came his
way. Begin another score? At eighty? Only a fool or a madman
would think of such a thing. No, he was through. Besides, he
was eager to devote his full attention to a very different sort of
undertaking—an undertaking which, already planned and
begun, gave him such satisfaction that he often said, "Of all
my works this is my favorite!"

[ 269 ]

# CHAPTER NINETEEN

# Beneath My Royal Mantle

## 1893-1901

WITH Peppina and the distinguished architect Camillo Boito, Arrigo's brother, Verdi leaned over the blueprints littering the big table in his study and beamed with satisfaction.

"Splendid! Excellent!" he exclaimed. "See, Peppina, how well the housekeeping arrangements have been planned: kitchen, scullery, laundry, and here, the storage space. These are the offices. And look at the fine courtyard where the old people can enjoy the sunshine. Here's the music room and the chapel. And these are the living quarters—the fifty double bedrooms."

"But, Verdi," said Peppina, "some of the inmates might prefer a single room."

"That's true, but at their age it's not good to be all alone. Suppose someone should suddenly be taken ill? Then his roommate can go for help. And there'll be screens for privacy. But, Camillo, why should these rooms have two windows each? They'd be bright and airy with only one, I'm sure. We must economize, you know. What with the taxes and Sant' Agata I'm not as rich as people imagine. Schemes of this sort so often end in failure because expenses have not been carefully foreseen. There's the upkeep to be considered—we can't risk running short of funds later on. I want these poor souls to have every comfort without useless extravagance."

The architect agreed. "Maestro, what do you intend to call the place?" he asked. " 'Home for Aged Musicians,' perhaps, or 'Retreat for Aged Artists'?"

Verdi shook his head. "No, nothing like that. Why remind these poor old people of their poverty? In a sense, of course, they'll be my guests, but I want them to feel that the place belongs to them, that it's their home. We'll call it the *Casa di Riposo* [House of Rest]."

Nowadays Verdi received so many appeals from charitable organizations that he had had a form letter prepared, politely declining to contribute. "Stingy!" the neighbors muttered, eyeing his vast estate and his fine crops. He let them talk. The fortune he had made was not to be scattered in small, futile donations to this and that cause, however worthy. All too often these charities were badly administered and the gifts served no purpose except to gratify the giver. No, he would save toward the fulfilment of a long-cherished idea.

Verdi had never forgotten the taste of misfortune, and in these days of his full success he could not help contrasting his own glowing fate with that of the singer who has lost her voice, the 'cellist grown too old and feeble to hold his orchestral job, the pianist whose fingers time has hopelessly stiffened, the composer who learned too late that he could not compose. . . . All of them had loved music, all dreamed great dreams not destined to come true. Though the broken careers were past mending, Verdi could and would save these unfortunates from anxiety and destitution, bring security and peace to their last years.

Now that the home he planned for them was about to become reality, Verdi decided that when his time came, instead of being walled away in some cold, marble monument, he would want to be buried among these humble old musicians who had struggled as he had done, but without reward—men like himself except for inscrutable fate. Some day both he and Peppina would lie here; for them, too, it would be the House of Rest.

The home was to be built on the outskirts of Milan. Back in 1889 Verdi had already bought land for the purpose, but so quietly that the newspapers did not discover and announce the fact till 1891. "At least," said the Maestro, "we managed to keep the secret for two years!" And, shunning publicity as always, he continued to plan this "favorite" of his works during the time that he composed *Falstaff*.

Not that he was entirely through with *Falstaff* even now. Paris was to hear it in the spring of 1894—at the Opéra Comique since, being a comedy, it was ineligible for the Opéra itself. Verdi, old though he was, planned to be present and even made a few tiny revisions in the score, destroying the earlier version with his usual care. Only the final form of a work of art, he believed, should be available to the public, and above all he was determined that no odds and ends of music should come to light after his death. He was aware how greedily a composer's papers are ransacked when he dies. Sometimes, of course, a treasure is unearthed; more often, however, unworthy fragments, experiments, and mistakes are published and performed simply because they are in a great man's handwriting. This Verdi considered unfair both to the composer and the public. He had mentioned the matter to his cousin Maria (now married to the son of his old friend, Dr. Carrara). There were his sketches, exercises, the shadowy hints of *Lear*—when the time came she would know what to do.

The news that *Falstaff* would appear at the Opéra Comique no sooner got about than the Opéra, jealous no doubt, asked permission to produce *Otello* first, in Italian! Never before had the rule forbidding performances in any language but French been considered breakable. No matter: for Verdi an exception would be made.

Though flattered, the Maestro firmly refused. Such an innovation, he said, could only bewilder and disappoint the audience. The Opéra must be patient until Boito and Du Locle had completed their translation. Meantime he added the inevitable ballet music (always omitted now) and, mistrusting the ability of the Parisian chorus, prepared a special, somewhat simpler version of the difficult third-act finale. *Otello* was definitely scheduled, in French, for October 1894 in spite of Verdi's exclamation of protest: "*Falstaff* and *Otello* within six months? Too much Verdi! Paris will never stand for it!"

He was mistaken. Each opera in turn was a triumph such as few composers, French or foreign, living or dead, had ever been accorded. Here, too, in "the capital of the world," Verdi had reached the summit. There were no further fields to conquer. On both occasions he was honored with even more banquets, speeches, decorations, what not, than on any of his previous visits. For a man close to eighty-one, all this was strenuous, but he enjoyed it intensely for he found in Paris not idle praise, but real appreciation, and knew that he had at last made himself understood there. It pleased him especially that among his most ardent worshipers were the Wagnerians, the very people who had hitherto believed that all opera should follow the great German's lead. Verdi himself, though he resented Wagner's influence and imitators, admired much of his music. Now it was good to see the world learning what he himself had always known: that there was room for both.

Even though there would be no more Verdian operas the old man could not drop his lifelong habit of putting notes on paper. He continued to work—"only a little, but every day" —on *Four Sacred Pieces* begun before *Falstaff* absorbed all his attention. One of these, the *Ave Maria*, composed on a so-called "enigmatic scale," the Maestro considered hardly more than a stunt, and it is sometimes omitted in performance. The others, a *Stabat Mater*, a *Hymn to the Virgin Mary*, and a *Te Deum*, he took more seriously. For the *Te Deum* especially he sought out and studied ancient scores, particularly those of Palestrina, whom he worshiped, the later Marcello, and Purcell. Not that Verdi wanted to produce a fake antique; rather, he was unwilling to put any musical form to his own use without a thorough knowledge of the roots from which it sprang. The eighty-year-old master was a pupil still.

As always, Verdi drew his inspiration directly from the text, and these *Sacred Pieces*, though they lack the immense vitality of the Requiem Mass, prove that his aging hand had lost none of its skill. The music, dramatic and deeply felt, has a pure, austere beauty all its own.

The *Te Deum*, for double chorus and orchestra, might have been composed expressly for a special, historic concert on May 11, 1946, so appropriate was it to that occasion. In World War II, La Scala was all but destroyed by bombs, and to raise funds with which to rebuild it Toscanini, then seventy-nine, returned to Milan after sixteen years of voluntary exile from Mussolini's régime. In the venerable opera house, cradle of so much great music, this greatest of living conductors led a series of concerts that filled the temporarily repaired auditorium with people of prominence and wealth who came from far and wide, and paid fabulous prices for tickets. The first program, broadcast to every European home and piped through loudspeakers to tens of thousands in the cathedral square, was symbolic of Italy's liberation and rebirth: Rossini's "Prayer" from *Moses*, the whole third act of Puccini's *Manon l'Escaut*, the magnificent "Prologue" to Boito's *Mefistofele*, and, of course, "Go, thought, on golden wings"—the beloved chorus that had ushered in the Verdian era and heralded the dawn of Italian freedom. The overtures to *Nabucco* and *The Sicilian Vespers* were also heard; and, unforgettably, the *Te Deum*, which is not only a song of grateful praise to God but, above all, a profoundly stirring prayer for salvation. For this rare and thrilling event, at Toscanini's request, certain guests of honor proudly occupied the Royal Box (now stripped of all its trimmings) and the adjacent boxes—twenty old musicians from Verdi's own beloved House of Rest.

This memorable performance was to take place fifty years after the Maestro, working slowly but steadily, brought his *Four Sacred Pieces* to completion. Absorbed in them, and busy with his innumerable affairs, he grumbled cheerfully that he seemed fated to labor till his last breath. Though he was beginning to tire easily he remained remarkably active, and took keen interest in the rising generation of composers—Mascagni, Puccini, and the rest—befriending and advising them with paternal kindness. Puccini even came to be spoken of as "the

Crown Prince," so highly did the Maestro think of him. On reading the libretto of *La Tosca*, Verdi envied Puccini the opportunity to set it. The old, infallible bait, a good story, could still lure the Maestro; on one occasion he actually considered composing opera again, but, being eighty-three, wisely put aside the temptation.

Verdi had mellowed and grown genial, but he could still say no. He refused to write his memoirs, protesting that his music was quite enough—no one should be condemned to read his prose. He declined to allow various musical institutions to use his name, as many were anxious to do. The Milan Conservatory wished to be called the Verdi Conservatory, but—"When I was young they didn't want me and they shan't have me now that I'm old!" said the Maestro wryly. Still shielding himself from the public eye, still focusing on the future rather than the past, he declared that "my name smells dusty—it bores even me." These days, however, there was a chuckle in his growl. He had acquired a serenity more to be desired than the thoughtless exuberance of youth; his was the seasoned happiness of an old man who had surmounted every obstacle in his destined path, and was justly and universally beloved.

But the sun always goes down, and every sunset, no matter how golden, fades at last. For Verdi twilight was to come suddenly and swiftly.

It was so perfect, this late rose that had opened to the still warm autumn air. Peppina must see it. She had aged recently—there had been a long attack of bronchitis from which she had only just recovered—and now, if she ventured as far as the garden, it was to walk with small, feeble steps, leaning on her Verdi's still stalwart arm. Carefully, so as not to spill the dewdrop quivering like a liquid diamond at its heart, he picked the rose and brought it to the house.

He found her lying on a couch, tired but wakeful. "Peppina, look," he said. "So beautiful! And such a fragrance! You must smell it."

She bent her feverish face to the cool petals. "What a pity—

I can't smell anything at all! You know, I seem to have a
little cold."

But the cold was pneumonia. A few days later, on November 14, 1897, Peppina died.

Immediately Verdi's lawyer hastened to Sant' Agata—so
many things must be attended to. He found the Maestro
alone in his study, standing motionless, tearless, erect.

"You must forgive me," said Verdi quietly; "I can't talk
to you now."

As the lawyer reverently turned to leave he noticed that the piano had been closed.

Once or twice during the following days Verdi wandered through the home that he and Peppina had so loved. In every doorway he paused, and, gazing at each familiar room as though he saw it now for the first time, he whispered: "Peppina's gone. She's not here . . . not any more . . ." Quietly, bravely, he struggled to grow used to this strange world without her, and as the weeks of impenetrable loneliness dragged on he wrote a friend, who also had suffered a bereavement, "The deepest sorrow does not seek expression." With a fresh pang the memory of his children in their tiny graves returned, and more than ever he envied other men their sons and daughters.

Not that the Maestro was literally alone. From this time onward his cousin, Maria Carrara, took devoted care of him and of the household. Teresa Stolz, too, and Boito were with him almost constantly. He loved them all, and yet—how young they seemed! Of his contemporaries he alone survived; there was no one left with whom he shared, as with Peppina, unspoken memories, and the weight of his years burdened him.

He still had work to do. The *Sacred Pieces* were to be presented at a concert in Paris in April 1898, and Verdi, though eighty-four years old, would have liked to supervise the performance himself. But his health, so remarkable until Peppina's death, had weakened; signs of heart trouble appeared, and the doctors would not permit him to undertake the fatiguing journey. The devoted Boito, therefore, went to Paris in his stead, and conscientiously carried out the Maestro's instructions. The old zeal for perfection had not slackened; Verdi wrote his friend last-minute advice sometimes at the rate of two letters a day. And he was still young enough to feel the familiar excitement. On the day before the event he murmured anxiously from time to time, "Tomorrow night's the night!" One might have supposed that this was his first venture.

To Verdi's relief and pleasure, the *Sacred Pieces* were enthusiastically received in Paris, and later in Turin under the baton of Arturo Toscanini. In preparation for this, the young conductor—a man cast in Verdi's own mold—studied the scores at the old composer's side, and a memorable performance resulted.

Toscanini's superb revival of *Falstaff* at La Scala the following year, 1899, delighted the Maestro. By this time people had grown accustomed to the opera; and, no longer dazzled and bewildered, they found it as lovable as it was brilliant. Again and again Verdi was told that this iridescent music seemed like the work of a much younger man—Rossini, after all, had written his immortal *Barber of Seville* at twenty-four— and this pleased him intensely. For by now he both felt and looked his age. Though he stood straight as ever, he no longer appeared tall, and his clothes seemed to hang loosely on his weakening body. His mind was keen and his memory unimpaired, but his eyesight began to dim and his hearing was no longer so acute as it had been. He dared not trust for any distance those long legs that had tramped so many miles in sun and wind, and took to visiting the beloved garden in a wheel chair. There had been many years when he dreamed of leisure as a blessing. Now it was forced upon him, and he despised his helplessness and inactivity.

Sometimes at Sant' Agata the piano sounded from Verdi's room, and he could be heard singing to himself in a thin, whispery old voice. "*Dormiro sol*'—I'll sleep only beneath my royal mantle, only in the dark vault of the tomb. . . ." It was a favorite aria from *Don Carlo*, sung by Philip, the sorrowful and lonely King, as he waits through the slow, wakeful hours for dawn.

Although Verdi still summered at Sant' Agata, he seldom went to Genoa these days. Without Peppina the Villa Doria was no longer the same, and he preferred to spend the winter months at Milan's Grand Hotel in the familiar suite. Here in the evenings his dearest friends gathered round him. Sometimes he merely listened to their talk; sometimes he took a lively part in the conversation, astonishing them with his immense musical knowledge and the ripe lucidity of his opinions. He spoke of everything—opera, the arts, world affairs—and looked always to the present and the future instead of recalling the past as so many old people do. In another mood he would enjoy a game of cards, but invariably he urged his friends to stay with him as late as possible. For an old man who slept but fitfully the nights were long . . . too long . . .

In July 1900 Verdi was shaken by an event that shocked the world: the brutal assassination of Italy's King Humbert by an anarchist. The widowed Queen Elena gave expression to her grief in a simple, heartfelt, and beautiful prayer which was published throughout the mourning nation. Verdi had seen much violence and disaster, but the well of compassion had not yet gone dry, and as he read those pure and touching words the embers of his creative power flickered once again. Hauntingly, the Queen's Prayer sang itself in his mind just as, long before, "Go, thought, on golden wings" had done. He took up his pen, ruled a sheet of paper into staves, and sketched a few measures. But how his hand shook! The writing, once so swift and sure, was barely legible. And the effort! Almost at once he wearied and, impatient at his own weakness, put the unfinished page aside. Though he could still hear music within himself, at eighty-six he lacked the strength to set it down.

Eighty-six, eighty-seven. . . . In spite of Verdi's amused denials, rumors of a new opera still persisted. People forgot that this marvelous old man was only mortal after all. But on January 21, 1901, the world realized with a shock that he, too, must die. He had had a stroke. The end, the doctors said, could not be far off—might come at any moment.

It had happened as the Maestro dressed himself that morning. His collar button slipped from his stiff fingers and, provokingly, rolled under a chest of drawers. To get down and look for it was no simple matter for his old bones, but Maria Carrara had just been called from the room. Should he summon help? No. This humiliating weakness—he must conquer it. Laboriously he stooped over, and crumpled on the floor,

The news spread rapidly, and a crowd soon gathered in front of the hotel. No cheers now, no serenades. Only a muffled silence, for the street, closed to all traffic, was ankle-deep in straw lest any sound disturb the dying man—a gesture touching in its futility. The minutes, the hours, ticked on— all day, all night, another day . . . Still Verdi breathed, and still the patient throng waited beneath his windows anxiously watching for the drawing of a curtain, the flicker of a light, something, anything. From time to time people wandered wearily away, melting down the hushed streets, but others took their places, whispering, "Have you heard anything? Is there any change?" And the answer was always "Nothing!" Day and night, night and day, they stood there scarcely knowing why, too concerned for this man they did not know to go about their normal occupations.

Inside the hotel several rooms were given over to the swarm of reporters who dozed and smoked and murmured drearily together, watching with tired eyes the comings and goings of the doctors, the Carraras, Boito, Teresa Stolz, the Ricordis, and many more. Telegrams were prepared, leaving blank only the day and hour of the Maestro's passing: telegrams to all the crowned heads of Europe and to the newspapers of Rome, Paris, London, Berlin, Vienna, St. Petersburg, Madrid, Cairo, New York. Runners stood ready, and twice, when the end seemed near, the telegraph office was kept open all night. And still Verdi breathed on.

The fourth day came, the fifth. People began to mention remarkable recoveries they had heard of. Perhaps . . . Yet the doctors insisted that there was no hope. The Maestro still lay unconscious, his eyebrows drawn together in the familiar frown of concentration as he fought his last battle, the only battle that he could not win. While the hours dragged by, his friends stood at his bedside, listening, listening to the labored breath that came and went and paused and came again. Boito, watching the grim struggle, was shaken with helpless anger. He had seen men die before, young men with much to live for, yet never had he so hated the blind, stupid, evil power called death as when it fastened on this old, old man, this victorious warrior whose days had been many and full and fine.

For a whole paralyzing week Verdi fought on. Then, at ten minutes before three on the morning of January 27, 1901, the breathing stopped and did not start again. The giant spirit passed, and with its passing the world became for all those waiting crowds a colder, darker place.

"Giuseppe Verdi is dead!" Around the globe wires hummed with the news. From the great of every land, and from the humble too, tributes at once poured in. And all the next day in Milan an interminable stream of people passed with bowed heads through the Maestro's bedroom—the hundreds, thousands, who wanted one last look at the sad, strong face, now so unutterably calm and still.

Italians love ceremonial pomp, and in their hands it becomes, not a vain, empty show, but impressive and dramatic. It was natural that they should plan for Italy's best-loved son a funeral of unequaled magnificence. But first—the will.

It was found at Sant' Agata—a simple document, clear, straightforward, typical of the man who wrote it. Half his fortune he left to Maria Carrara. With the rest he had remembered all for whom he cared. To each of his close friends went some keepsake, and to the faithful household servants substantial sums of money. Charities whose work appealed to him received generous gifts, especially his hospital at Villanova and Busseto's Monte di Pietà. But by far the largest amount, plus all his future royalties, was left to the House of Rest, where certain of his personal treasures were to be kept forever: his many trophies and decorations, and the battered spinet for which, nearly eighty years before, Carlo Verdi had bravely spent his savings. There, among the aged musicians, Verdi requested to be buried with Peppina. And the will ended thus:

I direct that my funeral shall be very modest, at dawn or at the time of the Ave Maria in the evening, without singing or music.

I do not wish my death to be announced with the usual formalities.

To the poor of the village of Sant' Agata six thousand lire shall
be distributed on the day after my death.

GIUSEPPE VERDI

Abruptly, and in shocked surprise, the elaborate funeral
preparations were brought to a halt, while horrified voices
were raised in protest. No longer, they cried, did Verdi have
a right to draw the veil of privacy. His wishes must be dis-
regarded—he belonged to the world. Italy should and would
pay fitting homage to her glorious son. But others declared
with equal vigor that his will must be respected, and a violent
controversy raged until a compromise solution was agreed
upon. Since some weeks would be required to make ready a
worthy tomb at the House of Rest, let Verdi be buried temporarily in Milan's vast cemetery, where Peppina already lay.
Then, when the time came, let both be transported to their
final resting place with all the pomp and splendor that anyone could desire.

Accordingly, before sunrise on January 30 the humble
procession set out: a priest carrying a cross, two more bearing
tall candles, the hearse without ornament, draped in somber
black, and, following, perhaps a hundred silent mourners.
No flowers, no music, nothing—not a sound. As Verdi wished.

But there was something he had not foreseen. Being the
man he was, he could not guess that from five o'clock of that
raw winter dawn the old woman who peddled flowers in the
Cathedral square would stand on a street corner waiting to
see him pass. The prosperous lawyer, too, who bought his
boutonnières from her; the waiter from the sidewalk café,
and the businessman he served; the shabby seamstress, and
the fine lady for whom she sewed; the poor student, and the
professor who taught him; the hack driver, the judge, the
newsboy, the senator, the engineer, the vagrant, the work-
man and his wife—her baby on her arm, a sleepy toddler
clinging to her skirt—the soldier, the Marquis, the grocer,
the banker, the fiddler, the clerk: they were all there. Thousands upon thousands, they waited in frozen silence, and as
the simple coffin came in sight pressed closer, closer, jamming

[ 282 ]

the way so that from time to time the slow procession wavered and halted, till a hastily summoned squad of cavalry, whose drawn swords glinted in the early, wintry sun, could force a passage through that mute, grieving throng.

Let the experts argue about theories of art; these people did not know about such things, or care. For them, as for Verdi himself, there was no right and wrong in music—there was only good and bad. Shoulder to shoulder they stood, heads bowed to honor the great dead, because this man had at one time or another flooded their souls unforgettably with beauty, because his ageless melodies had fallen on their hearts like rain after a drought. He was their voice, speaking the things that all men felt and none could say. The whole world revered him, and he was theirs, their very own. They did not want to let him go.

In Rome the Senate closed. Business all over Italy marked time. And the following evening La Scala, dark and empty since Verdi's illness, opened its doors for a memorial concert. Toscanini conducted; Tamagno sang; so did a remarkable new young tenor named Enrico Caruso, and many, many others. Gabriele d'Annunzio, Italy's poet laureate, was moved to write his *Ode to Verdi*, which closes with the line: "He wept and loved for all mankind."

In due time the peasant of Le Roncole and his gentle wife were borne in more than royal splendor to their last resting place. Velvet and gold, plumed horses, palm leaves, wreaths of flowers, soldiers in brilliant uniform, bemedaled diplomats from every land marching afoot, and gleaming ranks of cavalry—it was a not-to-be-forgotten spectacle. And as a climax Toscanini led a chorus of nine hundred. "Va, pensiero," they began—"Go, thought,"—and spontaneously three hundred thousand voices joined in the great song. This was Italy herself, full-throated, pouring out her soul.

Statues soon appeared everywhere, even in then distant New York. Verdi Societies, Verdi Theaters, flourished. Sant' Agata became a national museum, Le Roncole a place of pilgrimage. In 1913, centenary of the Maestro's birth, Italy staged a mammoth celebration with festivals and sports, agricultural contests, prizes for choral singing, and a deluge of opera throughout the land. And little towns, too poor to afford schools, hospitals, or water supply, nevertheless raised funds to erect a monument to *Il Nostro Grande*—Our Great One—in the public square. Surely Verdi himself would have frowned; yet every man who paid his pennies acquired a tiny share of immortality and walked forth with new dignity and pride.

The finest monument to the Maestro's memory, however, is neither marble nor bronze, but the living music. Verdi was no Beethoven before whom, as he said, "we must all bow." He was no Mozart, composing all the kinds of music that there are as if by heavenly dictation. Nor was he a Wagner, discovering a whole new world and changing the future course of music like a torrential storm shifting a riverbed. Verdi had limitations. But he was a superb craftsman; he had supremely the gift of melody—which he himself described as that element in music which ages least; and he was born with the mysterious power to transmute emotion into sound. In spite of varying fashions and new ways, he can still free his listeners from their care-weary selves, nourish the spirit, and enlarge the heart. Time has not altered his essential magic. Man and musician, his gigantic figure towers still, a symbol and a solace to his fellowmen.

# NOTE ON SOURCES, AND ACKNOWLEDGMENTS

How do we know that snow was falling on a certain night more than a century ago when Verdi, rounding a street corner, collided so fatefully with Merelli? Or that later, as he went home with the libretto of *Nabucco* in his pocket, he felt first a vague dread, then anger? Verdi himself tells us these things in his own much-quoted account of his early days. How do we know what went on behind the scenes at the première of *Macbeth*, back in 1847? The original Lady Macbeth has left us her recollection of that event. Verdi in Naples is vivid to us through the cartoons of his friend Melchiorre Delfico (the whole series is reproduced in Luzio's *Carteggi Verdiani*), that wittily reveal everyday aspects of the composer —and of Lulu—never set down in writing. We are familiar with the daily routine at Sant' Agata because Ghislanzoni, among others, has given us a detailed description of his visit there. We know how Verdi received those Christmas cakes of Ricordi's and can reconstruct the scene from Peppina's sprightly "thank-you" letters. Boito himself has told us how he felt when Verdi died. Thus, piece by piece, the picture is put together so that even thoughts and feelings, when they are stated, are based on evidence, not on invention.

The mosaic of description, anecdote, conversation, and contemporary opinion forming the background of this story is derived from sources too numerous to list in full, and many of them out of print, untranslated, or both. Most useful, however, among the older books were those by Pougin and Bellaigue. In *Verdi: Milan and "Othello"* (London, Ward and Downey, 1887) Blanche Roosevelt has given us a dazzled but priceless first-hand account of the birth of a masterpiece. Yet her biographical chapters are stuffed with inaccuracies that prove how little Verdi the human being was known to the public during his lifetime. Few men, indeed, perhaps none of his eminence, have been victims of so many confusions and misstatements, some of which tend to persist despite correction. The authority, therefore, for the facts as presented here is Carlo Gatti (brother of the late Giulio Gatti-Casazza, former director of the Metropolitan Opera Company) whose monumental but still untranslated *Verdi*, published in 1931, clarified the errors and discrepancies frequent in earlier works, besides bringing to light a wealth of new material. Nevertheless, for interest's sake, one or two likely but unproven anecdotes which Signor Gatti questions, have been included. Thus in 1914 a tablet was placed on the wall of the church at Le Roncole commemorating the infant Verdi's escape there from the marauding Cossacks in 1814. Yet this incident, of which the most plausible version is retold here, has never been traced to an eyewitness and consequently remains somewhat legendary.

It is, however, from Verdi's own story and, above all, from his letters that one comes best to know the man's true stature. Fortunately the legacy is vast: throughout most of his life he kept a private, business-like, and unself-conscious record of his correspondence. Furthermore his letters (and Peppina's) were treasured by those who received them. Several volumes have been published in Italian, and more may be expected; and Paul Stefan's excellent German collection, with a preface by Franz Werfel, has appeared in English (*Verdi, the Man in His Letters*, New York, Fischer, 1942).

Since a full record of Verdi's days would run to many tomes, much has necessarily been omitted, especially matters that seemed of musicological rather than of general interest. For instance the mysterious *Rocester* is not even listed here among his works. This opera, mentioned briefly in Verdi's early correspondence, has ever since baffled the scholars, many of whom considered it a first effort later destroyed. More probably (as Kathleen O'Donnell Hoover pointed out in the

*Musical Quarterly* for October 1942) *Rocester* was merely the original title of *Oberto,* the story's locale having been shifted from England to Italy during revision of the libretto.

Since in this informal account of Verdi's life the emphasis is on the man rather than the music, there is no serious attempt here to discuss his scores. The subject, however, is illuminatingly treated both by Francis Toye (*Giuseppe Verdi, the Man and His Works*, New York, Knopf, 1946) and by Dyneley Hussey (*Verdi*, New York, Dutton, 1940) whose invaluable biographies I have repeatedly and thankfully consulted.

To Miss Margherita de Vecchi and to Mr. Luigi Villa I am indebted for the loan of books which the war made unobtainable, and which they kindly and patiently permitted me to use for many months. I am also grateful to Mrs. John de Witt Peltz, Publications Director of the Metropolitan Opera Guild, for allowing me to consult the files of *Opera News* at will. And special thanks are due to Mrs. Elizabeth C. Moore for her indispensable editorial assistance.

# NOTE ON PRONUNCIATION

In pronouncing Italian names, it is well to remember that the letters k and j do not occur in the Italian alphabet. Therefore c and g must do double duty, as follows:

C and g are hard (as in *come*, *go*) except before i and e.
    Cavaletti = Kavaletti        Arrigo = Arrigo

C and g are soft (as in *church*, *gem*, *joy*) before i and e. This explains the pronunciation of some English words of Italian origin (for instance *'cello* = *chello*).
Fenice = Feniche    Giuseppe = Juseppe    Luigia = Luija

To indicate the hard sound before i and e, the Italians add h. (Thus ch = the English k.)
    Baistrocchi = Baistrocki    Merighi = Merigi

C never has the sound of s (as in *cell*).

Because g before n is ugly (for instance *ignore*), the Italians have softened the sound thus:
    Pugnatta = Punyatta    Lavigna = Lavinya

In Italian the vowel sounds do not vary as in English. They have approximately these values:
a = a in *and*  e = e in *end*  i = ee  o = o in *only*  u = u in *pull*

Unlike English, Italian is pronounced exactly as it is spelled. The pronunciation is therefore easy if the above rules are borne in mind.

# Stories of the Operas

AIDA

UN BALLO IN MASCHERA (THE MASKED BALL)

DON CARLO

FALSTAFF

LA FORZA DEL DESTINO (THE FORCE

OF DESTINY)

OTELLO

RIGOLETTO

SIMON BOCCANEGRA

LA TRAVIATA (THE ERRING ONE)

IL TROVATORE (THE TROUBADOUR)

# *Aida*

THE SCENE is laid in ancient Egypt. Although the background is historically authentic, characters and incidents are fictional.

*Act I.* In the King's palace at Memphis, Ramfis (bass), the High Priest, tells the young warrior Radames (tenor) that the Ethiopians are about to invade Egypt and that the goddess Isis has chosen a commander to lead the defending Egyptian armies. Ramfis goes to inform the King, and Radames, hoping that the honor will fall to him, dreams of winning glory and freeing his heavenly Aida, an Ethiopian slave whom he loves. Aida's mistress, the King's daughter Amneris (mezzo-soprano), herself loves Radames but suspects that his heart is Aida's, and, finding him alone, slyly questions him. When Aida (soprano), grieving over the approaching war, joins them, Amneris watches the lovers jealously. With priests, soldiers, and officials of his court, the King (bass) now enters to receive a messenger who announces that the Ethiopians are already threatening the city of Thebes. They are led by their king, the renowned warrior Amonasro, who, unknown to the Egyptians, is Aida's father. The King of Egypt then proclaims Radames the chosen general, Amneris presents him with the royal standard, and, with cheers for his victory, all but Aida depart. The homesick girl, aware that her rescue is the Ethiopians' objective, shudders for her countrymen. Torn between love of her father and love of Radames, she longs only for death as she implores the gods to take pity on her suffering.

At a solemn ceremony in the temple of Vulcan the sacred sword of Egypt is bestowed upon Radames while priests and priestesses chant and perform a ritual dance, praying the great god Ptah to grant victory to the Egyptians.

*Act II.* In the palace, slaves dance for the amusement of Amneris while her attendants adorn her for the festival in celebration of the Ethiopian defeat, and all sing praises of the hero, Radames. When the sorrowing Aida appears Amneris dismisses the others and, saying first that Radames is slain,

[ 291 ]

then that he lives, traps the girl into betraying her love. Hitherto the princess has treated Aida as a dear friend rather than a slave. Now, to Aida's despair, her hypocritical kindness turns to jealous fury.

Before the gates of Thebes the King and Amneris, enthroned amid a joyful throng, review the Egyptian troops, returning with trophies of victory. Amneris crowns Radames with laurel, and her father promises to grant him any boon. Among the Ethiopian prisoners who are now led before the King, Aida recognizes her father, Amonasro (baritone), but at his request she does not betray his royal identity. The priests demand death for the captives. The people, however, pity them and beg that their lives be spared. Radames, secretly moved by Aida's tears, asks the prisoners' release as his boon, and this the King grants, keeping only Aida's father as hostage. Then, as supreme reward, he gives Radames the hand of Amneris in betrothal.

*Act III.* With Ramfis, on the eve of her wedding, Amneris goes by boat to the temple of Isis on the Nile, and enters to pray that her bridegroom may love her as she loves him. Aida, coming to a secret rendezvous with Radames, is startled by the arrival of her father, who tells her that he has discovered their love and that, since the Ethiopians are again about to attack, she must induce Radames to betray the route by which the Egyptian army will march to battle. She refuses; but Amonasro, pleading with her to save her homeland from the ravages of war, then threatening to disown her, at last prevails upon the distracted girl. At Radames' approach, he hides among the palms. Since the unhappy lovers are powerless to prevent Radames' marriage to Amneris, Aida persuades him to flee with her to her beloved Ethiopia where an idyllic life awaits them. As they are about to depart she asks how they can avoid the Egyptian army. Radames replies that his soldiers will march by way of the Gorge of Napata, whereupon Amonasro comes forth and reveals himself as Ethiopia's dreaded king, whom he had tricked his captors into believing dead. Amneris, returning from the temple, has overheard and now denounces Radames as a traitor. Amonasro raises his dagger against the princess but Radames steps between them, and Amonasro and Aida disappear into the night as Ramfis summons the guards. Radames surrenders the sacred sword to him in disgrace.

*Act IV*. In a hall outside the palace courtroom, the remorseful Amneris orders Radames brought before her and pleads for his love. When he accuses her of Aida's death, she tells him that Amonasro has been slain but that Aida has vanished, and offers him freedom on condition that he renounce his beloved forever. Radames refuses, and is led back to his cell. In despair the princess watches the procession of priests enter the courtroom to pronounce judgment upon him. Radames is then led to trial, and Amneris hears the priests within solemnly call upon him three times to absolve himself of treason. He remains silent, and is declared guilty and condemned to be buried alive. As the priests march out Amneris frantically curses them for their cruelty.

Radames, in a rock-walled cell beneath the temple floor sees the slab of stone above him lowered into place. He dreams, sadly of his Aida, only to discover that she is there hiding in the tomb to die with him. Protesting that she is too young and fair for death, he tries in vain to move the stone, while above, in the temple, priests and priestesses go about their mystic rites. The lovers, growing faint, bid earth farewell in half-delirious ecstasy. As they lose consciousness, the stricken Amneris enters the temple and, kneeling above them, prays Isis for peace.

# Un Ballo in Maschera
## (THE MASKED BALL)

IN 1792, at a masked ball in Stockholm, King Gustave III of Sweden was murdered. The opera based on this historic incident is now presented with a Swedish setting, although the Italianized English names (due to the original shifting of the locale to Colonial Boston) are retained.

*Act I.* The popular Governor, Count Riccardo (tenor), is giving audience in his palace, while certain of his courtiers, led by Samuele and Tomaso (basses), for personal reasons plot his assassination. Oscar (soprano), a frivolous young page, submits for his approval the list of guests to be invited to a masked ball. Here the Count reads the name of his beloved, Amelia, wife of Renato, his secretary and closest friend. Renato (baritone) arrives to warn him of the conspiracy against his life, but Riccardo makes light of it. A judge then enters with a petition that a certain fortune-teller named Ulrica, who is suspected of witchcraft, be exiled. Riccardo decides to visit her himself in disguise and gaily urges his courtiers to do the same.

In her rude dwelling by the sea, Ulrica (contralto) is at her incantations while a crowd of fisherfolk wait to have their fortunes told. Riccardo, dressed as a simple sailor, mingles with them and hears her prophesy that Silvano (baritone), a real sailor, will soon be rewarded for his long, faithful service to the Governor. Thereupon Riccardo, unnoticed, slips a purse of gold and an officer's commission into Silvano's pocket. This the sailor promptly discovers amid general amazement at the sorceress's supernatural powers. Amelia's servant interrupts, announcing that his lady has come to consult Ulrica privately, and, while Ulrica dismisses the townspeople, Riccardo hides in order to witness the interview. Amelia (soprano) asks for a charm to cure her of unhappy love, and Ulrica bids her gather a certain herb at midnight, alone, in the hangman's field on the outskirts of the city. As she departs, Riccardo resolves to meet her there. The crowd, which now includes the courtiers in humble disguise, is readmitted. Ulrica reads the Count's palm and tells him, to the alarm of the conspirators, that he will soon be slain by the first man to shake his hand. Riccardo, scoffing and amused, offers his hand to everyone in vain—none dares touch it. A moment later Renato arrives, shakes hands with him, and calls him by name. Riccardo is thus revealed to the cheering townspeople as their beloved Governor.

*Act II.* At midnight beneath the gruesome gibbet, Amelia

is fearfully seeking the magic herb. Riccardo appears and, declaring his passion for her, begs for some word of love. She confesses that she has struggled vainly to put him out of her heart, but their rapture is interrupted by Renato, who has followed the Count to warn him that the conspirators have pursued and surrounded him. Amelia hastily draws her veil, the two men exchange cloaks, and Riccardo makes his escape after obtaining Renato's promise to escort the veiled lady back to the city without attempting to identify her. But Renato, in the Count's cloak, is set upon by the assassins and in the skirmish before he is recognized Amelia drops her veil. The conspirators are amused by this midnight rendezvous of man and wife. As they depart, Renato, heartbroken at Amelia's apparent infidelity, bids Samuele and Tomaso call on him next day.

*Act III.* True to his promise, Renato escorts Amelia home, but once there he informs her that she must die. At her entreaty, however, he permits her to kiss their child once more, and she goes, leaving him to vow vengeance as he contemplates a portrait of the Count and laments his ruined love. Samuele and Tomaso arrive. Renato tells them that he now wishes to join in their plot against Riccardo and, to convince them of his sincerity, offers his child as hostage. Since all three long to strike the fatal blow, they agree to draw lots for the privilege and place their names in a vase. When Amelia unexpectedly returns to announce Oscar, Renato forces her to draw a name from the vase. It is his own. At this dramatic moment Oscar enters with the invitation to the masked ball, and the conspirators arrange to murder Riccardo during the revelry. They will wear blue with red badges, and "Death" shall be their password.

Alone in his study Riccardo, resolved to part forever from his beloved, is signing an order sending Renato and Amelia to England, when Oscar brings a letter from an "unknown lady" (Amelia, of course) warning him of the attack to be made upon his life. Riccardo determines nevertheless to attend the ball, where he hopes to see Amelia once more.

In the magnificently decorated ballroom the conspirators,

disappointed by a rumor that the Count has been warned to absent himself, circulate anxiously among the masqueraders. Oscar, recognizing Renato, tells him that Riccardo is present but teasingly refuses to describe his costume. Renato, however, tricks the information from him. Amelia and Riccardo have found each other and are saying a last farewell when Renato rushes upon him and stabs him. The murderer is seized and unmasked while the Count, forgiving his enemies and protesting Amelia's innocence, dies surrounded by the horror-stricken courtiers.

# Don Carlo

THE SCENE is laid in the Forest of Fontainebleau, near Paris, and in Madrid, about the middle of the sixteenth century.

*Act I.* Elisabetta of Valois (soprano), daughter of Henry II of France, accompanied by her page, Teobaldo (soprano), and a party of hunters, rides past woodcutters in the forest. Watching unseen is her betrothed, Don Carlo (tenor), son of Philip II of Spain. The youth has come secretly to Paris for a glimpse of his bride-to-be, and falls passionately in love with her at first sight. The hunters vanish and, as night falls, the woodcutters go home. Elisabetta reappears on foot, with Teobaldo, who has lost the way. Don Carlo introduces himself as a member of the retinue of the Spanish Ambassador now concluding a peace treaty between France and Spain. When lights glow from the distant place, Elisabetta sends Teobaldo ahead, then questions the Spaniard about her unknown fiancé, who she fears will not love her. He already does, Don Carlo assures her, and, producing a miniature of himself, presents it to her as the gift of her betrothed. She at once recognizes the stranger to whom she has already lost her heart. The young lovers' rapture is interrupted by the sound of cannon, while the palace is suddenly illuminated in celebration of the signing of the treaty. Teobaldo returns and, hailing her as

Queen, announces that her father destines her to wed not Don Carlo, but the dread Philip himself. Courtiers, headed by the Spanish Envoy, now approach and Elisabetta, learning that this marriage is a condition of peace, has no choice but submission. The lovers' new-found joy turns to despair.

*Act II.* At daybreak in the Monastery of San Giusto, in Madrid, monks pray in the chapel where Philip's father, the great Charles V, lies buried; then go about their duties. The wretched Don Carlo, arriving at the cloister, is startled by a mysterious monk whose strangely familiar voice reminds him that his grandfather's ghost is said to haunt the spot. His friend Rodrigo, Marquis of Posa (baritone), now comes to urge him to rescue the conquered people of Flanders, perishing under Philip's fanatical persecution. Carlo confesses his unhappy love for his stepmother, whereupon Rodrigo, in shocked sympathy, counsels him to depart at once to lead the Flemish rebellion. Vowing eternal friendship, the two pledge their lives to the cause of liberty. Philip and Elisabetta then enter with attendants to pay homage at the tomb. When they have passed Carlo and Rodrigo renew their vow.

Meanwhile, outside the monastery, Princess Eboli (soprano) entertains the ladies of the Court with a Moorish song. When the Queen returns to them, Rodrigo slips her a message from Don Carlo requesting an interview, and at his friend's approach leads the others out of earshot. Carlo entreats Elisabetta to obtain his appointment as Governor of Flanders; then, overcome with emotion, begs her pity. Though admitting that she still loves him, she reminds him that she is his father's wife, and they sadly part. Philip, coming from the monastery, finds the Queen, whom he distrusts, alone, and insults her by dismissing the lady-in-waiting who should have been in attendance. He then bids the defiant di Posa, whom he cannot but admire, mend his rebellious ways for fear of the Inquisition and, confiding that he suspects Elisabetta and his son of guilty love, orders the Marquis to watch over them both.

*Act III.* At midnight in the Queen's garden, Don Carlo rereads the letter that has summoned him there. He believes

[ 297 ]

it to be from Elisabetta and therefore assumes that the veiled
lady who comes to meet him is she. To his dismay he discovers that it is Eboli, who loves him and has thought herself
loved in return. Di Posa comes upon them too late to prevent
Carlo from betraying his passion for the Queen, and Eboli,
as she departs, threatens in her jealousy to bring them all to
ruin. Rodrigo, realizing that she may denounce Carlo to the
Inquisition, persuades his friend to place all incriminating
papers in his hands for safekeeping.

In front of the Cathedral a festive crowd has gathered to
watch the burning of heretics at the stake. To the chanting of
prayers the condemned men are led to their doom; the Queen
arrives followed by the entire Court in full regalia, and the
King, wearing his crown and royal robes, comes from the
Cathedral. Don Carlo then presents six ragged deputies from
Flanders who throw themselves at Philip's feet imploring
leniency, but Philip replies that only through bloodshed can
peace be secured. The Prince thereupon demands the Flemish
governorship, Philip accuses him of rebellion and Carlo defiantly draws his sword. The King orders him disarmed, but
no one stirs until di Posa takes the sword from his astonished
friend and presents it to Philip, for which he is rewarded with
the title of Duke. As the royal procession moves on to witness
the executions, the fires are kindled and a Voice from Heaven
(soprano) welcomes the victims to the next world.

*Act IV*. In his library the lonely, fanatical King laments that
his young wife has never loved him and that, surrounded by
hatred and treachery, he will find rest only in the tomb. At his
request the Grand Inquisitor (bass), ninety years old and
blind, arrives to advise him on Carlo's punishment. Philip
agrees to surrender his only son to the Inquisition, and is even
forced by the old man's threats to consent to the death of di
Posa, who has become his trusted favorite. The Grand Inquisitor leaves him to bitter reflections on the dread power of
the Church. Elisabetta now comes begging retribution for the
theft of her jewel box, which Philip produces, commanding
her to open it. She refuses, whereupon he opens it himself and
discloses Carlo's portrait. He accuses her of infidelity and,

when she faints, summons Princess Eboli to her aid and angrily departs. Eboli, now remorseful, confesses that she stole the casket in order to betray Carlo's and Elisabetta's love to the King. Thereupon the Queen bids her choose between exile and the cloister. The distracted woman resolves to become a nun, but rejoices that one day is left her in which to rescue Carlo.

Rodrigo, visiting Carlo in prison, informs him that thanks to the treasonable documents found in his possession he, rather than Carlo, is now accused of instigating revolt, and he has arranged Carlo's escape. While his friend protests this sacrifice, two men descend the prison stairs, one in the habit of the Inquisition, the other armed. Without warning the latter shoots di Posa, thus fulfilling the Grand Inquisitor's will. Rodrigo dies exhorting Carlo to save Flanders, and later Spain itself, from Philip's tyranny. A rebellious mob incited by Princess Eboli now breaks into the dungeon demanding Carlo's release. Philip, arriving hastily, not only fails to quell them but is himself threatened, and only the intervention of the Grand Inquisitor saves the throne.

*Act V.* In the moonlit cloister of San Giusto, the sorrowful Queen prays by the tomb of Charles V while waiting for Don Carlo to bid her a secret farewell. He tells her that he is about to undertake his heroic mission in Flanders, thus carrying out di Posa's dying wish, and the lovers, at last resigned to fate's cruelty, look forward to reunion only in heaven. Suddenly the King appears and, assuming their guilt, demands justice. The Grand Inquisitor, who has accompanied Philip, orders Carlo's arrest, but the Prince resists with drawn sword. At that moment the mysterious monk who resembles Charles V emerges from behind the tomb and snatches Don Carlo to sanctuary while all stand frozen in superstitious terror.

# Falstaff

THE SCENE is laid in Windsor during the sixteenth century.

*Act I.* While the fat rascal, Sir John Falstaff (baritone), is
taking his ease at the Garter Inn, Dr. Caius (tenor) complains
that the knight's scoundrelly followers, Pistol (bass) and
Bardolf (tenor), have picked his pocket. Falstaff gets rid of
the fussy old physician, then upbraids his henchmen for stealing so clumsily. His purse being empty as usual, he proposes to
replenish it by courting not one, but two, wealthy burghers'
wives whom, in his infinite vanity, he believes smitten with his
charms. He has written to the ladies, Mistress Ford and
Mistress Page, amorous letters which he bids Bardolf and
Pistol deliver. They protest that honor prevents them from
taking part in such a scheme, whereupon Falstaff sends a
page-boy on the errand, and explains that honor is a much
overrated commodity.

In the garden by Ford's house Mrs. Ford (soprano) and her
daughter Nanetta (soprano) meet and gossip with Mrs. Page
(mezzo-soprano) and Dame Quickly (mezzo-soprano). They
soon discover that Falstaff has written the two ladies identical
letters and, with much hilarity, determine to punish the fat
rogue. Meantime Ford (baritone) appears with Pistol, Bardolf,
Dr. Caius, and young Fenton (tenor), who warn him that
Falstaff has designs upon his wife. The men decide that Ford,
whom Falstaff does not know, shall visit him under an assumed name; the ladies plan a rendezvous that shall be the fat
knight's undoing; and meantime Fenton and Nanetta, who
are in love, steal a few sweet words and hurried caresses.

*Act II.* Dame Quickly, calling upon Falstaff at the Inn, informs him with excessive politeness that both ladies pine for
him. Mrs. Ford bids him come to her between two and three,
when her husband is absent; Mrs. Page's husband, unfortunately, is seldom from home. Dame Quickly leaves, and
Bardolf announces Ford as "Signor Fontana" (Master Brook),
who presents the knight with a sack of gold and, explaining

that he has long loved Mrs. Ford in vain, entreats the irresistible Sir John to prepare the way for him by conquering the lady's scruples. Falstaff promises to win her and, boasting that he already has an appointment with her, withdraws to dress himself suitably. Ford, taken aback, begins to feel seriously jealous, but when Falstaff returns sumptuously attired the two go forth together with a great show of cordiality.

In Ford's house, while the ladies bustle about their preparations, Nanetta tearfully complains that her father intends her to marry Dr. Caius. Her mother, who is Fenton's ally, reassures her. All but Mrs. Ford vanish at Falstaff's approach and, according to plan, his courting is interrupted first by Dame Quickly, then by Mrs. Page, who warn that Ford, furiously jealous, is on the way home. This turns out to be no jest, but the truth. Falstaff is hastily concealed behind a screen; then, while the men search the house, he is transferred to an immense hamper full of soiled linen. The men return and, hearing Fenton kiss Nanetta behind the screen, are sure they have found their prey. The screen is overthrown, the young lovers stand revealed, and Ford, who has promised his daughter to Dr. Caius, angrily denounces them. Mrs. Ford summons four serving-men and bids them empty the abnormally heavy laundry basket out the window into the river. This is done, and Mrs. Ford mirthfully shows her husband the discomfited knight floundering in the water.

*Act III.* In front of the Inn, Falstaff meditates on the vileness of the world as he consoles himself with wine after his drenching. Dame Quickly brings word that Mrs. Ford still loves him and will meet him at midnight by Herne's Oak in Windsor Park. Sir John must disguise himself as the ghostly Sable Huntsman, said to haunt the spot, who according to legend is there tormented by fairies, elves, and witches. Peeking delightedly from the shrubbery, Ford, the two ladies, Nanetta, and Fenton watch the fat knight enter the Inn with Dame Quickly to arrange the rendezvous. Thereupon they plan to re-enact the legend by masquerading as the elfin tormentors. Nanetta shall be Queen of the Fairies. Ford bids Dr. Caius note her costume, since he intends to take advantage of darkness and disguise in order to marry her to the elderly doctor while the prank is in progress. All gleefully go about their preparations.

Beneath the great oak Fenton waits in the moonlight, dreaming of Nanetta. When the others assemble and don masks, Mrs. Ford gives him a cloak like that of Dr. Caius. Then all disappear as the village bell tolls midnight and Falstaff approaches. Mrs. Ford returns and while he is preposterously wooing her the pseudo fairies, witches, and hobgoblins (including the village children) surround him and with great mumbo-jumbo tumble, pinch and pummel him till he repents his sins. The fairies' true identity is then revealed to him, and "Signor Fontana" explains that he is Mrs. Ford's husband. Not one couple, but two, now present themselves to Ford to be married. He obliges only to find, when they cast off their disguises, that he has wedded Dr. Caius to Bardolf and his daughter to Fenton. At his wife's entreaty he nevertheless blesses the happy couple, and the whole company joyously proclaims that all life is a jest.

# La Forza del Destino
## (THE FORCE OF DESTINY)

THE ACTION takes place in Spain and Italy during the eighteenth century.

*Act I.* In his palace in Seville, the Marquis of Calatrava (bass) tenderly bids his daughter Leonora (soprano) goodnight and leaves her room. Her maid Curra (mezzo-soprano) at once hastens preparations for her mistress's elopement with Don Alvaro (tenor), a Peruvian nobleman whose mother was an Inca princess and whom the Marquis therefore will not countenance as Leonora's suitor. Leonora, loath to leave home and father for a strange land, half hopes her lover will not come, but at the last minute he enters by the balcony. Though the horses are ready, and a priest waits to marry them, she loses courage and tarries till Don Alvaro begins to doubt her love. Then, as they leave, the Marquis returns sword in hand and followed by servants. Don Alvaro, giving himself up, throws his pistol to the floor, whereupon it is accidentally discharged. The Marquis, mortally wounded, dies cursing his daughter.

*Act II.* In the kitchen of an inn in the Spanish village of Hornacuelos, peasants, muleteers, etc. are dancing and supping. Leonora, now disguised as a student, enters from an upper room and, recognizing her brother, Don Carlo di Vargas (baritone), also disguised as a student, immediately withdraws. Preziosilla (mezzo-soprano), a camp-follower, arrives and urges that all enlist to help Italy fight the German invaders. As she reads Don Carlo's palm, chanting pilgrims pass by on the way to the Monastery of the Madonna of the Angels. In the inn all kneel and pray, including Leonora, who has quietly reappeared. Concealing his identity, Don Carlo then tells the villagers that he has been helping his "friend, di Vargas" to seek his sister and her lover in order to avenge di Vargas' father's death upon them. From this Leonora learns that her brother intends to kill both her and Don Alvaro, whom she supposed already dead.

By moonlight Leonora comes to the monastery in the wilderness and, while the friars are heard chanting within, prays to the Virgin. She then begs the rascally Brother Melitone (baritone) to summon the Abbot, of whom she asks permission to spend the rest of her days in a hermit's abandoned cave near by, seeking peace and forgiveness. The Holy Father (bass), who knows her story, attempts to dissuade her until, convinced of her sincerity, he gives her a monk's habit and promises to leave food for her. Never again shall she see a human being, but, if in danger, or at her last hour, she may ring the hermit's bell. Then, summoning the friars, he orders them, under penalty of being accursed, not to approach the cave henceforth. All kneel and implore the Virgin to watch over the mysterious penitent.

*Act III.* In the woods near Velletri, Italy, soldiers can be heard gambling and drinking while Don Alvaro, now a captain in the Spanish Grenadiers, laments his fate. He was born in prison, his parents were unjustly beheaded, and now he has lost his only joy, Leonora; he calls upon her in heaven to pity him. Hearing a disturbance among the soldiers, he rushes off and returns with Don Carlo, whose life, endangered in a gamblers' brawl, he has just saved. The two men introduce themselves by their assumed names and, as the call to arms is heard, go side by side into battle vowing eternal friendship.

A military surgeon (tenor), watching from a house near the battlefield, sees Don Alvaro fall, and the wounded man, accompanied by Don Carlo, is borne in on a stretcher. At Don Alvaro's request Don Carlo swears, in the event of his friend's death, to burn a certain packet of letters unopened. After Don Alvaro is carried out, Don Carlo, who now suspects his friend's identity, is tempted to examine the packet, but honor prevails. Among Don Alvaro's possessions, however, he finds Leonora's portrait and realizes that this man is indeed his mortal enemy. When the surgeon, having removed Don Alvaro's bullet, announces that the patient will live, Don Carlo rejoices that he may yet punish his father's murderer.

At night near the battlefield, soldiers sleep while the patrol passes on its rounds; but Don Alvaro, now recovered, wanders, unable to rest. Don Carlo finds him, rejects his proffered friendship and, incidentally revealing that Leonora may be alive, taunts him into drawing his sword. The two fight fiercely until the patrol, returning, separates them and arrests Don Carlo. Alvaro, having now lost even his friend, resolves to become a monk, and sadly leaves. Meantime day has dawned and the camp comes to life. Among peddlers, food venders, etc., Preziosilla tells fortunes while Brother Melitone, who has also come from Spain, lectures one and all on their sins. The crowd turns on him, but Preziosilla, by beating a drum and singing a martial air, saves him from its wrath.

*Act IV.* In the courtyard of the monastery near Hornacuelos, Brother Melitone scolds a throng of beggars to whom he ladles soup. The Father Superior reproves him, but, when the beggars speak of their preference for gentle "Father Raffaele," Melitone angrily upsets the caldron and drives them away.

The Holy Father bids him not envy Father Raffaele, whom Melitone considers peculiar—perhaps mad. A knock is heard, the Holy Father withdraws, and Melitone admits Don Carlo who asks for Father Raffaele. When the latter (Don Alvaro) appears, Don Carlo declares that he has sought him five years and will now fight him to the death. Alvaro protests that his monk's vows forbid it but Carlo, with insults and blows, provokes him into seizing one of the swords he has brought and they rush forth in search of an isolated spot for their duel.

Outside her cave Leonora prays in vain to forget her love, then takes the bread the Holy Father has left for her, and retires. There is a noise of fighting, and Alvaro appears calling upon the hermit to absolve a man who lies near by, mortally wounded. Leonora rings her bell and comes forth to send the intruder away. The lovers recognize each other and Leonora, learning that the dying man is her brother, hastens to his aid. A cry is heard, and she returns supported by the Father Superior who has come in answer to her bell. Don Carlo, still intent on vengeance, has recognized and stabbed her. Telling Alvaro that Heaven forgives his crime, she dies, and the Holy Father announces that her soul has gone to God.

# *Otello*

THE SCENE is laid in Cyprus at the end of the fifteenth century, when the island was a Venetian colony coveted by the Turks. To defend it against Turkish attack, Venice has appointed the renowned Moorish general, Otello, as governor.

*Act I.* Before the Governor's castle, a crowd anxiously watches through darkness and a raging storm as Otello's ship fights off enemy vessels and reaches harbor safely. Upon disembarking, Otello (tenor) bids all exult over the Turkish rout, then enters the castle where Desdemona, his young Venetian bride, awaits his arrival. The storm is subsiding, and the townsfolk build a bonfire in celebration of victory. Meanwhile Otello's ensign, Iago (baritone), tells Roderigo, a love-sick Venetian who has followed Desdemona to Cyprus, that by doing his bidding he yet may win the lady. Iago then confides his hatred of the Moor, who has made Cassio his lieutenant in preference to himself (Iago), and easily persuades the young man to help him bring about Cassio's downfall. When a tavern-keeper serves them wine, they therefore induce the lieutenant to drink himself tipsy. A quarrel is soon started, and in the ensuing brawl Cassio (tenor) wounds his fellow officer, Montano (bass). Otello, roused by the turmoil, restores order and questions Iago who, with a show of reluctance, places the blame on Cassio. Desdemona, whom the uproar has also disturbed, now appears. Otello deprives Cassio of his rank and commands the crowd to disperse. The lovers, left alone under the now starry sky, tell each other of the immensity of their love.

*Act II.* In a room in the castle which opens into a garden, Iago advises the crestfallen Cassio to entreat Desdemona to plead with the Moor for his reinstatement. Seeing her in the garden with her maid Emilia (mezzo-soprano), Iago's wife, Cassio immediately does so, while Iago reflects that Cassio has become his tool even as he himself is the tool of the cruel god he worships. When Otello appears, Iago insinuates that Cassio and Desdemona are more than friendly, and bids the Moor beware of jealousy. In the garden sailors, village women, and children now bring Desdemona gifts and flowers. Otello, watching, cannot believe her false; yet, coming to him, she at once pleads Cassio's cause. In his distress the Moor complains of headache and angrily throws to the ground the handkerchief with which she tries to bind his brow. Emilia picks it up, and, while Desdemona renews her plea, Iago snatches it from his wife and pockets it. The women leave, and the tormented Moor threatens Iago with death, should the anguish he has caused him prove needless. Iago replies that he has heard Cassio in sleep murmur words of love to Desdemona, and furthermore has seen her handkerchief in Cassio's possession. At that Otello, almost convinced, swears he will punish the sinners, and Iago pledges himself to his aid.

*Act III.* In the great hall of the castle, a herald informs Otello and Iago of the landing of Venetian ambassadors. Iago goes to fetch Cassio, bidding Otello conceal himself and listen to their conversation. Meanwhile Desdemona comes to her husband, who answers her tender inquiries with cruel mockery and insults. Bewildered and weeping, she leaves, and Otello reflects that he could have borne any affliction but this, which nullifies all his past glory. Iago now returns with Cassio, whom he induces to talk of his affair with a woman of the town so that Otello, just out of earshot, believes he is speaking of Desdemona. Cassio then shows Iago a mysterious handkerchief found in his room, and Otello, recognizing it, is fully convinced of Desdemona's guilt. When trumpets signal the approach of the ambassadors, Cassio leaves. The Moor, now determined on revenge, agrees to Iago's suggestion that he murder Desdemona that night, while Iago himself undertakes to do away with Cassio. Courtiers, ladies, soldiers, etc. assemble as Lodovico (bass), the Venetian Envoy, arrives with his suite. Otello watches Desdemona suspiciously while he reads a letter summoning him back to Venice for new honors, and appointing Cassio Governor in his stead. Then, to the horror of all present, the Moor suddenly turns on his wife and throws her brutally to the ground. Taking advantage of the confusion this causes, Iago tells Roderigo to set upon Cassio in the street that night. Emilia leads the stricken Desdemona away, and Otello, now beside himself, drives everyone from the hall, then falls senseless. Iago lingers, and, as the crowd outside is heard cheering the "Lion of Venice," places his foot on the prostrate Moor in evil triumph and exclaims "Behold the Lion!"

*Act IV.* As Emilia prepares her mistress for the night, Desdemona is haunted by a wistful song of unhappy love remembered from her childhood. Full of vague foreboding, she bids Emilia good-night and, after praying to the Virgin Mary to pity all suffering mortals, goes to sleep. Otello, now calm and purposeful, quietly enters and wakes her with a kiss, then asks her if she is prepared to die. Terrified, she begs to know her sin, and he accuses her of loving Cassio. In vain she protests her innocence and implores him for an hour, a moment, of grace. He strangles her. Emilia comes crying that Cassio has slain Roderigo and himself escaped unhurt. From the bed Desdemona feebly murmurs that she has killed herself, and dies. Otello denounces the lie and Emilia's outcries bring Lodovico, Montano, Cassio, and Iago rushing in. The Moor declares that Iago has proven Desdemona faithless, whereupon Emilia reveals her husband's theft of the handkerchief and Iago, his villainy disclosed, hastily escapes. For Otello only death remains. He stabs himself, turning to Desdemona for a last kiss as he dies.

# *Rigoletto*

THE SCENE is laid in the Duchy of Mantua during the sixteenth century.

*Act I.* At a ball in his palace, the young Duke (tenor) speaks of his passion for an unknown beauty whom he has seen in church and followed to discover her home. He finds all women desirable, however, and, unabashed by her husband's presence, flirts with the Countess Ceprano (soprano). She leaves the ball escorted by the Count and the Duke and followed by Rigoletto (baritone), the hunchbacked court jester, who jeers openly at the outraged husband. Marullo (tenor) then informs his fellow courtiers that a woman has been seen in Rigoletto's house, and they assume with amusement that the hideous hunchback must be in love. Rigoletto, returning with the Duke and Count Ceprano, maliciously urges his master to have the Count's head chopped off. This shocks even the unprincipled Duke, and the licentious courtiers, who have all suffered from the evil jester's insolent cruelty, hope for an opportunity to punish him. The dancing is now interrupted by Monterone, an aged nobleman whose daughter the Duke has dishonored. The grieving father denounces the Duke, only to be mocked by Rigoletto. Thereupon Monterone, placed under arrest, pronounces a fearful curse upon the indifferent Duke and his suddenly terrified jester.

*Act II.* Rigoletto, profoundly troubled by the old man's curse, is approaching his modest dwelling next to the Ceprano palace, when a sinister figure steps from the shadows, introduces himself as Sparafucile (bass), a professional cutthroat, and offers, for a price, to do away with any enemy the jester may have. Sparafucile explains that he keeps a tavern outside the city, whither his attractive sister lures his victims. Rigoletto dismisses him and, reflecting that he himself is no better than the cutthroat, laments his deformity and his humiliating life. Entering his garden, he tenderly greets his beloved daughter, motherless Gilda (soprano), whose existence is his closely guarded secret. The girl, raised in ignorance even of her father's name and, for safety's sake, permitted to leave the house only to go to church with her companion, protests in vain against these restrictions. While she pleads with her father, her companion, Giovanna (mezzo-soprano), opens the gate to the Duke, from whom she accepts a bribe. The Duke conceals himself and, overhearing the conversation, is surprised to learn that the unknown beauty is not Rigoletto's mistress but his daughter. After cautioning Giovanna to watch over the girl faithfully, Rigoletto returns to the palace. The Duke thereupon comes forth and declares his love, telling Gilda, who has already lost her heart to him at church, that he is a poor student named Gualtier (Walter) Maldé. Hearing a disturbance in the street, he slips away, leaving her to repeat the name with shy rapture as she enters the house. Meanwhile the vengeful courtiers, in masks and cloaks, have assembled outside to kidnap her. When Rigoletto himself appears among them, they convince him that Countess Ceprano is their intended victim and, under cover of darkness, not only mask but blindfold him. It is he who holds the ladder while they climb his garden wall and carry away Gilda, bound and gagged. Rigoletto, left alone, discovers the blindfold, tears it off, and frantically seeks his vanished daughter. Monterone's curse has begun its work.

*Act III.* In an antechamber of the palace, the Duke is lamenting Gilda's disappearance when the courtiers arrive to tell him that they have stolen the jester's mistress (as they believe) and brought her to the palace. The Duke immediately goes to her. Rigoletto, who now comes to spy out her fate, tries to cover his anguish with mockery, but grief soon forces him to confess that he is seeking his daughter. When an inquiring page is informed that the Duke must not be disturbed, the jester at once realizes that Gilda is with him. He reviles, then pleads with, the courtiers who gloat over his misery as they forcibly restrain him from going to her. Gilda herself soon enters in agitation, whereupon Rigoletto sends the courtiers away and tries to comfort her while she confesses her love for her betrayer, whom she supposed a student. When Monterone, being led to prison, passes through the room, Rigoletto swears, in spite of Gilda's pleas, that he himself will bring fulfillment of the old man's curse upon the Duke.

*Act IV.* A month later Rigoletto's revenge is prepared, and, hoping to cure Gilda of her unhappy love, he leads her to Sparafucile's desolate and disreputable tavern by the river. There, unobserved, they hear the Duke, now dressed as a cavalry officer, proclaim the fickleness of womankind as he brazenly makes love to Sparafucile's sister, Maddalena (mezzo-soprano). Gilda, heartbroken, leaves at her father's orders to meet him later in Verona—dressed as a boy, since a girl dare not travel alone. After telling Sparafucile that he will come at midnight to claim the Duke's body, Rigoletto also leaves. A storm arises and the Duke, deciding to spend the night at the tavern, is shown to an upper room. Maddalena then begs her brother to spare the handsome young officer's life, and Sparafucile reluctantly agrees to substitute some other victim should one appear. Gilda, who, in man's attire, has come back for a last glimpse of her beloved, overhears this conversation with horror. Deliberately sacrificing her life to save the Duke, she knocks at the door and in the darkness is quietly stabbed. Through the storm Rigoletto returns, pays Sparafucile's fee, and receives the body in a sack. But, as he drags it triumphantly to the river, he hears the Duke's voice from the tavern. Panic-stricken, he tears away the sack and by a flash of lightning recognizes Gilda. She recovers conscious-ness and, as she dies, begs his forgiveness. The curse is now fulfilled.

## Simon Boccanegra

THE ACTION takes place in fifteenth-century Genoa during the long years of political strife between the Guelphs (patrician party) and the Ghibellines (plebeian party).

*Prologue.* In the square before the Fiesco palace, two am-bitious plebeians, Paolo (bass) and Pietro (baritone), fore-seeing wealth and influence for themselves, plot the election of their friend, Simon Boccanegra, a famed corsair, as Doge (ruler). Simon (baritone), meeting them, consents only be-cause the Doge's power will enable him to marry his long-loved Maria Fiesco, despite her patrician father's opposition. When he has withdrawn, his friends persuade the populace to vote for him in defiance of Fiesco, who holds Maria im-prisoned in his sinister abode. After the crowd disperses, Fiesco himself (bass) appears mourning her death while from within the palace dirgelike lamentations are heard. Simon, re-turning, encounters him and implores his pardon, but the proud patrician will forgive his archenemy only on condition that Boccanegra surrender his and Maria's daughter. This Simon cannot do, because the child, brought up near Pisa, vanished after the death of her old nurse. Learning this, Fiesco insists that there can be no end to the hostility between them. From the shadows he watches grimly while Simon boldly enters the palace, only to find Maria dead. Boc-canegra comes forth horror-stricken, and is confronted by a cheering crowd acclaiming him as Genoa's elected Doge.

*Act I.* Twenty-five years have passed, during which in-fluential patricians, including the men of the wealthy Grimaldi family, have suffered persecution and exile. In the garden of her palace, Amelia Grimaldi (soprano) awaits her lover,

Gabriele Adorno (tenor), a young patrician in league with Fiesco (who for safety has assumed the name Andrea) to overthrow Simon. Learning from her that she fears a forced marriage with the Doge's powerful favorite Paolo, Adorno plans to marry her at once and, since Fiesco acts as her guardian, he asks the old man's consent. This he obtains, after being told that the girl is not really Amelia Grimaldi but a nameless foundling substituted for the dead heiress to prevent the Doge from confiscating the family fortune. Boccanegra himself, bringing a pardon for her brothers, comes to ask her hand for Paolo. She thereupon tells him her story and, by means of a portrait of her mother, he discovers that she is his own missing daughter, Fiesco's grandchild. Since she has confided her love for another, he tells Paolo to abandon hope of winning her. Paolo considers this ingratitude, and angrily bids his friend Pietro arrange the girl's abduction.

In the Council Chamber of the Doge's palace, the twenty-four counselors representing both patricians and plebeians are assembled with other government officials. Simon, enthroned, reads a letter from the poet Petrarch (historically authentic) urging peace and unity on the warring Italian States. The deliberations are interrupted by tumult and cries of "Death to the Doge" from the street. A rebellion, led by Adorno, is in progress. All listen in suspense as a herald sent by Simon informs the mob that the Doge fearlessly welcomes it. This show of courage turns the threats to cheers and the crowd, bursting in, now demands the blood of Fiesco and Adorno. The latter, who has just killed the man who had abducted Amelia, attacks Simon as instigator of the crime. Amelia herself saves the Doge and insinuates that Paolo is to blame. To prevent Paolo's escape, Simon orders the doors barred, then forces the guilty wretch to lead the others in pronouncing a curse upon the criminal—himself.

*Act II.* In the Doge's apartments, Paolo, bent on revenge, empties a phial of poison into Simon's drinking cup. Fiesco and Adorno, whom he has had secretly released from prison, come to him and he urges them to murder Simon. Both refuse and Paolo orders Fiesco back to his cell, but detains

Adorno to tell him that Simon is guilty of an illicit love affair with Amelia. Then, confident that jealousy will take its course, he craftily locks the youth in and departs. Amelia soon enters from an inner room, but is unable to explain her presence there before the Doge himself approaches. While Adorno hides on the balcony, Amelia confesses to her father that the man she loves is the young rebel. Boccanegra promises to forgive Adorno if he will repent, and dismisses her. Amelia, however, conceals herself, fearing her lover's wrath. Simon then wearily pours water into the poisoned cup, drinks, and falls asleep. Adorno now re-enters and is about to stab the Doge when Amelia throws herself between them. Her relationship to Simon is soon revealed, and Adorno, won over, offers to fight for him against the insurgent mob heard nearing the palace. Simon thereupon bestows his blessing on the young couple's union.

*Act III.* The rebellion has been quelled. From a room in the palace, distant cheers are heard and the city can be seen brightly illuminated in celebration. Fiesco is brought in and set free, and Paolo, being led to execution, boasts to him of the slow poison he has given the Doge. Boccanegra enters and at once orders the festive lights extinguished out of respect for those who lost their lives in the struggle. Then, complaining of feeling weary and ill, he gazes out to sea and wishes that he had died in the glorious days when, as a corsair, he rid the ocean of Genoa's foes. One by one the lights begin to go out. Fiesco, whom Boccanegra believed long since dead, now approaches him with evil intent. Simon reveals that Fiesco's ward, Amelia, is in reality the lost child, Maria, and, since the condition of peace between them has long been fulfilled, the two are reconciled. Fiesco, however, tells the ailing Doge of Paolo's poison. Maria arrives with Adorno and various nobles of the Court, and the dying Simon informs her that Fiesco, whom she had known only as Andrea, is her mother's father. Then, blessing her and Adorno and proclaiming the latter his heir, Boccanegra expires as the last light in the harbor is extinguished. While bells toll his passing, Fiesco bids the populace outside acclaim Adorno as the new Doge.

# La Traviata

THE SCENE is Paris in mid-nineteenth century.

*Act I.* A friend brings young Alfredo Germont (tenor) to a party and introduces him to the hostess, a beautiful courtesan named Violetta (soprano). During her recent illness, Alfredo has called daily to inquire after her, and he confesses that for a year he has loved her from afar. Seated beside her at the supper table he proposes a toast to love. As the guests go to an adjoining room to dance, Violetta is seized with sudden faintness. Alfredo, remaining behind with her, begs her for her health's sake to give up the reckless gaiety of her life. Touched by his solicitude, she gives him a flower, bidding him return it to her next day. Left alone, she wonders whether she has at last found the man of her youthful dreams, but reflects that true love is not for her; she must live heart-free in a perpetual round of pleasure.

*Act II.* For three blissful months Alfredo has been living with Violetta in the country near Paris. He has just returned from riding when Annina (mezzo-soprano), Violetta's maid, interrupts his happy mood with the news that she has been to the city to sell her mistress's jewels. Full of remorse, he leaves at once for Paris to obtain funds. Meantime Violetta receives an invitation from her friend Flora, but parties no longer attract her. Alfredo's father (baritone), intent on rescuing his son, whom he imagines to be in the clutches of a coarse, grasping woman, calls unexpectedly. Though surprised by Violetta's gracious dignity, he entreats her to part from Alfredo, whom he says she is ruining. She protests that she truly loves Alfredo and that it is she, not he, who pays the bills. The elder Germont then tells her that Alfredo has a sister whose fiancé is about to break their engagement because of Violetta's scandalous reputation. At this Violetta agrees to make the sacrifice, and Germont leaves, having obtained her promise to part from her lover. She writes a farewell note and is about to start for Paris when Alfredo returns saying that he expects a visit from his father. Violetta replies that Germont must not see her and, concealing her sorrow, departs. Germont returns to find his son reading her letter, and urges him to seek comfort at the family home in Provence. But Alfredo, assuming that she has tired of him and returned to her former protector, Baron Douphol, is maddened with jealousy and hastens in pursuit of her.

At Flora's party, dancers entertain the guests, who gossip about Violetta's and Alfredo's separation. Alfredo arrives alone and sullenly begins to play cards. Violetta enters with the Baron (baritone), who forbids her to speak to her lover; he then joins the gamblers and loses heavily to Alfredo. The two men are on the point of quarreling when the guests are summoned to supper. Violetta detains Alfredo and warns him to avoid Douphol, whom she says she loves. Alfredo thereupon calls the guests back and publicly insults her, throwing his winnings at her feet. Violetta faints, and Germont, who has followed Alfredo to the party, denounces his son. The guests reproach Alfredo, and Douphol challenges him to a duel as Violetta, now recovered, is led away by Flora (mezzo-soprano) and Dr. Grenville (bass).

*Act III.* Some time has passed, and Violetta is now dying of consumption. Dr. Grenville calls on her and, before he leaves, informs Annina that her mistress has but a few hours to live. Violetta rereads a letter from Germont telling her that the Baron, wounded in the duel, is recovering and that Alfredo has gone away. Germont has told his son of her sacrifice and both are coming to ask her forgiveness. Fearing she may not live to see them, she sadly recalls the bright past. It is carnival time and from the street come sounds of revelry that contrast with her despair. Annina enters with news of Alfredo's arrival, and the lovers are reunited. In their rapture they are certain that Violetta will now recover, and plan to leave Paris. She wishes to go at once to church and give thanks for his return, but the effort proves too great and her strength fails. Annina hastens to summon the doctor. He arrives with Germont, who is overwhelmed with remorse at the sight of the dying Violetta. Giving Alfredo her picture, she bids him marry some innocent young girl and remember always that she is praying for them both in heaven. Alfredo implores her not to leave him. With a sudden sense of well-being she joyously arises, only to fall back dead.

# Il Trovatore
## (THE TROUBADOUR)

THE SCENE is laid in Spain early in the fifteenth century while a feudal war rages between the principalities of Aragon and Biscay. The Queen of Aragon is at Aliferia, a castle belonging to the Count di Luna.

*Act I.* At night in the hall of the castle, the soldiers of the guard await the Count's return. To keep them awake, their captain, Ferrando (bass), tells them the following story: Long ago a gypsy hag had been found muttering over the cradle of the Count's younger brother. Though she vowed that she sought only to divine the child's future, she was accused of witchcraft. The child soon sickened and the gypsy, protesting her innocence and calling upon her daughter to avenge her, was therefore burned at the stake. Shortly thereafter the infant disappeared, and among the ashes where the old gypsy had died, tiny bones were discovered. It was assumed that the gypsy's daughter had stolen and burned the child. Yet, as proof was lacking, hope of finding the missing boy and punishing the gypsy's vanished daughter had never been abandoned.

Meanwhile in the castle garden, Leonora (soprano), lady-in-waiting to the Queen, tells her friend Inez (soprano) that she loves a mysterious, black-clad knight whom she had crowned with laurel after his victory in a tournament. Since then he sometimes comes beneath her balcony at night to sing of his love for her. She knows of him only that he is a troubadour. The ladies retire, and the Count di Luna (baritone) enters the garden seeking Leonora, whom he also loves. He is about to follow her into the castle when the troubadour's lute and voice are heard. Leonora returns and in the darkness mistakes di Luna for her lover. The troubadour appears and, in the ensuing quarrel with his rival, reveals that he is Manrico (tenor), a warrior of Biscay. Instead of taking him prisoner, di Luna challenges him to a duel and, despite Leonora's attempt to intervene, the two men rush off with drawn swords. In her distress Leonora faints.

*Act II.* Manrico, wounded in battle, has returned after years of chivalrous adventures to his gypsy mother, Azucena (contralto), to be healed. They are living at an encampment in the mountains of Biscay, where the gypsies forge weapons. Azucena, gazing as in a trance at the campfire, relives her own mother's last moments at the stake, and echoes the dying woman's cry for vengeance. Left alone with Manrico, she shudders as she recalls how, crazed with grief, she had thrown to the flames not the stolen infant, but her own! Manrico cries "Then whose child am I?" By way of answer she reminds him of her devotion, then urges him to slay the Count, whose life he had spared in obedience to a strange impulse after worsting him in their duel. The troubadour's friend Ruiz (tenor) interrupts with news that Manrico has been appointed commander of the fortress of Castellor, and that Leonora, believing her lover dead, is about to enter a convent. Despite Azucena's protests, Manrico hastens away to prevent his beloved from becoming a nun.

In the cloister of the convent, di Luna, determined to kidnap Leonora before she takes the veil, places his men in ambush. The bell tolls for the ceremony and nuns are heard chanting as Leonora arrives, accompanied by other ladies-in-waiting to whom she bids farewell. Di Luna rushes forth from hiding to seize her, but at that moment Manrico appears and steps between them. A skirmish follows, the Count is defeated, and Manrico carries Leonora away.

*Act III.* The soldiers of Aragon, encamped before Castellor, prepare to assault the fortress. A gypsy woman, suspected of spying, is captured by sentinels and brought before the Count. It is Azucena. Questioning her, di Luna discovers that she is the mother of his mortal enemy, Manrico, and guesses that it was she who long ago stole his brother. Azucena is brutally bound and led away.

Within the fortress, Manrico and Leonora, their happiness menaced by the approaching battle, are preparing for a hurried wedding when Ruiz brings word of Azucena's capture. She has been condemned to the stake, and Manrico, explaining to Leonora that the woman is his mother, dashes to the rescue.

*Act IV.* Manrico's attempt has failed. With Azucena he is now a condemned prisoner in the dungeon of Aliferia. Thither comes Leonora, with Ruiz, to plead for her lover's life. Dismissing Ruiz, she awaits di Luna in the courtyard while priests within chant a prayer for the soul of the doomed man in the dungeon whom she hears singing of his eternal love. The Count appears and gives orders for Manrico's execution and Azucena's death by fire. Leonora throws herself at his feet imploring him to spare Manrico, which only hardens di Luna's jealous heart. She then offers herself to him on condition that he set Manrico free. Di Luna is overjoyed, while Leonora, in an ecstasy of self-sacrifice, secretly sucks poison from a ring on her finger.

In their prison cell, Manrico tries to comfort Azucena who, weakened and crazed with suffering, imagines that they are in their mountain home and thus falls asleep. Leonora brings word of Manrico's release, but he guesses the price she has paid for his freedom and turns upon her with a curse. The poison, however, takes effect sooner than expected and, with failing strength, she explains that she has chosen death rather than marriage to di Luna who, appearing in the doorway, sees her die in Manrico's arms. The Count, furious at the deception, has Manrico led off to instant execution and forces Azucena to the window to witness his end. In horror she tells him that the troubadour was the stolen child—his own brother. And with the cry "Mother, thou art avenged!" she too falls dead. Only di Luna remains, his life in ruins.

# Verdi's Works

## OPERAS

| TITLE | LIBRETTIST AND SOURCE | FIRST PERFORMANCE |
|---|---|---|
| Oberto, Conte di San Bonifacio (Oberto, Count of St. Boniface) | Piazza and Solera | La Scala, Milan Nov. 17, 1839 |
| Un giorno di regno. Revived under original title of libretto, Il finto Stanislao (The False Stanislaus) | Romani | La Scala, Milan Sept. 5, 1840 |
| Nabucodonosor, better known as Nabucco | Solera, from Old Testament | La Scala, Milan March 9, 1842 |
| I Lombardi alla prima crociata (The Lombards at the First Crusade) | Solera | La Scala, Milan Feb. 11, 1843 |
| Ernani | Piave, from Hugo's *Hernani* | La Fenice, Venice March 9, 1844 |
| I due Foscari (The Two Foscari) | Piave, from Byron's *The Two Foscari* | L'Argentina, Rome Nov. 3, 1844 |
| Giovanna d'Arco (Joan of Arc) | Solera, from Schiller's *Die Jungfrau von Orleans* | La Scala, Milan Feb. 15, 1845 |
| Alzira | Cammarano, from Voltaire's *Alzire* | San Carlo, Naples Aug. 12, 1845 |
| Attila | Solera | La Fenice, Venice March 17, 1846 |
| Macbeth | Piave, from Shakespeare's *Macbeth* | La Pergola, Florence March 14, 1847 |

[ 319 ]

| TITLE | LIBRETTIST AND SOURCE | FIRST PERFORMANCE |
|---|---|---|
| Revised version | Nuittier and Beaumont (French) | Lyrique, Paris April 21, 1865 |
| I masnadieri (The Robbers) | Maffei, from Schiller's *Die Räuber* | Her Majesty's, London July 22, 1847 |
| Jérusalem (I Lombardi revised) | Royer and Vaëz (French) | L'Opéra, Paris Nov. 26, 1847 |
| Il corsaro (The Corsair) | Piave, from Byron's *The Corsair* | Teatro Grande, Trieste Oct. 25, 1848 |
| La battaglia di Legnano (The Battle of Legnano). Also produced as L'Assedio di Haarlem (The Siege of Harlem) * | Cammarano | L'Argentina, Rome Jan. 27, 1849 |
| Luisa Miller | Cammarano, from Schiller's *Kabale und Liebe* | San Carlo, Naples Dec. 8, 1849 |
| Stiffelio | Piave, from play by Souvestre and Bourgeois | Teatro Grande, Trieste Nov. 16, 1850 |
| Rigoletto | Piave, from Hugo's *Le Roi s'amuse* | La Fenice, Venice March 11, 1851 |
| Il Trovatore (The Troubador) | Cammarano and Bardare, from Gutierrez' *El Trovador* | L'Argentina, Rome Jan. 19, 1853 |
| La Traviata (The Erring One) | Piave, from Dumas' (the younger) *La Dame aux camélias* | La Fenice, Venice March 6, 1853 |
| Les Vêpres siciliennes (The Sicilian Vespers) Also produced as Giovanna di Guzman * | Scribe and Duveyrier (French) | L'Opéra, Paris June 13, 1855 |
| Simon Boccanegra | Piave, from play by Gutierrez | La Fenice, Venice March 12, 1857 |
| Revised version | Boito | La Scala, Milan March 24, 1881 |
| Aroldo (Stiffelio revised) | Piave | Rimini Aug. 16, 1857 |

* Censors objected to original setting.

| TITLE | LIBRETTIST AND SOURCE | FIRST PERFORMANCE |
|---|---|---|
| Un ballo in maschera (The Masked Ball) | Somma, from Scribe's *Gustave III ou le bal masqué* | L'Argentina, Rome Feb. 17, 1859 |
| La forza del destino (The Force of Destiny) | Piave, from the Duke de Rivas' *Don Alvaro* | St. Petersburg Nov. 10, 1862 |
| Revised version | Ghislanzoni | La Scala, Milan Feb. 20, 1869 |
| Don Carlos | Méry and du Locle (French) from Schiller's *Don Carlos* | L'Opéra, Paris March 11, 1867 |
| Revised version | | La Scala, Milan Jan. 10, 1884 |
| Aida | Ghislanzoni, from unpublished novelette by Mariette | Cairo Dec. 24, 1871 |
| Otello | Boito, from Shakespeare's *Othello* | La Scala, Milan Feb. 5, 1887 |
| Falstaff | Boito, from Shakespeare's *The Merry Wives of Windsor and Henry IV* | La Scala, Milan Feb. 9, 1893 |

## CHORAL WORKS

| | | |
|---|---|---|
| Suona la tromba (Sound the trumpet) | Mameli | Composed 1848 |
| Inno delle nazioni (Hymn of the Nations) | Boito | Her Majesty's, London May 24, 1862 |
| Messa da Requiem per Alessandro Manzoni (Requiem Mass for Manzoni) | | St. Mark's Church, Milan May 22, 1874 |
| Pater Noster, for 5 voices | Italian version by Dante | Milan April 18, 1880 |

| TITLE | LIBRETTIST AND SOURCE | FIRST PERFORMANCE |
|---|---|---|
| Ave Maria, for 4 voices (on so-called "enigmatic" scale) | | Composed about 1889 |
| Stabat Mater, for chorus and orchestra | | Paris April 7, 1898 |
| Laudi alla Vergine Maria (Hymn to the Virgin Mary) for 4 voices | Verses from Dante's *Paradiso* | Paris April 7, 1898 |
| Te Deum, for double chorus and orchestra | | Paris April 7, 1898 |

## CHAMBER MUSIC

| | |
|---|---|
| String Quartet in E minor | Naples April 1, 1873 |

## SONGS

Sei romanze (Six Romances), published 1838
L'esule (The Exile), song for bass, 1839
La seduzione (The Seduction), song for bass, 1839
Notturno a 3 voci (Nocturne for 3 voices), 1839
Album di sei romanze (Album of Six Romances), 1845
Il poveretto (Poor Little One), 1847
Tu dici che non m'ami (You say you do not love me), for album in honor of Piave, 1869
Ave Maria (Italian version by Dante), for soprano and strings, 1880

# Verdi on Records

SINCE the earliest days of the phonograph Verdi has been well represented on records, partly because the human voice could at first
be better reproduced than could orchestral music, and partly because of the perennial and widespread popularity of his operas and
the fame of the stars who sang them. His best loved arias therefore
appeared in profusion on discs at a time when recorded symphonies
were still few and far between. There exist, for example, excerpts
from *Otello* made in the early nineteen hundreds by Tamagno and
Maurel of the original cast, but, like most records of that vintage,
they are more interesting than enjoyable. The bulk of these early
attempts are often so crudely recorded as to be of historical rather
than musical interest, yet they have value, sometimes as glimpses
of operas no longer in the repertory, sometimes as samples of super-
lative singing. The best of these are being reissued, usually with a
modern orchestra dubbed in. The others are for the most part col-
lectors' items, to be found in old collections, libraries, and occasionally at a dealer's.

A complete list of Verdi recordings would almost fill a separate
book. There are for instance at least a dozen modern versions of
"Ah! fors è lui" from *La Traviata*, to say nothing of earlier acoustical
recordings. The following list is therefore limited to American recordings that are easily available. Imported records are also becoming increasingly obtainable in this country. Verdi has been recorded
in English, French, German, Russian, Swedish, and Danish, but the
Italian versions are musically preferable. HMV, however, offers
some of the best known arias sung in English for those who enjoy
opera in their own tongue. A better solution to the problem of understanding is to follow with a libretto giving both Italian and
English texts—even though the standard translations often fail ab-
surdly to convey whatever beauty and poetry the original may have.

Though some of the older items are now difficult to obtain every month brings new releases, both domestic and imported. It is easier today for nonmusicians to familiarize themselves with Verdi's scores than it has ever been before.

| | |
|---|---|
| *AIDA* | RECORD NO. |
| Complete recording by D. Giannini, I. Minghini-Cattaneo, A. Pertile, G. Inghilleri, L. Manfrini, G. Masini, G. Nessi, with Chorus and Orchestra of La Scala of Milan under Carlo Sabajno | VMC-100 |
| Complete recording by G. Arangi-Lombardi, M. Capuana, A. Lindi, A. Borgioli, T. Pasero, S. Baccaloni, G. Nessi, with Chorus and Orchestra of La Scala of Milan under Lorenzo Molajoli | C-OP. 3 |
| "Celeste Aida" | |
| J. Bjoerling | V-12039 |
| G. Martinelli | V-14206 |
| E. Caruso | V-7770 |
| "Ritorno vincitor" | |
| Z. Milanov | V-11-9288 in VM-1074 |
| R. Ponselle | V-7438 |
| H. Traubel | CM-675 |
| "Nume, custode e vincici" (Temple Scene) | |
| E. Pinza and G. Martinelli | V-8111 |
| Grand March | |
| Boston Pops Orchestra under Arthur Fiedler | V-11885 |
| Ballet Music | |
| Boston Pops Orchestra under Arthur Fiedler | V-11985 |
| Columbia Broadcasting Symphony under Howard Barlow | C-71401-D |
| "Quest' assisa ch' io vi dica" | |
| D. Giannini, A. Pertile, G. Inghilleri | V-8994 |

| AIDA | RECORD NO. |
|---|---|
| "O patria mia," E. Rethberg | V-8994 |
| "Fuggiam gli ardori," D. Giannini and A. Pertile | V-11898 |
| "La fatal pietra," R. Ponselle and G. Martinelli | V-1744/5 |

### ATTILA

| "Te sol quest' anima," E. Rethberg, B. Gigli, E. Pinza | V-8194 |
|---|---|

### UN BALLO IN MASCHERA

| "Di' tu se fedele" (Barcarola), J. Bjoerling | V-10-1323 |
|---|---|
| "Eri tu che macchiavi" L. Tibbett | V-7353 |
| L. Warren | V-11-9292 |
| "Ma se m'e forza," J. Peerce | V-11-9292 |

### DON CARLOS

| "O don fatale," B. Castagna | C-71276-D |
|---|---|

### ERNANI

| "Infelice, e tu credevi," E. Pinza | V-7552 |
|---|---|

### FALSTAFF

Complete recording by G. Rimini, P. Tassinari,
I. Alfani Tellini, A. Buades, R. d'Alessio, R.

## FALSTAFF

Monticone, E. Ghirardini, S. Baccaloni, E. Venturini, G. Nessi, with Chorus and Orchestra of
La Scala of Milan under Lorenzo Molajoli    C-op. 16

"E sogna? o realta?" (Ford's Monologue), L. Warren    V-18293

## LA FORZA DEL DESTINO

Overture, NBC Symphony Orchestra under
Arturo Toscanini    V-11-9010

"La Vergine degli angeli," R. Ponselle and E.
Pinza    V-8097

"Solenne in quest' ora," B. Gigli and G. de Luca    V-8069

"Pace, pace mio dio"
Z. Milanov    V-11-8927
C. Muzio    C-9106-M and in
   CM-259

## I LOMBARDI ALLA PRIMA CROCIATA

"Qual voluttà trascorrere," E. Rethberg, B. Gigli, E.
Pinza    V-8194

"O Signore, dal tetto natio," Chorus and Orchestra
of La Scala of Milan under Carlo Sabajno    V-25-7071

## NABUCCO

"Va pensiero sull' ali dorate," Chorus and Orchestra
of La Scala of Milan under Carlo Sabajno    V-25-7071

OTELLO

Complete recording by N. Fusati, A. Granforte,
M. Carbone, P. Girardi, N. Palai, C. Zambelli,
E. Spada, T. Beltacchi, with Chorus and Or-
chestra of La Scala of Milan under Carlo
Sabajno      VMC-115

"Inaffia l'ugola" (Drinking song), L. Tibbett      V-15801 in VM-620

Love Duet
    T. Lemnitz and T. Ralf (in German)      V-18363 in VM-860
    H. Jepson and G. Martinelli      V-15801/2 in VM-620

"Credo in un Dio cruel"
    J. C. Thomas      V-17639
    L. Warren      V-11-9292 in VM-1074
    L. Tibbett      V-15802 in VM-620
    R. Stracciari      C-7299-M

"Ora e per sempre addio," G. Martinelli      V-15803 in VM-620

"Era la notte" (Iago's Dream), L. Tibbett      V-15803 in VM-620

"Si, pel ciel marmoreo giuro!"
    G. Martinelli and L. Tibbett      V-15804 in VM-620

"Dio! mi potevi scagliar" (Othello's Monologue)
    L Melchior      C-71389-D
    G. Martinelli      V-15804 in VM-620

"Vieni, l'aula e deserta," L. Tibbett, G. Martinelli,
    N. Massuer      V-15805 in VM-620

"Salce, salce," and "Ave Maria"
    T. Lemnitz      V-18364 in VM-860
    H. Jepson      V-15805/6 in VM-620

"Ave Maria" only, H. Traubel      In CM-675

"Niun mi tema" (Death of Othello)
    L. Melchior      C-71389-D
    G. Martinelli      V-15806 in VM-620

## REQUIEM MASS

Complete recording by M. Caniglia, E. Stignani,
B. Gigli, E. Pinza, with Chorus and Orchestra
of the Rome Opera under Tullio Serafin                    VM-734

"Ingemisco," J. Bjoerling                                 V-13588


## RIGOLETTO

Complete recording by R. Stracciari, M. Capsir,
D. Borgioli, E. Dominici, A. Masetti Bassi,
I. Mannarini, E. dall' Argine, D. Baronti,
A. Baracchi, with Chorus and Orchestra of La
Scala of Milan under Lorenzo Molajoli                    C-OP. 18

Complete recording by L. Piazza, L. Pagluighi,
T. Folgar, S. Baccaloni, O. de Cristoff, A.
Baracchi, G. Nessi, with Chorus and Orchestra
of La Scala of Milan under Carlo Sabajno                 VM-32

"Questa o quella"
   J. Bjoerling                                          V-10-1200
   N. Martini                                            C-17191-D

"Pari siamo!" (Rigoletto's Monologue)
   L. Warren                                             V-11-9413

"Il nome vostro ditemi"
   L. Pons and G. de Luca                          V-17233 in VM-702

"È il sol dell' anima"
   H. Schymberg and J. Bjoerling                        V-11-8440

"Caro nome"
   L. Pons                                       C-17370-D in CM-582
   L. Pons                                               V-7383
   A. Galli-Curci                                        V-7655

"Parmi veder le lagrime," J. Peerce                      V-11-8926

| RIGOLETTO | RECORD NO. |
|---|---|

"Cortigiani vil razza"
R. Weede — C-71261-D
L. Warren — V-11-9413

"Tutte le feste al tempio," L. Pons — V-7383

"La donna è mobile"
J. Bjoerling — V-4372
E. Caruso — V-1616
T. Schipa — V-1099

"Bella figlia dell' amore" (Quartet), B. Gigli, G. de Luca, A. Galli-Curci, L. Homer — V-10012

*SIMON BOCCANEGRA*

"Il lacerato spirito" (Prologue)
A. Kipnis — V-8684
E. Pinza — CM-676

"Dinne, alcun la non vedesti?", L. Tibbett and R. Bampton — V-15642

"Figlia, tal nome palpita," L. Tibbett and R. Bampton — V-15642

"Plebe, Patrizi," L. Tibbett, R. Bampton, R. Nicholson — V-15642

"Piango su voi," L. Tibbett, R. Bampton, R. Nicholson — V-15642

*LA TRAVIATA*

Complete recording by A. Guerini, M. Huder, L. Infantino, P. Silveri, A. Zagonara, P. Rakowsky, C. Plantania, B. Giusti, with Chorus and Orchestra of the Rome Opera under Vincenzo Bellezza — C-op. 25

## LA TRAVIATA

Complete recording by A. Rosza, O. de Franco,
A. Ziliani, L. Borgonovo, G. Callegari, A.
Gelli, A. Lenzi, with Chorus and Orchestra of
La Scala of Milan under Carlo Sabajno     VM-112

Prelude to Act I.
NBC Symphony Orchestra under Arturo Toscanini     V-18080
Milan Symphony Orchestra under Lorenzo Molajoli     C-69064-D

"Un di felice"
L. Albanese and J. Peerce     V-11-9290 in VM-1074
A. Galli-Curci and T. Schipa     V-1754

"A! fors' è lui" and "Sempre libera"
B. Sayao     C-71451-D
L. Albanese     V-11-9331
L. Pons     in CM-638

L. Bori     $\begin{cases} \text{V-7438} \\ \text{V-11-8569} \end{cases}$

"De' miei bollenti spiriti," J. Peerce     V-11-8926

"Dite alla giovine" and "Imponete"
L. Albanese and R. Merrill     V-11-9175

"Di provenza il mar"
G. de Luca     V-7086
J. C. Thomas     V-15850 in VM-645

Prelude to Act III.
NBC Symphony Orchestra under Arturo Toscanini     V-18080
Milan Symphony Orchestra under Lorenzo Molajoli     C-69064-D

"Addio del passato," C. Muzio     C-9106-M

IL TROVATORE                                           RECORD NO.

Complete recording by M. Carena, I. Minghini-
Cattaneo, A. Pertile, A. Granforte, B. Carmassi,
O. de Franco, G. Callegari, A. Gelli, with
Chorus and Orchestra of La Scala of Milan
under Carlo Sabajno                                    VMC-103

Complete recording by B. Scacciati, G. Zinetti,
F. Merli, E. Molinari, C. Zambelli, I. Mannarini, E. Venturini, E. Arnaldi, with Chorus
and Orchestra of La Scala of Milan under
Lorenzo Molajoli                                       C-OP. 9

Anvil Chorus, RCA Victor Chorale and Orches-
tra under Robert Shaw                                  V-11-9294

"Mal reggendo all' aspro assalto"
G. Martinelli and L. Homer                             V-8105

"Ah! si, ben mio, coll' essere," J. Bjoerling          V-2136

"Di quella pira"
J. Bjoerling                                           V-2136
G. Martinelli (with chorus)                            V-8109

"Miserere"
Z. Milanov and J. Peerce                               V-11-8782
R. Ponselle and G. Martinelli                          V-8097

"Ai nostri monti"
K. Thorborg and J. Peerce                              V-11-8782
L. Homer and G. Martinelli                             V-8105

# Index

## Date Due

| | | | |
|---|---|---|---|
| OCT 1 1 1955 | | | |